Italian

PHRASEBOOK & DICTIONARY

Acknowledgments
Product Editor Tracy Whitmey
Book Designer Gwen Cotter
Production Support Chris Love
Language Writers Pietro Iagnocco, Karina Coates, Susie Walker, Mirna Cicioni, Anna Beltrami
Cover Image Researcher Naomi Parker

Thanks
James Hardy, Kirsten Rawlings, Angela Tinson

Published by Lonely Planet Global Limited
CRN 554153

7th Edition – June 2017
ISBN 978 1 78657 450 3

Cover Image Sofie Delauw/Getty©

Printed in China 10 9 8 7 6 5 4 3 2 1

Contact lonelyplanet.com/contact

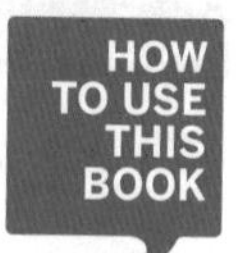

Look out for the following icons throughout the book:

'Shortcut' Phrase
Easy-to-remember alternative to the full phrase

Q&A Pair
'Question-and-answer' pair – we suggest a response to the question asked

Look For
Phrases you may see on signs, menus etc

Listen For
Phrases you may hear from officials, locals etc

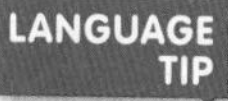

Language Tip
An insight into the foreign language

Culture Tip
An insight into the local culture

How to read the phrases:

- Coloured words and phrases throughout the book are phonetic guides to help you pronounce the foreign language.
- Lists of phrases with tinted background are options you can choose to complete the phrase above them.

These abbreviations will help you choose the right words and phrases in this book:

f	feminine	**m**	masculine	**sg**	singular
inf	informal	**pl**	plural		
lit	literal	**pol**	polite		

Contents

PAGE 6

About Italian

Learn about Italian, build your own sentences and pronounce words correctly.

Introduction 6
Top Phrases 8
Pronunciation 10
Grammar 14

PAGE 29

Travel Phrases

Ready-made phrases for every situation – buy a ticket, book a hotel and much more.

Basics **29**
Understanding 30
Numbers & Amounts 32
Time & Dates 34

Practical **39**
Transport 40
Border Crossing 53
Directions 55
Accommodation 58
Shopping 70
Communications 80
Money & Banking 87
Business 91

Sightseeing ... 93
Senior & Disabled Travellers ... 99
Travel with Children ... 101

Social ... 103

Meeting People ... 104
Interests ... 114
Feelings & Opinions ... 118
Going Out ... 122
Romance ... 128
Beliefs & Culture ... 133
Sports ... 135
Outdoors ... 140

Safe Travel ... 145

Emergencies ... 146
Police ... 148
Health ... 150

Food ... 159

Eating Out ... 160
Self-Catering ... 176
Vegetarian & Special Meals ... 181

PAGE 184

Menu Decoder

Dishes and ingredients explained – order with confidence and try new foods.

PAGE 204

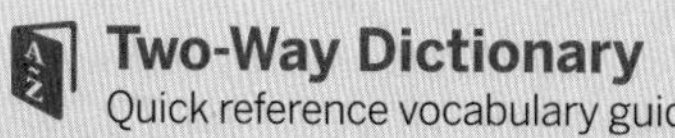

Two-Way Dictionary

Quick reference vocabulary guide – 3500 words to help you communicate.

English–Italian Dictionary ... 204
Italian–English Dictionary ... 236

Index ... 267

Italian

italiano ee·ta·*lya*·no

Who speaks Italian?

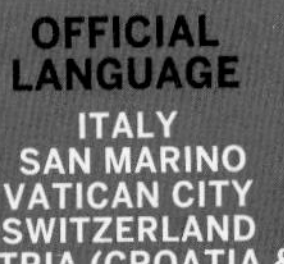

Widely Understood Eritrea – Malta – Monaco

Why Bother

When even a simple sentence sounds like an aria, it's difficult to resist striking up a conversation. Besides, all you need for *la dolce vita* is to be able to tell your Moschino from your *macchiato* and your Fellini from your *fettuccine*!

Distinctive Sounds

The rolled r, stronger than in English; most other consonants can have a more emphatic pronunciation too (in which case they're written as double letters).

65 MILLION speak Italian as their first language

20 MILLION speak Italian as their second language

Italian in the World

Thanks to widespread migration and the enormous popularity of Italian culture and cuisine – from 'spaghetti Western' to opera – Italian is often a language of choice in schools all over the world, despite the fact that Italy never established itself as a colonial power.

Italian in Italy

Italians are very proud of their language's rich history and influence – rightly so, since it claims the closest relationship with the language spoken by the Romans. For example, Italy is one of the few countries in Europe where dubbing of foreign-language movies is preferred to subtitling.

False Friends

Warning: many Italian words look like English words but have a different meaning altogether, eg *camera* *ka*·me·ra is a room, not a camera (which is *macchina fotografica* *ma*·kee·na fo·to·*gra*·fee·ka in Italian).

Language Family

Romance (developed from Latin, the language of the Roman Empire). Close relatives include Spanish, Portuguese, French and Romanian.

Must-Know Grammar

Italian has a formal and informal word for 'you' (*Lei* lay and *tu* too respectively); the verbs have a different ending for each person, like the English 'I do' vs 'he/she does'.

Donations to English

Numerous – most of us are familiar with *ciao, pasta, bella, maestro, mafia...*

5 Phrases to Learn Before You Go

1 What's the local speciality?

Qual'è la specialità di questa regione?

kwa·*le* la spe·cha·lee·*ta* dee *kwes*·ta re·*jo*·ne

A bit like the rivalry between medieval Italian city-states, these days the country's regions compete in specialty foods and wines.

2 Which combined tickets do you have?

Quali biglietti cumulativi avete?

kwa·lee bee·*lye*·tee koo·moo·la·*tee*·vee a·*ve*·te

Make the most of your euro by getting combined tickets to various sights; they are available in all major Italian cities.

3 Where can I buy discount designer items?

C'è un outlet in zona? che oon *owt*·let in *zo*·na

Discount fashion outlets are big business in major cities – get bargain-priced seconds, samples and cast-offs for *la bella figura*.

4 I'm here with my husband/boyfriend.

Sono qui con il mio marito/ragazzo.

so·no kwee kon eel *mee*·o ma·*ree*·to/ra·*ga*·tso

Solo women travellers may receive unwanted attention in some parts of Italy; if ignoring fails have a polite rejection ready.

5 Let's meet at 6pm for pre-dinner drinks.

Ci vediamo alle sei per un aperitivo.

chee ve·*dya*·mo *a*·le say per oon a·pe·ree·*tee*·vo

At dusk, watch the main *piazza* get crowded with people sipping colourful cocktails and snacking the evening away: join your new friends for this authentic Italian ritual!

10 Phrases to Sound Like a Local

What's up?	**Cosa c'é?**	*ko*·za che
All OK?	**Tutto a posto?**	*too*·ta *pos*·to
It's OK.	**Va bene.**	va *be*·ne
Great!	**Fantastico!**	fan·*tas*·tee·ko
That's true.	**È vero.**	e *ve*·ro
Sure.	**Certo.**	*cher*·to
No way!	**Per niente!**	per *nyen*·te
You're kidding!	**Scherzi!**	*sker*·tsee
If only!	**Magari!**	ma·*ga*·ree
Really?	**Davvero?**	da·*ve*·ro

ABOUT Italian

Pronunciation

The Italian sound system will be familiar to most English-speakers: almost all of the sounds you'll hear exist in English. You might notice slight differences, particularly with the vowel sounds, but there's nothing to stop you from having a go and being understood. Standard Italian pronunciation is given in this book – the same form that's used in education and the media.

Vowel Sounds

Italian vowel sounds are generally shorter than in English. They normally do not run together to form vowel sound combinations (diphthongs), though it can often sound that way to English-speakers. There are four vowel sounds that roughly correspond to diphthongs in English (ai, ay, ow, oy).

SYMBOL	ENGLISH EQUIVALENT	ITALIAN EXAMPLE	TRANSLITERATION
a	father	pane	*pa*·ne
ai	aisle	mai	mai
ay	say	vorrei	vo·*ray*
e	red	letto	*le*·to
ee	bee	vino	*vee*·no
o	pot	molto	*mol*·to
oo	took	frutta	*froo*·ta
ow	cow	ciao, autobus	chow, *ow*·to·boos
oy	boy	poi	poy

Consonant Sounds

SYMBOL	ENGLISH EQUIVALENT	ITALIAN EXAMPLE	TRANSLITERATION
b	big	bello	*be*·lo
ch	chilli	centro	*chen*·tro
d	din	denaro	de·*na*·ro
dz	lids	mezzo, zaino	*me*·dzo, *dzai*·no
f	fun	fare	*fa*·re
g	go	gomma	*go*·ma
j	jam	cugino	koo·*jee*·no
k	kick	cambio, quanto	*kam*·byo, *kwan*·to
l	loud	linea	*lee*·ne·a
ly	million	figlia	*fee*·lya
m	man	madre	*ma*·dre
n	no	numero	*noo*·me·ro
ny	canyon	bagno	*ba*·nyo
p	pig	pronto	*pron*·to
r	run (strong and rolled)	ristorante	rees·to·*ran*·te
s	so	sera	*se*·ra
sh	show	capisce	ka·*pee*·she
t	tin	teatro	te·*a*·tro
ts	hits	grazie, sicurezza	*gra*·tsye, see·koo·*re*·tsa
v	van	viaggio	vee·*a*·jo
w	win	uomo	*wo*·mo
y	yes	italiano	ee·tal·*ya*·no
z	zoo	casa	*ka*·za

As well as the pronunciation described above, Italian consonant sounds have an additional form: a stronger, almost emphatic pronunciation. The actual sounds are basically the same, though meaning can be altered between a normal consonant sound and this double consonant sound. It's referred to as a 'double consonant' because usually, if the word is written with a double letter, that's the cue to use the stronger form.

Here are some examples where this 'double consonant' effect can make a difference:

sonno	*son*·no	sleep
sono	*so*·no	I am
pappa	*pap*·pa	baby food
papa	*pa*·pa	pope

Unlike the above examples, the pronunciation guides in this book don't distinguish between the two forms. Refer to the written Italian beside each transliteration as the cue to making the consonant sounds a little stronger. Even if you never distinguish them, you'll always be understood in context – your audience will work out if you're talking about the pope or baby food!

Reading & Writing

~ ITALIAN ALPHABET ~

A a a	**B b** bee	**C c** chee
D d dee	**E e** e	**F f** *e*·fe
G g jee	**H h** *a*·ka	**I i** ee
L l *e*·le	**M m** *e*·me	**N n** *e*·ne
O o o	**P p** pee	**Q q** koo
R r *e*·re	**S s** *e*·se	**T t** tee
U u oo	**V v** voo	**Z z** *tse*·ta

The relationship between Italian sounds and their spelling is straightforward and consistent. The table below will help you read the Italian that you come across in your travels.

~ SPELLBOUND ~

c, g, sc	before *a*, *o*, *u* and *h* they sound hard like the 'k' in 'kick', 'g' in 'go' and 'sc' in 'scooter' respectively; before *e* and *i* they sound soft like the 'ch' in 'chilli', 'j' in 'jam' and 'sh' in 'show' respectively	bianco, gomma, fresco; centro, gelato, ascensore
ci, gi, sci	before *a*, *o* and *u*, the 'i' is not pronounced	ciao, giallo, prosciutto
h	never pronounced	traghetto
j, w, k, x, y	only found in foreign words that have been adopted by Italian	jogging, weekend, kosher, fax, yogurt
z	pronounced as 'dz' or as 'ts'	zaino, grazie
s	pronounced as 'z' between vowels; pronounced as 's' elsewhere	casa; sì, essere, scatola
gli, gn	pronounced as the 'll' in 'million' and 'ny' in 'canyon' respectively	figlia, bagno

Word Stress

In Italian, you generally emphasise the second-last syllable in a word. However, when a written word has an accent marked on a vowel, the stress is on that syllable. The characteristic sing-song quality of an Italian sentence is created by pronouncing the syllables evenly and rhythmically, then swinging down on the last word. The stressed syllable is always italicised in our pronunciation guides, so you can't go wrong!

ABOUT Italian Grammar

This chapter is designed to explain the main grammatical structures you need in order to make your own sentences. Look under each heading – listed in alphabetical order – for information on functions which these grammatical categories express in a sentence. For example, demonstratives are used for giving instructions, so you'll need them to tell the taxi driver where your hotel is etc.

Adjectives & Adverbs

Describing People/Things • Doing Things

Adjectives generally come after the noun in Italian. However, adjectives expressing quantity (eg 'much', 'few') always precede the noun.

black cat	gatto nero (lit: cat black-**m-sg**) *ga*·to *ne*·ro
many cats	molti gatti (lit: many-**m-pl** cats) *mol*·tee *ga*·tee

The adjective endings change depending on whether the noun is masculine or feminine, singular or plural (see **gender** and **plurals**).

	~ SINGULAR ~		~ PLURAL ~	
m	bello	*be*·lo	belli	*be*·lee
f	bella	*be*·la	belle	*be*·le

Adjectives ending in *-e* in the singular – eg *felice* fe·*lee*·che (happy) – take the ending *-i* in the plural, regardless of the noun's gender:

happy cats	gatti felici (lit: cats happy-**m-pl**) *ga*·tee fe·*lee*·chee

Many adverbs in Italian are derived from adjectives by adding the ending *-mente* ·*men*·te to the singular feminine form of the adjective (ie the form ending in *-a*), just like you add the ending '-ly' to the adjective in English. In Italian, adverbs are generally placed after the verb they refer to.

a slow train	un treno lento (lit: a-**m-sg** train slow-**m-sg**) oon *tre*·no *len*·to
to speak slowly	parlare lentamente (lit: to-speak slowly) par·*la*·re len·ta·*men*·te

Articles

Naming People/Things

There are four words for the definite article (ie equivalents of 'the' in English) in Italian. Which one you use depends on the gender and number of the noun (see **gender** and **plurals**).

~ DEFINITE ARTICLES ~			
m sg	**the train**	il treno	eel *tre*·no
m pl	**the trains**	i treni	ee *tre*·nee
f sg	**the receipt**	la ricevuta	la ree·che·*voo*·ta
f pl	**the receipts**	le ricevute	le ree·che·*voo*·te

Note that the forms *lo* lo and *gli* lyee are used before masculine nouns starting with 's' plus a consonant, or with *z-*, *gn-*, *pn-*, *ps-*, *x-* or *y-*. The form *l'* is used before masculine and feminine nouns starting with a vowel (*l'* is joined in pronunciation with the noun).

m sg	**the backpack**	lo zaino	lo *dzai*·no
m pl	**the backpacks**	gli zaini	lyee *dzai*·nee
f sg	**the exit**	l'uscita	loo·*shee*·ta
f pl	**the exits**	le uscite	le oo·*shee*·te

The definite article in Italian is joined with some prepositions when it's used after them, eg *di* dee (of) + *il* eel becomes *del* del, and *a* a (to) + *la* la becomes *alla* *a*·la. See also **prepositions**.

Italian has two words for the indefinite article (ie 'a/an'), depending on the noun's gender (*un* oon/*una* *oo*·na). Two other forms are used depending on the first letter of the next word: *uno* *oo*·no (for masculine nouns starting with 's' plus a consonant, or with *z-*, *gn-*, *pn-*, *ps-*, *x-* or *y-*) and *un'* oon (for feminine nouns starting with a vowel).

~ INDEFINITE ARTICLES ~

m sg	**a sandwich**	un panino	oon pa·*nee*·no
	a stadium	uno stadio	*oo*·no *sta*·dyo
f sg	**an apple**	una mela	*oo*·na *me*·la
	a friend	un'amica	oon·a·*mee*·ka

Be

Describing People/Things • Making Statements

There are two equivalents of the English verb 'be' in Italian – *essere* *e*·se·re and *stare* *sta*·re – which are used depending on the context. For negative forms with 'be', see **negatives**.

~ USE OF ESSERE (TO BE) ~

permanent characteristics of persons/things	Sei molto bella. say *mol*·to *be*·la	You're very beautiful.
occupations or nationality	Sono dall'Inghilterra. *so*·no da·leen·geel·*te*·ra	I am from England.
time or location of events	È l'una. e *loo*·na	It's one o'clock.
mood of a person	Sei felice? say fe·*lee*·che	Are you happy?
possession	Non è mio. non e *mee*·o	It's not mine.

~ USE OF STARE (TO BE) ~

temporary characteristics of persons/things	È malato. e ma·*la*·to	He is sick.
time or location of events	Stai a casa? stai a *ka*·za	Are you at home?

~ ESSERE (TO BE) – PRESENT TENSE ~

I	**am**	io	sono	yo	*so*·no
you sg inf	**are**	tu	sei	too	say
you sg pol	**are**	Lei	è	lay	e
he/ she/ it	**is**	lui/ lei	è	looy/ lay	e
we	**are**	noi	siamo	noy	*sya*·mo
you pl inf	**are**	voi	siete	voy	*sye*·te
you pl pol	**are**	Loro	sono	*lo*·ro	*so*·no
they	**are**	loro	sono	*lo*·ro	*so*·no

~ STARE (TO BE) – PRESENT TENSE ~

I	**am**	io	sto	yo	sto
you sg inf	**are**	tu	stai	too	stai
you sg pol	**are**	Lei	sta	lay	sta
he/she/it	**is**	lui/lei	sta	looy/lay	sta
we	**are**	noi	stiamo	noy	*stya*·mo
you pl inf	**are**	voi	state	voy	*sta*·te
you pl pol	**are**	Loro	stanno	*lo*·ro	*sta*·no
they	**are**	loro	stanno	*lo*·ro	*sta*·no

Demonstratives

Giving Instructions • Indicating Location • Pointing Things Out

To point something out, just use the phrase *È* ... e ... (it-is ...):

It's a local custom. È una tradizione locale.
(lit: it-is a-**f-sg** custom local-**f-sg**)
e *oo*·na tra·dee·*tsyo*·ne lo·*ka*·le

To refer to or to point out a person or object, use one of the following demonstratives before the noun. Each of these words changes form depending on the gender and number of the noun it refers to. See also **gender** and **plurals**.

~ DEMONSTRATIVES ~

	m sg			m pl	
this	questo	*kwe*·sto	**these**	questi	*kwe*·stee
that	quel/ quello	kwel/ *kwe*·lo	**those**	quei/ quegli/ quelli	kway/ *kwe*·lyee/ *kwe*·lee
	f sg			f pl	
this	questa	*kwe*·sta	**these**	queste	*kwe*·ste
that	quella	*kwe*·la	**those**	quelle	*kwe*·le

Demonstratives can also be used on their own:

How much is this?	Quanto costa questo? (lit: how-much costs this-**m-sg**) *kwan*·to *kos*·ta *kwe*·sto

Gender

Naming People/Things

In Italian, all nouns are either masculine or feminine. You can recognise the noun's gender by the article, demonstrative, possessive or any other adjective used with the noun, as they all change form to agree with the noun's gender. The gender of words is also indicated in the dictionary, but here are some general rules:

» A word is masculine/feminine if it refers to a man/woman.
» Words ending in *-o*, *-ore* or a consonant are usually masculine.
» Words ending in *-a* or *-ione* are generally feminine.

The masculine and feminine forms of words are indicated with the abbreviations **m** and **f** throughout this phrasebook where relevant. See also the box **masculine & feminine** (p130).

Have

Possessing

Possession can be indicated in various ways in Italian (see also **possessives**). One way is by using the verb *avere* a·*ve*·re (have). For negative forms with 'have', see **negatives**.

~ AVERE (TO HAVE) – PRESENT TENSE ~

I	**have**	io	ho	yo	o
you sg inf	**have**	tu	hai	too	ai
you sg pol	**have**	Lei	ha	lay	a
he/ she/ it	**has**	lui/ lei	ha	looy/ lay	a
we	**have**	noi	abbiamo	noy	a·*bya*·mo
you pl inf	**have**	voi	avete	voy	a·*ve*·te
you pl pol	**have**	Loro	hanno	*lo*·ro	*a*·no
they	**have**	loro	hanno	*lo*·ro	*a*·no

You can also use the phrases *c'è* che (there is) and *ci sono* chee *so*·no (there are) to say or ask if something is available:

Is there hot water?

C'è acqua calda?
(lit: there-is water hot-**f-sg**)
che *a*·kwa *kal*·da

Negatives

Negating

To make a negative statement in Italian, just add the word *non* non (not) before the main verb of the sentence. Unlike English, Italian uses double negatives.

I don't understand.

Non capisco.
(lit: not I-understand)
non ka·*pee*·sko

I don't understand anything.

Non capisco niente.
(lit: not I-understand nothing)
non ka·*pee*·sko *nyen*·te

Personal Pronouns

Making Statements • Naming People/Things

Personal pronouns ('I', 'you' etc) change form in Italian depending on whether they're the subject or the object in a sentence. It's the same in English, which has 'I' and 'me' as the subject and object pronouns respectively (eg 'I see her' vs 'She sees me'). Note, however, that the subject pronoun is usually omitted in Italian as the subject is understood from the corresponding verb form.

I'm a student.	Sono studente. (lit: I-am student) *so*·no stoo·*den*·tee

~ SUBJECT PRONOUNS ~

I	io	yo	**we**	noi	noy
you sg inf	tu	too	**you** pl inf	voi	voy
you sg pol	Lei	lay	**you** pl pol	Loro	*lo*·ro
he/ she/ it	lui/ lei	looy/ lay	**they**	loro	*lo*·ro

When talking to people familiar to you or younger than you, it's usual to use the informal form of 'you', *tu* too, rather than the polite form, *Lei* lay. Phrases in this book use the form of 'you' that is appropriate to the situation you're likely to encounter as a traveller. Where both forms are used, they are indicated by the abbreviations pol and inf. See also the box **addressing people** (p107).

~ OBJECT PRONOUNS ~

me	mi	mee	**us**	ci	chee
you sg inf	ti	tee	**you** pl inf	vi	vee
you sg pol	La/ Le	la/ le	**you** pl pol	Li/ Loro **m** Le/ Loro **f**	lee/ *lo*·ro **m** le/ *lo*·ro **f**
him **it**	lo/ gli	lo/ lyee	**them**	li/ loro **m** le/ loro **f**	lee/ *lo*·ro **m** le/ *lo*·ro **f**
her **it**	la/ le	la/ le			

In the table above, the forms separated by a slash are direct/ indirect object pronouns.

The direct and indirect object pronouns differ only for the third person ('he', 'she', 'it', 'they') and the polite 'you' form.

I've seen him.

Lo ho visto.
(lit: him I-have seen)
lo o *vee*·sto

I've talked to him.

Gli ho parlato.
(lit: to-him I-have talked)
lyee o par·*la*·to

The object pronouns generally come before the verb. The indirect object pronoun comes before the direct object pronoun.

I'll give it to you.

Ti lo darò.
(lit: to-you-**sg inf** it I-will-give)
tee lo da·*ro*

Plurals

Naming People/Things

General rules for forming plurals in Italian are pretty simple: words ending in *-a* in the singular end in *-e* in the plural, and words ending in *-o* or *-e* in the singular end in *-i* in the plural. See also the box **irregular plurals** (p97).

~ SINGULAR ~			~ PLURAL ~		
a person	una persona	*oo*·na per·*so*·na	**three people**	tre persone	tre per·*so*·ne
a ticket	un biglietto	oon bee·*lye*·to	**two tickets**	due biglietti	*doo*·e bee·*lye*·tee
a country	un paese	oon pa·*e*·se	**five countries**	cinque paesi	*cheen*·kwe pa·*e*·see

Possessives

Possessing

A common way of indicating possession is by using possessive adjectives before the noun they refer to. Like other adjectives, they agree with the noun in number and gender, and they are preceded by the definite article (see **articles**).

It's my ticket.	È il mio biglietto. (lit: it-is the-**m-sg** my-**m-sg** ticket) e eel *mee*·o bee·*lye*·to

In Italian, posessive adjectives (ie 'my', 'your' etc) and possessive pronouns (ie 'mine', 'yours' etc) are the same – if what is being talked about is clear from the context, the noun can be omitted:

It's mine.	È il mio. (lit: it-is the-**m-sg** mine-**m-sg**) e eel *mee*·o

~ POSSESSIVE ADJECTIVES & PRONOUNS ~

my/ mine	il mio i miei la mia le mie	eel *mee*·o ee *mye*·ee la *mee*·a le *mee*·e	**our/ ours**	il nostro i nostri la nostra le nostre	eel *nos*·tro ee *nos*·tree la *nos*·tra le *nos*·tre
your/ yours sg inf	il tuo i tuoi la tua le tue	eel *too*·o ee *two*·ee la *too*·a le *too*·e	**your/ yours** pl inf	il vostro i vostri la vostra le vostre	eel *vos*·tro ee *vos*·tree la *vos*·tra le *vos*·tre
your/ yours sg pol	il Suo i Suoi la Sua le Sue	eel *soo*·o ee *swo*·ee la *soo*·a le *soo*·e	**your/ yours** pl pol	il Loro i Loro la Loro le Loro	eel *lo*·ro ee *lo*·ro la *lo*·ro le *lo*·ro
his/ her(s)/ its	il suo i suoi la sua le sue	eel *soo*·o ee *swo*·ee la *soo*·a le *soo*·e	**their/ theirs**	il loro i loro la loro le loro	eel *lo*·ro ee *lo*·ro la *lo*·ro le *lo*·ro

The four alternatives given in the table above are used with m sg, m pl, f sg and f pl nouns.

Ownership can also be expressed with the verb *avere* a·*ve*·re (see **have**) or the construction '*di* dee (of) + noun/pronoun':

It's Lorenzo's backpack.	È lo zaino di Lorenzo. (lit: it-is the-m-sg backpack of Lorenzo) e lo *dzai*·no dee lo·*ren*·dzo
Whose seat is this?	Di chi è questo posto? (lit: of who is this-m-sg place) dee kee e *kwe*·sto *pos*·to

Prepositions

Giving Instructions • Indicating Location • Pointing Things Out

Like English, Italian uses prepositions to explain where things are in time or space. Common prepositions are listed on the following page; more can be found in the **dictionary**.

When certain prepositions are followed by a definite article, they are contracted into a single word (see **articles**).

~ PREPOSITIONS ~

after	dopo	*do*·po	**in (place)**	in	een
at (time)	a	a	**of**	di	dee
before	prima	*pree*·ma	**to**	a	a
from	da	da	**with**	con	kon

Questions

Asking Questions • Negating

The easiest way of forming 'yes/no' questions in Italian is to add the phrase *è vero* e *ve*·ro (literally 'is-it true') to the end of a statement, similar to 'isn't it?' in English.

This seat is free, isn't it?
Questo posto è libero, è vero?
(lit: this-m-sg seat is free-m-sg is-it true)
kwe·sto *po*·sto e *lee*·be·ro e *ve*·ro

You can also turn a statement into a question by putting the verb before the subject of the sentence, just like in English.

Is this seat free?
È libero questo posto?
(lit: is free-m-sg this-m-sg seat)
e *lee*·be·ro *kwe*·sto *po*·sto

As in English, there are also question words for more specific questions. These words go at the start of the sentence.

~ QUESTION WORDS ~

how	come	*ko*·me	**where**	dove	*do*·ve
what	che cosa	ke *ko*·za	**who**	chi	kee
when	quando	*kwan*·do	**why**	perché	per·*ke*

Verbs

Doing Things

There are three verb categories in Italian – those whose infinitive (dictionary form) ends in *-are, -ere* or *-ire*, eg *parlare* par·*la*·re (talk), *scrivere skree*·ve·re (write), *capire* ka·*pee*·re (understand). Tenses are formed by adding various endings for each person to the verb stem (the part of the verb that remains after removing *-are, -ere* or *-ire* from the infinitive), and for most verbs these endings follow regular patterns according to the verb category. The verb endings for the present, past and future tenses are presented in the following tables.

As in any language, there are also irregular verbs in Italian. The most important ones are *essere, stare* and *avere* (see **be** and **have**). For negative forms of verbs, see **negatives**.

I speak, write and understand Italian.

Parlo, scrivo e capisco italiano. (lit: I-speak, I-write and I-understand Italian)
par·lo *skree*·vo e ka·*pee*·sko ee·ta·*lya*·no

Note that before the endings for the present tense, some verbs ending in *-ire* (eg *capire*) also change their verb stem slightly.

~ PRESENT TENSE ~

		parlare	scrivere	capire
I	io	parlo	scrivo	capisco
you sg inf	tu	parli	scrivi	capisci
you sg pol	Lei	parla	scrive	capisce
he/she	lui/lei	parla	scrive	capisce
we	noi	parliamo	scriviamo	capiamo
you pl inf	voi	parlate	scrivete	capite
you pl pol	Loro	parlano	scrivono	capiscono
they	loro	parlano	scrivono	capiscono

The main past tense in Italian, used for a completed action, is a compound tense, which means it is made up of an auxiliary verb – either *essere* *e*·se·re (be) or *avere* a·*ve*·re (have) – in the present tense, plus a form of the main verb, called 'past participle'. The past participle is formed by replacing the infinitive endings *-are, -ere* or *-ire* with *-ato, -uto* or *-ito* respectively. Some past participles are irregular. See also **be** and **have**.

	~ INFINITIVE ~		~ PAST PARTICIPLE ~	
love	amare	a·*ma*·re	amato	a·*ma*·to
believe	credere	*kre*·de·re	creduto	*kre*·doo·to
follow	seguire	se·*gee*·re	seguito	se·*gee*·to

Past participles taking *essere* agree in gender and number with the subject, while those taking *avere* agree with the object.

I went there.	Sono andato/andata là. m/f (lit: I-am gone-m-sg/-f-sg there) *so*·no an·*da*·to/an·*da*·ta la
I saw her yesterday.	La ho vista ieri. (lit: her I-have seen-f-sg yesterday) la o *vee*·sta *ye*·ree

~ FUTURE TENSE ~

		parlare	scrivere	capire
I	io	parlerò	scriverò	capirò
you sg inf	tu	parlerai	scriverai	capirai
you sg pol	Lei	parlerà	scriverà	capirà
he/she	lui/lei	parlerà	scriverà	capirà
we	noi	parleremo	scriveremo	capiremo
you pl inf	voi	parlerete	scriverete	capirete
you pl pol	Loro	parleranno	scriveranno	capiranno
they	loro	parleranno	scriveranno	capiranno

You can also express future plans by using the present tense with some indication of time referring to the future:

Tomorrow we're going to Rome.	Domani andiamo a Roma. (lit: tomorrow we-go to Rome) do·*ma*·nee an·*dya*·mo a *ro*·ma

Word Order

Making Statements

Italian has a basic word order of subject–verb–object, just like English. However, the subject pronoun (eg 'I' or 'you') is usually omitted in Italian as the subject is understood from the corresponding verb form (see **verbs**) – so the second example below is more common.

We're waiting for the bus.	Noi aspettiamo l'autobus. (lit: we wait the-**m-sg**-bus) noy as·pe·*tya*·mo *low*·to·boos
We're waiting for the bus.	Aspettiamo l'autobus. (lit: we-wait the-**m-sg**-bus) as·pe·*tya*·mo *low*·to·boos

See also **negatives** and **questions**.

UNDERSTANDING 30
NUMBERS & AMOUNTS 32
TIME & DATES 34

Understanding

KEY PHRASES

Do you speak English?	Parla/Parli inglese? **pol/inf**	*par*·la/*par*·lee een·*gle*·ze
I don't understand.	(Non) Capisco.	(non) ka·*pee*·sko
What does ... mean?	Che cosa vuol dire ...?	ke *ko*·za vwol *dee*·re ...

Q **Do you speak English?**	Parla/Parli inglese? **pol/inf** *par*·la/*par*·lee een·*gle*·ze
Q **Does anyone speak English?**	C'è qualcuno che parla inglese? che kwal·*koo*·no ke *par*·la een·*gle*·ze
A **I speak English.**	Parlo inglese. *par*·lo een·*gle*·ze
I need an interpreter who speaks English.	Ho bisogno di un interprete che parla l'inglese. o bee·*so*·nyo dee oon een·*ter*·pre·te ke *par*·la leen·*gle*·ze
Q **Do you understand?**	Capisce/Capisci? **pol/inf** ka·*pee*·she/ka·*pee*·shee
A **I (don't) understand.**	(Non) Capisco. (non) ka·*pee*·sko
I (don't) speak Italian.	(Non) Parlo italiano. (non) *par*·lo ee·ta·*lya*·no
I speak a little.	Parlo un po'. *par*·lo oon po

I'd like to practise Italian.	Vorrei fare pratica con l'italiano. vo·*ray* *fa*·re *pra*·tee·ka kon lee·ta·*lya*·no
I'd like to learn some of your local dialects.	Vorrei imparare qualche dialetto regionale. vo·*ray* eem·pa·*ra*·re *kwal*·ke dee·a·*le*·to re·jo·*na*·le
Would you like me to teach you some English?	Vuole che le insegni un po' d'inglese? *vwo*·le ke le een·*se*·nyee oon po deen·*gle*·ze
What does ... mean?	Che cosa vuol dire ...? ke *ko*·za vwol *dee*·re ...
How do you pronounce this?	Come si pronuncia questo? *ko*·me see pro·*noon*·cha *kwe*·sto
How do you write ...?	Come si scrive ...? *ko*·me see *skree*·ve ...
Could you please repeat that?	Può/Puoi ripeterlo, per favore? **pol/inf** pwo/pwoy ree·*pe*·ter·lo per fa·*vo*·re
Could you please write it down?	Può/Puoi scriverlo, per favore? **pol/inf** pwo/pwoy *skree*·ver·lo per fa·*vo*·re
Could you please speak more slowly?	Può/Puoi parlare più lentamente, per favore? **pol/inf** pwo/pwoy par·*la*·re pyoo len·ta·*men*·te per fa·*vo*·re

Slowly, please!	Più lentamente, per favore!	pyoo len·ta·*men*·te per fa·*vo*·re

BASICS UNDERSTANDING

Numbers & Amounts

KEY PHRASES

How much?	Quanto/a? **m/f**	*kwan*·to/a
some	alcuni/e **m/f**	al·*koo*·nee/al·*koo*·ne
less/more	di meno/più	dee *me*·no/pyoo

Cardinal Numbers

0	zero	*dze*·ro
1	uno	*oo*·no
2	due	*doo*·e
3	tre	tre
4	quattro	*kwa*·tro
5	cinque	*cheen*·kwe
6	sei	say
7	sette	*se*·te
8	otto	*o*·to
9	nove	*no*·ve
10	dieci	*dye*·chee
11	undici	*oon*·dee·chee
12	dodici	*do*·dee·chee
13	tredici	*tre*·dee·chee
14	quattordici	kwa·*tor*·dee·chee
15	quindici	*kween*·dee·chee
16	sedici	*se*·dee·chee
17	diciassette	dee·cha·*se*·te

18	diciotto	dee·*cho*·to
19	diciannove	dee·cha·*no*·ve
20	venti	*ven*·tee
21	ventuno	ven·*too*·no
30	trenta	*tren*·ta
40	quaranta	kwa·*ran*·ta
50	cinquanta	cheen·*kwan*·ta
60	sessanta	se·*san*·ta
70	settanta	se·*tan*·ta
80	ottanta	o·*tan*·ta
90	novanta	no·*van*·ta
100	cento	*chen*·to
200	duecento	doo·e·*chen*·to
1000	mille	*mee*·le
2000	duemila	doo·e·*mee*·la
1,000,000	un milione	oon mee·*lyo*·ne

Ordinal Numbers

1st	primo/a **m/f**	*pree*·mo/a
2nd	secondo/a **m/f**	se·*kon*·do/a
3rd	terzo/a **m/f**	*ter*·tso/a

Useful Amounts

How much?	Quanto/a? **m/f**	*kwan*·to/a
How many?	Quanti/e? **m/f**	*kwan*·tee/*kwan*·te
less	di meno	dee *me*·no
more	di più	dee pyoo
some	alcuni/e **m/f**	al·*koo*·nee/al·*koo*·ne

For more amounts, see **self-catering** (p177).

Time & Dates

KEY PHRASES

What time is it?	Che ora è?	ke o·ra e
At what time?	A che ora...?	a ke o·ra ...
What date?	Che data?	ke *da*·ta

Telling the Time

When telling the time in Italian, 'It is ...' is expressed by *Sono le so*·no le followed by a number. However, 'one o'clock' is *È l'una* e *loo*·na, and 'midday' is *È mezzogiorno* e me·dzo·*jor*·no. Note that in Italy the 24-hour clock is commonly used.

Q **What time is it?**	Che ora è? ke *o*·ra e
A **It's one o'clock.**	È l'una. e *loo*·na
A **It's (two) o'clock.**	Sono le (due). *so*·no le (*doo*·e)
A **Quarter past (one).**	(L'una) e un quarto. (*loo*·na) e oon *kwar*·to
A **Half past (one).**	(L'una) e mezza. (*loo*·na) e *me*·dza
A **Quarter to (eight).**	(Le otto) meno un quarto. (le *o*·to) *me*·no oon *kwar*·to
in the morning	di mattina dee ma·*tee*·na
in the afternoon	di pomeriggio dee po·me·*ree*·jo
in the evening	di sera dee *se*·ra

at night	di notte dee *no*·te
midday	mezzogiorno me·dzo·*jor*·no
midnight	mezzanotte me·dza·*no*·te
Q **At what time ...?**	A che ora ...? a ke *o*·ra ...
A **At one.**	All'una. a·*loo*·na
A **At (7.57pm).**	Alle (19.57). *a*·le (dee·cha·*no*·ve e cheen·kwan·ta·*se*·te)

The Calendar

Monday	lunedì **m**	loo·ne·*dee*
Tuesday	martedì **m**	mar·te·*dee*
Wednesday	mercoledì **m**	mer·ko·le·*dee*
Thursday	giovedì **m**	jo·ve·*dee*
Friday	venerdì **m**	ve·ner·*dee*
Saturday	sabato **m**	*sa*·ba·to
Sunday	domenica **f**	do·*me*·nee·ka
January	gennaio **m**	je·*na*·yo
February	febbraio **m**	fe·*bra*·yo
March	marzo **m**	*mar*·tso
April	aprile **m**	a·*pree*·le
May	maggio **m**	*ma*·jo
June	giugno **m**	*joo*·nyo
July	luglio **m**	*loo*·lyo
August	agosto **m**	a·*gos*·to
September	settembre **m**	se·*tem*·bre

October	ottobre **m**	o·*to*·bre
November	novembre **m**	no·*vem*·bre
December	dicembre **m**	dee·*chem*·bre

summer	estate **f**	es·*ta*·te
autumn	autunno **m**	ow·*too*·no
winter	inverno **m**	een·*ver*·no
spring	primavera **f**	pree·ma·*ve*·ra

What date?	Che data? ke *da*·ta
Q What date is it today?	Che giorno è oggi? ke *jor*·no e o·jee
A It's (3 March).	È (il terzo) marzo. e (eel *ter*·tso *mar*·tso)

Present

now	adesso a·*de*·so
this morning	stamattina sta·ma·*tee*·na
this afternoon	oggi pomeriggio *o*·jee po·me·*ree*·jo
today	oggi *o*·jee
tonight	stasera sta·*se*·ra
this month	questo mese *kwe*·sto *me*·ze
this week	questa settimana *kwe*·sta se·tee·*ma*·na
this year	quest'anno kwe·*sta*·no

Past

day before yesterday	l'altro ieri *lal*·tro *ye*·ree
yesterday	ieri *ye*·ree
yesterday morning	ieri mattina *ye*·ree ma·*tee*·na
yesterday afternoon	ieri pomeriggio *ye*·ree po·me·*ree*·jo
yesterday evening	ieri sera *ye*·ree *se*·ra
last night	ieri notte *ye*·ree *no*·te
last week	la settimana scorsa la se·tee·*ma*·na *skor*·sa
last month	il mese scorso eel *me*·ze *skor*·so
last year	l'anno scorso *la*·no *skor*·so
(three days) ago	(tre giorni) fa (tre *jor*·nee) fa
since (May)	da (maggio) da (*ma*·jo)

Future

day after tomorrow	dopodomani do·po·do·*ma*·nee
tomorrow	domani do·*ma*·nee
tomorrow morning	domani mattina do·*ma*·nee ma·*tee*·na

LISTEN FOR

You'll often hear the centuries referred to as follows, particularly when talking about periods in history and art:

Il Duecento	eel doo·e·*chen*·to	13th century (lit: the 200)
Il Trecento	eel tre·*chen*·to	14th century (lit: the 300)
Il Quattrocento	eel kwa·tro·*chen*·to	15th century (lit: the 400)
Il Cinquecento	eel cheen·kwe·*chen*·to	16th century (lit: the 500)

tomorrow afternoon	domani pomeriggio do·*ma*·nee po·me·*ree*·jo
tomorrow evening	domani sera do·*ma*·nee *se*·ra
next week	la settimana prossima la se·tee·*ma*·na *pro*·see·ma
next month	il mese prossimo eel *me*·ze *pro*·see·mo
next year	l'anno prossimo *la*·no *pro*·see·mo
in (six days)	fra (sei giorni) fra (say *jor*·nee)
until (June)	fino a (giugno) *fee*·no a (*joo*·nyo)

Practical

TRANSPORT	40
BORDER CROSSING	53
DIRECTIONS	55
ACCOMMODATION	58
SHOPPING	70
COMMUNICATIONS	80
MONEY & BANKING	87
BUSINESS	91
SIGHTSEEING	93
SENIOR & DISABLED TRAVELLERS	99
TRAVEL WITH CHILDREN	101

Transport

KEY PHRASES

When's the next bus?	A che ora passa il prossimo autobus?	a ke *o*·ra *pa*·sa eel *pro*·see·mo *ow*·to·boos
One ticket to ..., please.	Un biglietto per ..., per favore.	oon bee·*lye*·to per ..., per fa·*vo*·re
Can you tell me when we get to ...?	Mi sa dire quando arriviamo a ...?	mee sa *dee*·re *kwan*·do a·ree·*vya*·mo a ...
Please take me to (this address).	Mi porti a (questo indirizzo), per piacere.	mee *por*·tee a (*kwe*·sto een·dee·*ree*·tso) per pya·*che*·re

Getting Around

At what time does the ... leave/arrive?	A che ora parte/arriva ...? a ke *o*·ra *par*·te/a·*ree*·va ...

boat	la nave	la *na*·ve
bus	l'autobus	*low*·to·boos
ferry	il traghetto	eel tra·*ge*·to
hydrofoil	l'aliscafo	la·lees·*ka*·fo
metro	la metropolitana	la me·tro·po·lee·*ta*·na
plane	l'aereo	la·e·re·o
train	il treno	eel *tre*·no

Can we get there by public transport?	Possiamo arrivarci con i mezzi pubblici? po·*sya*·mo a·ree·*var*·chee kon ee *me*·dzee *poo*·blee·chee
At what time's the first bus?	A che ora passa il primo autobus? a ke *o*·ra *pa*·sa eel *pree*·mo *ow*·to·boos
At what time's the last bus?	A che ora passa l'ultimo autobus? a ke *o*·ra *pa*·sa *lool*·tee·mo *ow*·to·boos
At what time's the next bus?	A che ora passa il prossimo autobus? a ke *o*·ra *pa*·sa eel *pro*·see·mo *ow*·to·boos
That's my seat.	Quel posto è mio. kwel *pos*·to e *mee*·o
Is this seat free?	È libero questo posto? e *lee*·be·ro *kwe*·sto *pos*·to

Is it free?	È libero?	e *lee*·be·ro

For phrases on disabled access, see **senior & disabled travellers** (p99).

Buying Tickets

Where can I buy a ticket?	Dove posso comprare un biglietto? *do*·ve *po*·so kom·*pra*·re oon bee·*lye*·to
Do I need to book?	Bisogna prenotare (un posto)? bee·*zo*·nya pre·no·*ta*·re (oon *pos*·to)

LISTEN FOR

Deve cambiare a (Parma).	*de*·ve kam·*bya*·re a (*par*·ma)	You'll have to change at (Parma).
Il treno è cancellato.	eel *tre*·no e kan·che·*la*·to	The train is cancelled.
La prossima fermata è ...	la *pro*·see·ma fer·*ma*·ta e ...	The next stop is ...
Questa fermata è ...	*kwe*·sta fer·*ma*·ta e ...	We're arriving at ...

Can I get a stand-by ticket?	Posso essere messo/a in lista d'attesa? **m/f** *po*·so *e*·se·re *me*·so/a een *lee*·sta da·*te*·sa
What time do I have to check in?	A che ora devo presentarmi per l'accettazione? a ke *o*·ra *de*·vo pre·zen·*tar*·mee per la·che·ta·*tsyo*·ne
I'd like a sleeping berth.	Vorrei una cuccetta, per favore. vo·*ray oo*·na koo·*che*·ta per fa·*vo*·re
I'd like to ... my ticket, please.	Vorrei ... il mio biglietto, per favore. vo·*ray* ... eel *mee*·o bee·*lye*·to per fa·*vo*·re

cancel	cancellare	kan·che·*la*·re
change	cambiare	kam·*bya*·re
collect	ritirare	ree·tee·*ra*·re
confirm	confermare	kon·fer·*ma*·re

Buying a Ticket

When does the ... leave?

A che ora parte il/la prossimo/a ...? **m/f**
a ke o·ra par·te eel/la pro·see·mo/a ...

boat
nave **f**
na·ve

bus
autobus **m**
ow·to·boos

train
treno **m**
tre·no

One ... ticket, please.

Un biglietto di..., per favore.
oon bee·lye·to dee... per fa·vo·re

one-way
sola andata
so·la an·da·ta

return
andata e ritorno
an·da·ta e ree·tor·no

I'd like a/an ... seat.

Vorrei un posto ...
vo·ray oon pos·to ...

aisle
sul corridoio
sool ko·ree·do·yo

window
vicino al finestrino
vee·chee·no al fee·nes·tree·no

Which platform does it depart from?

Da quale binario parte?
da kwa·le bee·na·ryo par·te

One ... ticket (to Rome), please.	Un biglietto ... (per Roma), per favore.	oon bee·*lye*·to ... (per *ro*·ma) per fa·*vo*·re

1st-class	di prima classe	dee *pree*·ma *kla*·se
2nd-class	di seconda classe	dee se·*kon*·da *kla*·se
child's	per bambini	per bam·*bee*·nee
one-way	di sola andata	dee *so*·la an·*da*·ta
return	di andata e ritorno	dee an·*da*·ta e ree·*tor*·no
student's	per studenti	per stoo·*den*·tee

I'd like an aisle seat, please.	Vorrei un posto sul corridoio, per favore.	vo·*ray* oon *pos*·to sool ko·ree·*do*·yo per fa·*vo*·re
I'd like a window seat, please.	Vorrei un posto vicino al finestrino, per favore.	vo·*ray* oon *pos*·to vee·*chee*·no al fee·nes·*tree*·no per fa·*vo*·re

For phrases about getting through customs and immigration, see **border crossing** (p53).

Si fermi qui, per favore.

see *fer*·mee kwee per fa·*vo*·re

Please stop here.

Luggage

My luggage hasn't arrived.	Non è arrivato il mio bagaglio. non e a·ree·*va*·to eel *mee*·o ba·*ga*·lyo
My luggage has been damaged.	Il mio bagaglio è stato danneggiato. eel *mee*·o ba·*ga*·lyo e *sta*·to da·ne·*ja*·to
My luggage has been stolen.	Il mio bagaglio è stato rubato. eel *mee*·o ba·*ga*·lyo e *sta*·to roo·*ba*·to
I'd like a luggage locker.	Vorrei un armadietto per il bagaglio. vo·*ray* oon ar·ma·*dye*·to per eel ba·*ga*·lyo

Bus, Tram & Metro

Which bus goes to (Rome)?	Quale autobus va a (Roma)? *kwa*·le *ow*·to·boos va a (*ro*·ma)
Where's the bus stop?	Dov'è la fermata dell'autobus? do·*ve* la fer·*ma*·ta del *ow*·to·boos
What's the next stop?	Qual'è la prossima fermata? kwa·*le* la *pro*·see·ma fer·*ma*·ta
I want to get off here/at ...	Voglio scendere qui/a ... *vo*·lyo *shen*·de·re kwee/a ...

Fermata del Tram	fer·*ma*·ta del tram	Tram Stop
Fermata dell'autobus	fer·*ma*·ta de·*low*·to·boos	Bus Stop
Stazione della Metropolitana	sta·*tsyo*·ne *de*·la me·tro·po·lee·*ta*·na	Metro Station
Uscita	oo·*shee*·ta	Way Out

How many stops to (the museum)?	Quante fermate mancano (al museo)? *kwan*·te fer·*ma*·te *man*·ka·no (al moo·*ze*·o)
Can you tell me when we get to (the market)?	Mi sa dire quando arriviamo (al mercato)? mee sa *dee*·re *kwan*·do a·ree·*vya*·mo (al mer·*ka*·to)

For bus numbers, see **numbers & amounts** (p32).

Train

What station is this?	Che stazione è questa? ke sta·*tsyo*·ne e *kwe*·sta
What's the next station?	Qual'è la prossima stazione? kwa·*le* la *pro*·see·ma sta·*tsyo*·ne
Does this train stop at (Milan)?	Questo treno si ferma a (Milano)? *kwe*·sto *tre*·no see *fer*·ma a (mee·*la*·no)

Is it a direct route?	È un itinerario diretto? e oon ee·tee·ne·*ra*·ryo dee·*re*·to
How long does the trip take?	Quanto ci vuole? *kwan*·to chee *vwo*·le
Where's the dining car?	Dov'è il vagone ristorante? do·*ve* eel va·*go*·ne rees·to·*ran*·te
Which carriage is 1st class?	Quale carrozza è di prima classe? *kwa*·le ka·*ro*·tsa e dee *pree*·ma *kla*·se
Which carriage is for (Rome)?	Quale carrozza è per (Roma)? *kwa*·le ka·*ro*·tsa e per (*ro*·ma)
Do I need to change trains?	Devo cambiare treno? *de*·vo kam·*bya*·re *tre*·no

LISTEN FOR

diretto	dee·*re*·to	direct – no need to change trains
espresso	es·*pre*·so	express – stops only at major stations
Eurostar Italia (ES)	e·oo·ro·*star* ee·*ta*·lya	very fast
Inter City	*een*·ter *see*·tee	runs between large cities
locale	lo·*ka*·le	local – usually stops at all stations
rapido	*ra*·pee·do	fast – runs between large cities

LOOK FOR

Borgo (B.go)	*bor*·go	district
Corso (C.so)	*kor*·so	main street/avenue
Largo (L.go)	*lar*·go	little square
Piazza (P.za)	*pya*·tsa	square
Strada (Str.)	*stra*·da	street
Via (V.)	*vee*·a	road/street
Viale (V.le)	vee·*a*·le	avenue/boulevard
Vicolo (V.lo)	*vee*·ko·lo	alley/lane

Taxi

I'd like a taxi at (9am).	Vorrei un tassì alle (nove di mattina). vo·*ray* oon ta·*see* *a*·le (*no*·ve dee ma·*tee*·na)
Is this taxi free?	È libero questo tassì? e *lee*·be·ro *kwe*·sto ta·*see*

Is it free?	È libero?	e *lee*·be·ro

How much is it to ...?	Quant'è per ...? kwan·*te* per ...
Please put the meter on.	Usi il tassametro, per favore. *oo*·zee eel ta·*sa*·me·tro per fa·*vo*·re
Please take me to (this address).	Mi porti a (questo indirizzo), per piacere. mee *por*·tee a (*kwe*·sto een·dee·*ree*·tso) per pya·*che*·re

To ...	A ...	a ...

Please slow down.	Rallenti, per favore. ra·*len*·tee per fa·*vo*·re
Please stop here.	Si fermi qui, per favore. see *fer*·mee kwee per fa·*vo*·re
Please wait here.	Mi aspetti qui, per favore. mee as·*pe*·tee kwee per fa·*vo*·re

Car & Motorbike

I'd like to hire a/an ...	Vorrei noleggiare ... vo·*ray* no·le·*ja*·re ...

4WD	un fuoristrada	oon fwo·ree·*stra*·da
automatic (car)	una macchina automatica	*oo*·na *ma*·kee·na ow·to·*ma*·tee·ka
car	una macchina	*oo*·na *ma*·kee·na
manual (car)	una macchina manuale	*oo*·na *ma*·kee·na ma·noo·*a*·le
motorbike	una moto	*oo*·na *mo*·to

How much is it daily?	Quanto costa al giorno? *kwan*·to *kos*·ta al *jor*·no
How much is it weekly?	Quanto costa alla settimana? *kwan*·to *kos*·ta *a*·la se·tee·*ma*·na
Does that include insurance?	E' compresa l'assicurazione? e kom·*pre*·sa la·see·koo·ra·*tsyo*·ne
Does that include mileage?	E' compreso il chilometraggio? e kom·*pre*·so eel kee·lo·me·*tra*·jo

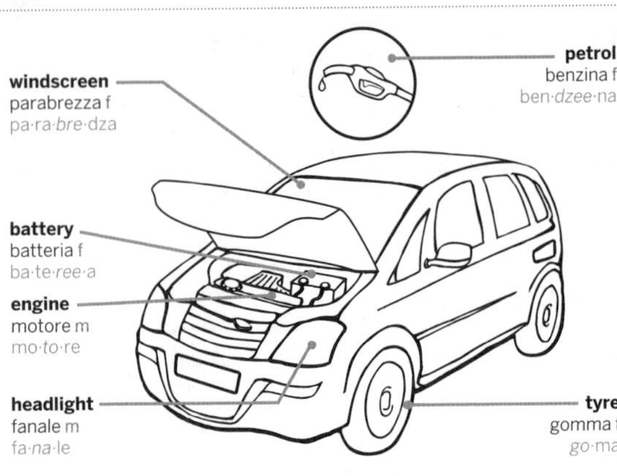

What's the city/country speed limit?	Qual'è il limite di velocità in città/campagna? kwa·*le* eel *lee*·mee·te dee ve·lo·chee·*ta* een chee·*ta*/kam·*pa*·nya
Is this the road to (Venice)?	Questa strada porta a (Venezia)? *kwe*·sta *stra*·da *por*·ta a (ve·*ne*·tsya)
Where's a service station?	Dov'è una stazione di servizio? do·*ve oo*·na sta·*tsyo*·ne dee ser·*vee*·tsyo
(How long) Can I park here?	(Per quanto tempo) Posso parcheggiare qui? (per *kwan*·to *tem*·po) *po*·so par·ke·*ja*·re kwee
I need a mechanic.	Ho bisogno di un meccanico. o bee·*zo*·nyo dee oon me·*ka*·nee·ko

LOOK FOR

benzina f **con/ senza piombo**	ben·*dzee*·na kon/ *sen*·tsa *pyom*·bo	leaded/unleaded petrol
gasauto m	ga·*zow*·to	LPG
gasolio/diesel m	ga·*zo*·lyo/*dee*·zel	diesel

I had an accident.	Ho avuto un incidente. o a·*voo*·to oon een·chee·*den*·te
The car/motorbike has broken down.	La macchina/moto si è guastata. la *ma*·kee·na/*mo*·to see e gwas·*ta*·ta

Bicycle

Can we get there by bike?	Possiamo arrivarci in bicicletta? po·*sya*·mo a·ree·*var*·chee een bee·chee·*kle*·ta
Where can I hire a bicycle?	Dove posso noleggiare una bicicletta? *do*·ve *po*·so no·le·*ja*·re *oo*·na bee·chee·*kle*·ta
How much per day?	Quanto costa al giorno? *kwan*·to *kos*·ta al *jor*·no
How much per hour?	Quanto costa all'ora? *kwan*·to *kos*·ta a·*lo*·ra
I'd like to have my bicycle repaired.	Vorrei fare riparare la mia bicicletta. vo·*ray fa*·re ree·pa·*ra*·re la *mee*·a bee·chee·*kle*·ta
I have a puncture.	Ho una gomma bucata. o *oo*·na *go*·ma boo·*ka*·ta

LOOK FOR

Alt	alt	Stop
Attenzione	a·ten·*tsyo*·ne	Caution
Autostrada	ow·to·*stra*·da	Freeway
Dare la Precedenza	*da*·re la pre·che·*den*·tsa	Give Way
Deviazione	de·vya·*tsyo*·ne	Detour
Divieto di Accesso	dee·*vye*·to dee a·*che*·so	No Entry
Divieto di Sorpasso	dee·*vye*·to dee sor·*pa*·so	No Overtaking
Divieto di Sosta	dee·*vye*·to dee *sos*·ta	No Parking
Entrata	en·*tra*·ta	Entrance
Lavori in Corso	la·*vo*·ree een *kor*·so	Roadworks
Parcheggio	par·*ke*·jo	Parking
Passo Carrabile	*pa*·so ka·*ra*·bee·le	Keep Clear
Pedaggio	pe·*da*·jo	Toll
Pericolo	pe·*ree*·ko·lo	Danger
Rallentare	ra·len·*ta*·re	Slow Down
Rimozione Forzata	ree·mo·*tsyo*·ne for·*tsa*·ta	Tow-Away Zone
Senso Unico	*sen*·so *oo*·nee·ko	One Way
Uscita	oo·*shee*·ta	Exit

Are there cycling paths?
Ci sono piste ciclabili?
chee *so*·no *pee*·ste chee·*kla*·bee·lee

Can I take my bike on the train?
Posso portare la bicicletta in treno?
po·so por·*ta*·re la bee·chee·*kle*·ta een *tre*·no

Border Crossing

KEY PHRASES

I'm here for ... days.	Sono qui per ... giorni.	so·no kwee per ... *jor*·nee
I'm staying at ...	Alloggio a ...	a·*lo*·jo a ...
I have nothing to declare.	Non ho niente da dichiarare.	non o *nyen*·te da dee·kya·*ra*·re

Passport Control

I'm here ... Sono qui ...
so·no kwee ...

in transit	in transito	een *tran*·see·to
on business	per affari	per a·*fa*·ree
on holiday	in vacanza	een va·*kan*·tsa
to study	per motivi di studio	per mo·*tee*·vee dee *stoo*·dyo
to visit relatives	per visitare parenti	per vee·zee·*ta*·re pa·*ren*·tee

I'm here for (six) days. Sono qui per (sei) giorni.
so·no kwee per (say) *jor*·nee

I'm here for (three) weeks. Sono qui per (tre) settimane.
so·no kwee per (tre) se·tee·*ma*·ne

I'm here for (two) months. Sono qui per (due) mesi.
so·no kwee per (*doo*·e) *me*·zee

LISTEN FOR

Il Suo visto, per favore.	eel *soo*·o *vees*·to per fa·*vo*·re	Your visa, please.
Viaggia da solo/a? m/f	vee·*a*·ja da *so*·lo/a	Are you travelling on your own?

I have a residency/work permit.	Ho un permesso di soggiorno/lavoro. o oon per·*me*·so dee so·*jor*·no/la·*vo*·ro
I'm going to (Perugia).	Vado a (Perugia). *va*·do a (pe·*roo*·ja)
I'm staying at the ...	Alloggio al ... a·*lo*·jo al ...

At Customs

I have nothing to declare.	Non ho niente da dichiarare. non o *nyen*·te da dee·kya·*ra*·re
I have something to declare.	Ho delle cose da dichiarare. o *de*·le *ko*·ze da dee·kya·*ra*·re
Do you have this form in English?	Avete questo modulo in inglese? a·*ve*·te *kwe*·sto *mo*·doo·lo een een·*gle*·ze

LOOK FOR

Controllo Passaporti	kon·*tro*·lo pa·sa·*por*·tee	Passport Control
Dogana	do·*ga*·na	Customs
Immigrazione	ee·mee·gra·*tsyo*·ne	Immigration

Directions

KEY PHRASES

Where's ...?	Dov'è ...?	do·*ve* ...
What's the address?	Qual'è l'indirizzo?	kwa·*le* leen·dee·*ree*·tso
How far is it?	Quant'è distante?	kwan·*te* dees·*tan*·te

I'm looking for (the public toilets).	Cerco (i servizi igienici). *cher*·ko (ee ser·*vee*·tsee ee·*je*·nee·chee)
Q **Which way's (the post office)?**	Dove si trova (l'ufficcio postale)? *do*·ve see *tro*·va (loo·*fee*·cho pos·*ta*·le)
Q **Where's (the bank)?**	Dov'è (la banca)? do·*ve* (la *ban*·ka)
A **It's ...**	È ... e ...
How do I get there?	Come ci si arriva? *ko*·me chee see a·*ree*·va
How far is it?	Quant'è distante? kwan·*te* dees·*tan*·te
Can you show me (on the map)?	Può mostrarmi (sulla pianta)? pwo mos·*trar*·mee (*soo*·la *pyan*·ta)
What's the address?	Qual'è l'indirizzo? kwa·*le* leen·dee·*ree*·tso

Turn at the corner.	Giri all'angolo. *jee*·ree a·*lan*·go·lo
Turn at the traffic lights.	Giri al semaforo. *jee*·ree al se·*ma*·fo·ro
Turn left.	Giri a sinistra. *jee*·ree a see·*nee*·stra
Turn right.	Giri a destra. *jee*·ree a *de*·stra
It's (100) metres.	È a (cento) metri. e a (*chen*·to) *me*·tree
It's (30) minutes.	È a (trenta) minuti. e a (*tren*·ta) mee·*noo*·tee

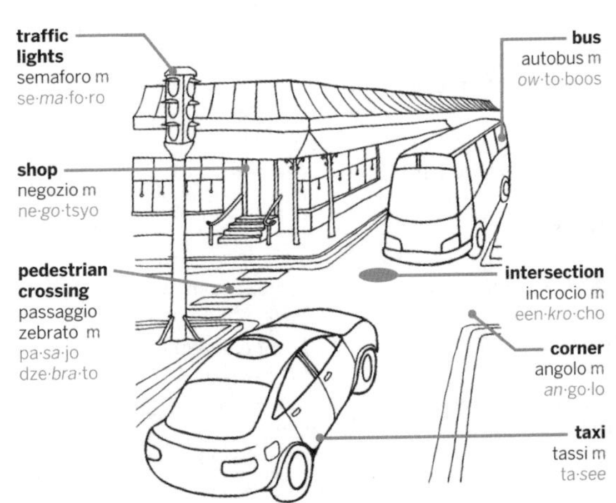

LISTEN FOR

a destra	a *de*·stra	right
a sinistra	a see·*nee*·stra	left
accanto a ...	a·*kan*·to a ...	next to ...
all'angolo	a·*lan*·go·lo	on the corner
davanti a ...	da·*van*·tee a ...	in front of ...
di fronte a ...	dee *fron*·te a ...	opposite ...
dietro ...	*dye*·tro ...	behind ...
là	la	there
lontano	lon·*ta*·no	far away
qui	kwee	here
sempre diritto	*sem*·pre dee·*ree*·to	straight ahead
vicino (a ...)	vee·*chee*·no (a ...)	near (to ...)

by bus	con l'autobus kon *low*·to·boos
by taxi	con il tassì ko·*neel* ta·*see*
by train	con il treno ko·*neel* *tre*·no
on foot	a piedi a *pye*·dee

Accommodation

KEY PHRASES

Where's a hotel?	Dov'è un albergo?	do·*ve* oo·nal·*ber*·go
Do you have a room?	Avete una camera?	a·*ve*·te *oo*·na *ka*·me·ra
How much is it per night?	Quanto costa per una notte?	*kwan*·to *kos*·ta per *oo*·na *no*·te
Is breakfast included?	La colazione è compresa?	la ko·la·*tsyo*·ne e kom·*pre*·sa
What time is checkout?	A che ora si deve lasciar libera la camera?	a ke o·*ra* see *de*·ve la·*shar lee*·be·ra la *ka*·me·ra

Finding Accommodation

Can you recommend a place?
Può consigliare qualche posto?
pwo kon·see·*lya*·re *kwal*·ke *pos*·to

Where's a/an ...?
Dov'è ...?
do·*ve* ...

campsite	un campeggio	oon kam·*pe*·jo
guesthouse	una pensione	*oo*·na pen·*syo*·ne
hotel	un albergo	oo·nal·*ber*·go
inn	una locanda	*oo*·na lo·*kan*·da
youth hostel	un ostello della gioventù	oo·nos·*te*·lo *de*·la jo·ven·*too*

For phrases on how to get there, see **directions** (p55).

Booking Ahead & Checking In

I'd like to book a room, please.	Vorrei prenotare una camera, per favore. vo·*ray* pre·no·*ta*·re *oo*·na *ka*·me·ra per fa·*vo*·re

Are there rooms?	Avete camere libere?	a·*ve*·te *ka*·me·ray *lee*·be·ray

Do you have a single room?	Avete una camera singola? a·*ve*·te *oo*·na *ka*·me·ra *seen*·go·la
Do you have a twin room?	Avete una camera doppia a due letti? a·*ve*·te *oo*·na *ka*·me·ra *do*·pya a *doo*·e *le*·tee
How much is it per night/ week?	Quanto costa per una notte/settimana? *kwan*·to *kos*·ta per *oo*·na *no*·te/se·tee·*ma*·na
How much is it per person?	Quanto costa per persona? *kwan*·to *kos*·ta per per·*so*·na
I have a reservation.	Ho una prenotazione. o *oo*·na pre·no·ta·*tsyo*·ne
Is breakfast included?	La colazione è compresa? la ko·la·*tsyo*·ne e kom·*pre*·sa
Is there parking?	C'è il parcheggio? chay eel par·*ke*·jo
Is there wireless internet access here?	Qui c'è il collegamento Wi-Fi? kwee chay eel ko·le·ga·*men*·to wai·fai

LISTEN FOR

Ha una prenotazione?	a *oo*·na pre·no·ta·*tsyo*·ne	Do you have a reservation?
Mi dispiace, è completo.	mee dees·*pya*·che e kom·*ple*·to	I'm sorry, we're full.
Per quante notti?	per *kwan*·te *no*·tee	For how many nights?

For (three) nights/weeks.	Per (tre) notti/settimane. per (tre) *no*·tee/se·tee·*ma*·ne
From (July 2) to (July 6).	Dal (due luglio) al (sei luglio). dal (*doo*·e *loo*·lyo) al (say *loo*·lyo)
Can I see it?	Posso vederla? *po*·so ve·*der*·la
It's fine. I'll take it.	Va bene. La prendo. va *be*·ne la *pren*·do

For methods of payment, see **money & banking** (p87).

Requests & Queries

When's breakfast served?	A che ora è la prima colazione? a ke *o*·ra e la *pree*·ma ko·la·*tsyo*·ne
Where's breakfast served?	Dove si prende la prima colazione? *do*·ve see *pren*·de la *pree*·ma ko·la·*tsyo*·ne
Please wake me at (seven).	Mi svegli (alle sette), per favore. mee *sve*·lyee (*a*·le *se*·te) per fa·*vo*·re

Booking a Room

Do you have a ... room?

Avete una camera ...?
a·ve·te oo·na ka·me·ra ...

double
doppia
do·pya

single
singola
seen·go·la

How much is it per ...?

Quanto costa per ...?
kwan·to kos·ta per ...

night
una notte
oo·na no·te

person
persona
per·so·na

Is breakfast included?

La colazione è compresa?
la ko·la·tsyo·ne e kom·pre·sa

Can I see the room?

Posso vederla?
po·so ve·der·la

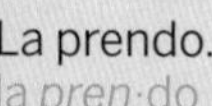

I'll take it.

La prendo.
la pren·do

I won't take it.

Non la prendo.
non la pren·do

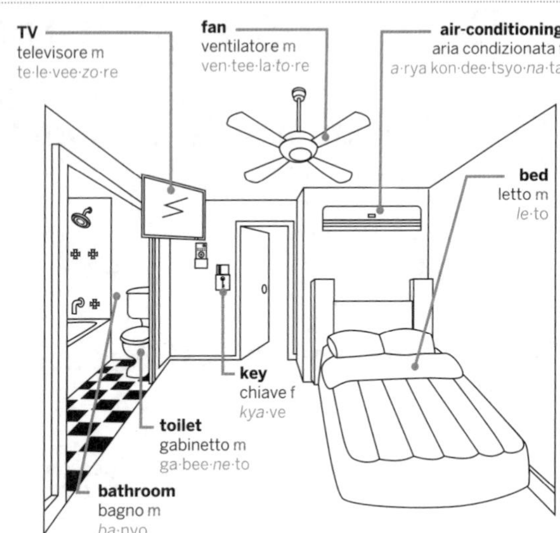

Can I get another ...?	Può darmi un altro/a ... **m/f** pwo *dar*·mee oon·*al*·tro/a ...
Can I use the ...?	Posso usare ...? *po*·so oo·*za*·re ...

internet	l'Internet	*leen*·ter·net
kitchen	la cucina	la koo·*chee*·na
laundry	la lavanderia	la la·van·de·*ree*·a
telephone	il telefono	eel te·*le*·fo·no

Do you have an elevator?	C'è un ascensore? che oo·na·shen·*so*·re

Do you have a laundry service?	C'è il servizio lavanderia? che eel ser·*vee*·tsyo la·van·de·*ree*·a
Do you have a safe?	C'è una cassaforte? che *oo*·na ka·sa·*for*·te
Do you arrange tours here?	Si organizzano le gite qui? see or·ga·*nee*·dza·no le *jee*·te kwee
Do you change money here?	Si cambiano i soldi qui? see *kam*·bya·no ee *sol*·dee kwee
Can I leave a message for someone?	Posso lasciare un messaggio per qualcuno? *po*·so la·*sha*·re oon me·*sa*·jo per kwal·*koo*·no
Is there a message for me?	C'è un messaggio per me? che oon me·*sa*·jo per me

Ho una prenotazione
o oo·na pre·no·ta·*tsyo*·ne
I have a reservation

I'm locked out of my room.

Mi sono chiuso/a fuori dalla mia camera. **m/f**
mee so·no kyoo·zo/a fwo·ree da·la mee·a ka·me·ra

The (bathroom) door is locked.

La porta (del bagno) è chiusa a chiave.
la por·ta (del ba·nyo) e kyoo·za a kya·ve

Complaints

The room is too ...

La camera è troppo ...
la ka·me·ra e tro·po ...

cold	fredda	*fre·da*
dark	scura	*skoo·ra*
light/bright	luminosa	*loo·mee·no·za*
small	piccola	*pee·ko·la*

This ... isn't clean.

Questo/a ... non è pulito/a. **m/f**
kwe·sto/a ... no·ne poo·lee·to/a

There's no hot water.

Non c'è acqua calda.
non chay ak·wa kal·da

The ... doesn't work.

... non funziona.
... non foon·tsyo·na

air-con	L'aria condizionata	*la·rya kon·dee·tsyo·na·ta*
fan	Il ventilatore	*eel ven·tee·la·to·re*
heater	La stufa	*la stoo·fa*
toilet	Il gabinetto	*eel ga·bee·ne·to*

For more things you might have in your room, see the **dictionary**.

Answering the Door

Who is it?	Chi è? kee e
Just a moment.	Un momento. oon mo·*men*·to
Come in.	Avanti. a·*van*·tee
Come back later, please.	Torni più tardi, per favore. *tor*·nee pyoo *tar*·dee per fa·*vo*·re

Checking Out

What time is checkout?	A che ora si deve lasciar libera la camera? a ke o·*ra* see *de*·ve la·*shar lee*·be·ra la *ka*·me·ra
Can I have a late checkout?	Posso liberare la camera più tardi? *po*·so lee·be·*ra*·re la *ka*·me·ra pyoo *tar*·dee
Can I leave my luggage here?	Posso lasciare il mio bagaglio qui? *po*·so la·*sha*·re eel *mee*·o ba·*ga*·lyo kwee
Can you call a taxi for me (for 11 o'clock)?	Può chiamarmi un tassì (per le undici)? pwo kya·*mar*·mee oon ta·*see* (per le *oon*·dee·chee)
Could I have my deposit, please?	Posso avere la caparra, per favore? *po*·so a·*ve*·re la ka·*pa*·ra per fa·*vo*·re

LISTEN FOR

La chiave è alla reception.	la *kya*·ve e *a*·la ray·sep·*shon*	The key is at reception.
Qual'è il Suo numero di camera?	kwa·*le* eel *soo*·o *noo*·me·ro dee *ka*·me·ra	What's your room number?
Ha usato il frigobar?	a oo·*za*·to eel *free*·go·bar	Did you use the mini-bar?

Could I have my passport, please?	Posso avere il mio passaporto, per favore? *po*·so a·*ve*·re eel *mee*·o pa·sa·*por*·to per fa·*vo*·re
Could I have my valuables, please?	Posso avere i miei oggetti di valore, per favore? *po*·so a·*ve*·re ee myay o·*je*·tee dee va·*lo*·re per fa·*vo*·re
I'll be back on (Tuesday).	Torno (martedì). *tor*·no (mar·te·*dee*)
I had a great stay, thank you.	Sono stato/a benissimo/a, grazie. **m/f** *so*·no *sta*·to/a be·*nee*·see·mo/a *gra*·tsye

Camping

Can I camp here?	Si può campeggiare qui? see pwo kam·pe·*ja*·re kwee
Where's the nearest campsite?	Dov'è il campeggio più vicino? do·*ve* eel kam·*pe*·jo pyoo vee·*chee*·no

Where's the nearest shop?	Dov'è il negozio più vicino? do·*ve* eel ne·*go*·tsyo pyoo vee·*chee*·no
Where's the nearest shower facility?	Dov'è il servizio doccia più vicino? do·*ve* eel ser·*vee*·tsyo *do*·cha pyoo vee·*chee*·no
Where's the nearest toilet block?	Dove sono i servizi igienici più vicini? *do*·ve *so*·no ee ser·*vee*·tsee ee·*je*·nee·chee pyoo vee·*chee*·nee
Is the water drinkable?	L'acqua è potabile? *la*·kwa e po·*ta*·bee·le
Do you have ...?	Avete ...? a·*ve*·te ...

a site	un sito	oon *see*·to
electricity	la corrente	la ko·*ren*·te
shower facilities	servizio doccia	ser·*vee*·tsyo *do*·cha
tents for hire	tende da noleggiare	*ten*·de da no·le·*ja*·re

How much is it per ...?	Quant'è per ...? kwan·*te* per ...

caravan	roulotte	roo·*lot*
person	persona	per·*so*·na
tent	tenda	*ten*·da
vehicle	veicolo	ve·*ee*·ko·lo

Renting

I'm here about the ... for rent.	Sono qui per il/la ... che date in affitto. m/f *so*·no kwee per eel/la ... ke *da*·te ee·na·*fee*·to
Do you have a/an ... for rent?	Avete ... d'affittare? a·*ve*·te ... da·fee·*ta*·re

apartment	un appartamento	oo·na·par·ta·*men*·to
cabin	una cabina	*oo*·na ka·*bee*·na
house	una casa	*oo*·na *ka*·za
room	una camera	*oo*·na *ka*·me·ra
villa	una villa	*oo*·na *vee*·la

(partly) furnished	(in parte) ammobiliato/a m/f (een *par*·te) a·mo·bee·*lya*·to/a
unfurnished	non ammobiliato/a m/f no·na·mo·bee·*lya*·to/a
How much is it for (one) week?	Quant'è per (una) settimana? kwan·*te* per (*oo*·na) se·tee·*ma*·na
How much is it for (two) months?	Quant'è per (due) mesi? kwan·*te* per (*doo*·e) *me*·zee
Are bills extra?	Sono extra le bollette? *so*·no *ek*·stra le bo·*le*·te

Staying with Locals

Can I stay at your place?	Posso stare da Lei/te? pol/inf *po*·so *sta*·re da lay/te

Thanks for your hospitality.	Grazie per la Sua/tua ospitalità. **pol/inf** *gra*·tsye per la *soo*·a/*too*·a os·pee·ta·lee·*ta*
Is there anything I can do to help?	Posso aiutare in qualche modo? *po*·so a·yoo·*ta*·re een *kwal*·ke *mo*·do
I have my own mattress.	Ho il mio proprio materasso. o eel *mee*·o *pro*·pryo ma·te·*ra*·so
I have my own sleeping bag.	Ho il mio proprio sacco a pelo. o eel *mee*·o *pro*·pryo *sa*·ko a *pe*·lo
Can I ...?	Posso ...? *po*·so ...

bring anything for the meal	portare qualcosa per il pasto	por·*ta*·re kwal·*ko*·za per eel *pas*·to
do the dishes	lavare i piatti	la·*va*·re ee *pya*·tee
set/clear the table	apparecchiare/ sparecchiare	a·pa·re·*kya*·re/ spa·re·*kya*·re
take out the rubbish	gettare la spazzatura	je·*ta*·re la spa·tsa·*too*·ra

For compliments to the chef, see **eating out** (p168).

Shopping

KEY PHRASES

I'd like to buy ...	Vorrei comprare ...	vo·*ray* kom·*pra*·re ...
Can I look at it?	Posso dare un'occhiata?	*po*·so *da*·re oo·no·*kya*·ta
Can I try it on?	Potrei provarmelo/a? **m/f**	po·*tray* pro·*var*·me·lo/a
How much is it?	Quanto costa?	*kwan*·to *kos*·ta
That's too expensive.	È troppo caro/a. **m/f**	e *tro*·po *ka*·ro/a

Looking For ...

Where's (a travel agency)?	Dov'è (un'agenzia di viaggi)? do·*ve* (oo·na·jen·*tsee*·a dee vee·*a*·jee)
Where can I buy (bread)?	Dove posso comprare (pane)? *do*·ve *po*·so kom·*pra*·re (*pa*·ne)

For more on shops and services, see the **dictionary**.

Making a Purchase

I'd like to buy ...	Vorrei comprare ... vo·*ray* kom·*pra*·re ...
I'm just looking.	Sto solo guardando. sto *so*·lo gwar·*dan*·do

LOOK FOR

Aperto	a·*per*·to	Open
Chiuso	*kyoo*·zo	Closed
Spingere	*speen*·je·re	Push
Tirare	tee·*ra*·re	Pull

What is this made of?
Questo con che cosa è fatto?
kwe·sto kon ke *ko*·za e *fa*·to

How much is this?
Quanto costa questo?
kwan·to *kos*·ta *kwes*·to

How much? | Quanto? | *kwan*·to

Can you write down the price?
Può scrivere il prezzo?
pwo *skree*·ve·re eel *pre*·tso

Do you have any others?
Ne avete altri?
ne a·*ve*·te *al*·tree

Can I look at it?
Posso dare un'occhiata?
po·so *da*·re oo·no·*kya*·ta

Could I have it wrapped, please?
Può incartarlo, per favore?
pwo een·kar·*tar*·lo per fa·*vo*·re

Does it have a guarantee?
Ha la garanzia?
a la ga·ran·*tsee*·a

Can you order it for me?
Me lo può ordinare, per favore?
me lo pwo or·dee·*na*·re per fa·*vo*·re

Can I pick it up later?
Posso ritirarlo più tardi?
po·so ree·tee·*rar*·lo pyoo *tar*·dee

It's faulty.
È difettoso.
e dee·fe·*to*·zo

It's broken.	È rotto. e *ro*·to
Do you accept credit/ debit cards?	Accettate la carta di credito/debito? a·che·*ta*·te la *kar*·ta dee *kre*·dee·to/*de*·bee·to
Could I have a bag, please?	Può darmi un sacchetto, per favore? pwo *dar*·mee oon sa·*ke*·to per fa·*vo*·re
I don't need a bag, thanks.	Non mi serve la busta, grazie. non mee *ser*·ve la *boos*·ta *gra*·tsye
Could I have a receipt, please?	Può darmi una ricevuta, per favore? pwo *dar*·mee *oo*·na ree·che·*voo*·ta per fa·*vo*·re

Receipt, please.	La ricevuta, per favore.	la ree·che·*voo*·ta per fa·*vo*·re

I'd like my money back, please.	Vorrei un rimborso, per favore. vo·*ray* oon reem·*bor*·so per fa·*vo*·re
I'd like to change this, please.	Vorrei cambiare questo/a, per favore. **m/f** vo·*ray* kam·*bya*·re *kwe*·sto/a per fa·*vo*·re

LISTEN FOR

Posso aiutarla?	*po*·so a·yoo·*tar*·la	Can I help you?
No, non ne abbiamo.	no non ne a·*bya*·mo	No, we don't have any.

Making a Purchase

I'd like to buy ...

Vorrei comprare...

vo·ray kom·pra·re ...

How much is it?

Quanto costa?

kwan·to kos·ta

OR

Can you write down the price?

Può scrivere il prezzo?

pwo skree·ve·re eel pre·tso

Do you accept credit cards?

Accettate la carta di credito?

a·che·ta·te la kar·ta dee kre·dee·to

Could I have a ...., please?

Può darmi ...., per favore?

pwo dar·mee ... per fa·vo·re

receipt
una ricevuta
oo·na ree·che·voo·ta

bag
un sacchetto
oon sa·ke·to

I'd like to return this, please.	Vorrei restituire questo/a, per favore. **m/f** vo·*ray* res·tee·*twee*·re *kwe*·sto/a per fa·*vo*·re

Bargaining

That's too expensive.	È troppo caro/a. **m/f** e *tro*·po *ka*·ro/a
The price is very high.	Il prezzo è molto alto. eel *pre*·tso e *mol*·to *al*·to
Can you lower the price?	Può farmi lo sconto? pwo *far*·mee lo *skon*·to
Do you have something cheaper?	Ha qualcosa di meno costoso? a kwal·*ko*·za dee *me*·no kos·*to*·zo
I'll give you ...	Le offro ... le *o*·fro ...

Clothes

Can I try it on?	Potrei provarmelo/a? **m/f** po·*tray* pro·*var*·me·lo/a
It doesn't fit.	Non va bene. non va *be*·ne

CULTURE TIP

Shop Etiquette

In style-conscious Italy, though shop window displays may look good enough to eat, they're absolutely not to be touched. Disrupting a window display could jeopardise a shop's *bella figura* *be*·la fee·*goo*·ra – that all-important Italian preoccupation with creating a good impression.

LISTEN FOR

affare m	a·*fa*·re	bargain
affarista m	a·fa·*ree*·sta	bargain hunter
fregatura f	fre·ga·*too*·ra	rip-off
occasioni f pl	o·ka·*zyo*·nee	specials
saldi m pl	*sal*·dee	sales

My size is large.	Sono una taglia forte. *so*·no *oo*·na *ta*·lya *for*·te
My size is medium.	Sono una taglia media. *so*·no *oo*·na *ta*·lya *me*·dya
My size is small.	Sono una taglia piccola. *so*·no *oo*·na *ta*·lya *pee*·ko·la

For clothing items see the **dictionary**, and for sizes see **numbers & amounts** (p32).

Repairs

Can I have my backpack repaired here?	Posso far aggiustare il mio zaino qui? *po*·so far a·joo·*sta*·re eel *mee*·o *dzai*·no kwee
Can I have my camera repaired here?	Posso far aggiustare la mia macchina fotografica qui? *po*·so far a·joo·*sta*·re la *mee*·a *ma*·kee·na fo·to·*gra*·fee·ka kwee
When will it be ready?	Quando sarà pronto? *kwan*·do sa·*ra* *pron*·to

Books & Reading

Is there an English-language bookshop?	C'è una libreria specializzata in lingua inglese? che *oo*·na lee·bre·*ree*·a spe·cha·lee·*dza*·ta een *leen*·gwa een·*gle*·ze
Is there an (English-language) entertainment guide?	C'è una guida agli spettacoli (in inglese)? che *oo*·na *gwee*·da *a*·lyee spe·*ta*·ko·lee (ee·neen·*gle*·ze)
Do you have a book by (Alberto Moravia)?	C'è un libro di (Alberto Moravia)? che oon *lee*·bro dee (al·*ber*·to mo·*ra*·vee·a)

Music & DVD

I'd like a CD/DVD.	Vorrei un CD/DVD. vo·*ray* oon chee·*dee*/ dee·voo·*dee*
I'd like headphones.	Vorrei delle cuffia. vo·*ray* *de*·le *koo*·fya
I heard a band called (Marlene Kuntz).	Ho sentito un gruppo chiamato (Marlene Kuntz). o sen·*tee*·to oon *groo*·po kya·*ma*·to (mar·*le*·ne koonts)
What's his/her best recording?	Qual'è la sua migliore incisione? kwa·*le* la *soo*·a mee·*lyo*·re een·chee·*zyo*·ne
Can I listen to this?	Potrei ascoltare questo? po·*tray* as·kol·*ta*·re *kwe*·sto
Will this work on any DVD player?	Funzionerà con tutti i lettori di DVD? foon·tsyo·ne·*ra* kon *too*·tee ee le·*to*·ree dee dee·voo·*dee*

Video & Photography

I need a cable to connect my camera to a computer.	Mi serve un cavo per collegare la mia macchina a un computer. mee *ser*·ve oon *ka*·vo per ko·le·*ga*·re la *mee*·a *ma*·kee·na a oon komp·*yoo*·ter
I need a cable to recharge this battery.	Mi serve un cavo per ricaricare questa batteria. mee *ser*·ve oon *ka*·vo per ree·ka·ree·*ka*·re *kwe*·sta ba·te·*ree*·a
Do you have memory cards for this camera?	Avete schede di memoria per questa macchina fotografica? a·*ve*·te *ske*·de dee me·*mo*·rya per *kwe*·sta *ma*·kee·na fo·to·*gra*·fee·ka
Do you have batteries for this camera?	Avete batterie per questa macchina fotografica? a·*ve*·te ba·te·*ree*·e per *kwe*·sta *ma*·kee·na fo·to·*gra*·fee·ka
Can you print digital photos?	Potete stampare foto digitali? po·*te*·te stam·*pa*·re *fo*·to dee·jee·*ta*·lee

LANGUAGE TIP

Addressing People

The plural polite form has become virtually obsolete in modern Italian. If you want to show respect to more than one person, use *voi* voy. See also **personal pronouns** in the **grammar** chapter (p21).

Can you transfer my photos from camera to CD?	Potete trasferire le mie foto dalla macchina su un CD? po·*te*·te tra·sfe·*ree*·re le *mee*·e *fo*·to *da*·la *ma*·kee·na soo oon chee·*dee*
I need a ... film for this camera.	Vorrei un rullino ... per questa macchina fotografica. vo·*ray* oon roo·*lee*·no ... per *kwe*·sta *ma*·kee·na fo·to·*gra*·fee·ka

B&W	in bianco e nero	een *byan*·ko e *ne*·ro
colour	a colori	a *ko*·lo·ree
slide	per diapositive	per dya·po·zee·*tee*·ve
(100) speed	da (cento) ASA	da (*chen*·to) *a*·za

Could you develop this film?	Potrebbe sviluppare questo rullino? po·*tre*·be svee·loo·*pa*·re *kwe*·sto roo·*lee*·no

For more photographic equipment, see the **dictionary**.

Souvenirs

antiques	pezzi **m** d'antiquariato *pe*·tsee dan·tee·kwa·*rya*·to
blown glass	vetro **m** soffiato *ve*·tro so·*fya*·to
ceramics/pottery	ceramiche **f pl** che·*ra*·mee·ke
embroidery	ricamo **m** ree·*ka*·mo
glassware	vetrame **m** ve·*tra*·me

handicrafts	ogetti **m pl** d'artigianato o·*je*·tee dar·tee·ja·*na*·to
jewellery	gioielli **m pl** jo·*ye*·lee
lace	merletto **m** mer·*le*·to
leather goods	pelletterie **f pl** pe·le·te·*ree*·e
marbled paper	carta **f** marmorizzata *kar*·ta mar·mo·ree·*tsa*·ta
masks	maschere **f pl** *ma*·ske·re
paper goods	articoli **m pl** di carta ar·*tee*·ko·lee dee *kar*·ta
woodcarvings	legno **m** intagliato *le*·nyo een·ta·*lya*·to

Ne avete altri?
ne a·*ve*·te *al*·tree
Do you have any others?

Communications

KEY PHRASES

Where's the local internet cafe?	Dove si trova l'Internet point?	*do*·ve see *tro*·va *leen*·ter·net poynt
I'd like to check my email.	Vorrei controllare il mio email.	vo·*ray* kon·tro·*la*·re eel *mee*·o e·mayl
I'd like a SIM card.	Vorrei un SIM card.	vo·*ray* oon seem kard

Post Office

I want to send a ...

Vorrei mandare ...
vo·*ray* man·*da*·re ...

letter	una lettera	*oo*·na *le*·te·ra
parcel	un pacchetto	oon pa·*ke*·to
postcard	una cartolina	*oo*·na kar·to·*lee*·na

I want to buy an envelope.

Vorrei comprare una busta.
vo·*ray* kom·*pra*·re *oo*·na *boo*·sta

I want to buy stamps.

Vorrei comprare dei francobolli.
vo·*ray* kom·*pra*·re day fran·ko·*bo*·lee

LISTEN FOR

dichiarazione f **doganale**	dee·kya·ra·*tsyo*·ne do·ga·*na*·le	customs declaration
indirizzo m **postale**	een·dee·*ree*·tso po·*sta*·le	postal address
posta f **prioritaria**	*pos*·ta pryo·ree·*ta*·rya	express mail
posta f **raccomandata**	*pos*·ta ra·ko·man·*da*·ta	registered mail

Please send it by airmail (to Denmark).	Lo mandi via aerea (in Danimarca), per favore. lo *man*·dee *vee*·a a·e·re·a (een da·nee·*mar*·ka) per fa·*vo*·re
It contains ...	Contiene ... kon·*tye*·ne ...
Where's the poste restante section?	Dov'è il fermo posta? do·*ve* eel *fer*·mo *pos*·ta
Is there any mail for me?	C'è posta per me? che *pos*·ta per me

Phone

Q **What's your phone number?**	Qual'è il Suo/tuo numero di telefono? **pol/inf** kwa·*le* eel *soo*·o/*too*·o *noo*·me·ro dee te·*le*·fo·no
A **The number is ...**	Il numero è ... eel *noo*·me·ro e ...
A **I don't have a contact number.**	Non ho un numero fisso. non o oon *noo*·me·ro *fee*·so

Where's the nearest public phone?	Dov'è il telefono pubblico più vicino? do·*ve* eel te·*le*·fo·no *poo*·blee·ko pyoo vee·*chee*·no
I'd like to know the number for ...	Vorrei sapere il numero di ... vo·*ray* sa·*pe*·re eel *noo*·me·ro dee ...
I want to make a/an ...	Vorrei fare una chiamata ... vo·*ray* *fa*·re *oo*·na kya·*ma*·ta ...

call to (Belgium)	in (Belgio)	een (*bel*·jo)
internet call	via Internet	*vee*·a *een*·ter·net
local call	urbana	oor·*ba*·na
reverse-charge/ collect call	a carico del destinatario	a *ka*·ree·ko del des·tee·na·*ta*·ryo

I want to buy a phone card.	Vorrei comprare una scheda telefonica. vo·*ray* kom·*pra*·re *oo*·na *ske*·da te·le·*fo*·nee·ka
How much does a (three)-minute call cost?	Quanto costa una telefonata di (tre) minuti? *kwan*·to *kos*·ta *oo*·na te·le·fo·*na*·ta dee (tre) mee·*noo*·tee
What's the area/country code for ...?	Qual'è il prefisso per ...? kwa·*le* eel pre·*fee*·so per ...
It's engaged.	La linea è occupata. la *lee*·ne·a e o·koo·*pa*·ta
I've been cut off.	È caduta la linea. e ka·*doo*·ta la *lee*·ne·a
The connection's bad.	La linea non è buona. la *lee*·ne·a no·*ne* *bwo*·na

Hello.	Pronto. *pron*·to
It's ...	Sono ... *so*·no ...
Can I speak to ...?	Posso parlare con ...? *po*·so par·*la*·re kon ...
Can I leave a message?	Posso lasciare un messaggio? *po*·so la·*sha*·re oon me·*sa*·jo
Please tell him/her I called.	Gli/Le dica che ho telefonato, per favore. lyee/le *dee*·ka ke o te·le·fo·*na*·to per fa·*vo*·re
I'll call back later.	Richiamerò più tardi. ree·kya·me·*ro* pyoo *tar*·dee

For telephone numbers, see **numbers & amounts** (p32).

Qui c'è il collegamento Wi-Fi?

kwee chay eel ko·le·ga·men·to wai·fai

Is there wi-fi here?

LISTEN FOR

Con chi parlo?	kon kee *par*·lo	Who's calling?
Con chi vuole parlare?	kon kee *vwo*·le par·*la*·re	Who do you want (to speak to)?
Si, è qui.	see e kwee	Yes, he/she is here.
Glielo/Gliela passo.	*lye*·lo/*lye*·la *pa*·so	I'll put him/her on.
Mi dispiace, (lui/lei) non c'è.	mee dees·*pya*·che (*loo*·ee/lay) non che	I'm sorry, he/she is not here.
Mi dispiace, ha sbagliato numero.	mee dees·*pya*·che a sba·*lya*·to *noo*·me·ro	Sorry, wrong number.

Mobile/Cell Phone

What are the rates?	Quali sono le tariffe? *kwa*·lee *so*·no le ta·*ree*·fe
I'd like a/an ...	Vorrei ... vo·*ray* ...

adaptor plug	un adattatore	oo·na·da·ta·*to*·re
charger for my phone	un caricabatterie	oon ka·ree·ka·ba·te·*ree*·e
mobile/cell phone for hire	un cellulare da noleggiare	oon che·loo·*la*·re da no·le·*ja*·re
recharge card for ...	una ricarica telefonica per ...	*oo*·na re·*ka*·ree·ka te·le·*fo*·nee·ka per ...
SIM card for your network	un SIM card per la vostra rete telefonica	oon seem kard per la *vos*·tra *re*·te te·le·*fo*·nee·ka

The Internet

Where's the local internet cafe?	Dove si trova l'Internet point? *do*·ve see *tro*·va *leen*·ter·net poynt
Do you have public internet access here?	Qui c'è il collegamento a Internet? kwee chay eel ko·le·ga·*men*·to a *een*·ter·net
Is there wireless internet access here?	Qui c'è il collegamento Wi-Fi? kwee chay eel ko·le·ga·*men*·to wai·fai
Can I connect my laptop here?	Posso collegare il mio portatile? *po*·so ko·le·*ga*·re eel *mee*·o por·ta·*tee*·le
Do you have headphones (with a microphone)?	Avete una cuffia (con microfono)? a·*ve*·te *oo*·na *koo*·fya (kon mee·*kro*·fo·no)
I'd like to ...	Vorrei ... vo·*ray* ...

burn a CD	masterizzare un CD	mas·te·ree·*tsa*·re oon chee·*dee*
check my email	controllare il mio email	kon·tro·*la*·re eel *mee*·o e·mayl
download my photos	scaricare le mie foto	ska·ree·*ka*·re le *mee*·e *fo*·to
use a printer	usare una stampante	oo·*za*·re *oo*·na stam·*pan*·te
use a scanner	scandire	skan·*dee*·re
use Skype	usare Skype	oo·*za*·re skaip

How much per hour?	Quanto costa all'ora? *kwan*·to *kos*·ta a·*lo*·ra
How much per page?	Quanto costa a pagina? *kwan*·to *kos*·ta a *pa*·jee·na
How do I log on?	Come posso accedere? *ko*·me *po*·so a·*che*·de·re
It's crashed.	Si è bloccato. see e blo·*ka*·to
I've finished.	Ho finito. o fee·*nee*·to
Can I connect my ... to this computer?	Posso collegare ... a questo computer? *po*·so ko·le·*ga*·re ... a *kwe*·sto kom·*pyoo*·ter

camera	la mia macchina fotografica	la *mee*·a *ma*·kee·na fo·to·*gra*·fee·ka
iPod	il mio iPod	eel *mee*·o *ai*·pod
media player (MP3)	il mio lettore MP3	eel *mee*·o le·*to*·re e·me·pee·tre
portable hard drive	il mio hard drive portatile	eel *mee*·o hard draiv por·*ta*·tee·le
PSP	la mia consolle PSP portatile	la *mee*·a kon·*so*·le pee·e·se·pee por·*ta*·tee·le
USB flash drive (memory stick)	la mia chiavetta USB	la *mee*·a kya·*ve*·ta oo·e·se·bee

Money & Banking

KEY PHRASES

How much is this?	Quanto costa questo?	*kwan*·to *kos*·ta *kwe*·sto
What's the exchange rate?	Quant'è il cambio?	kwan·*te* eel *kam*·byo
Where's the nearest ATM?	Dov'è il Bancomat più vicino?	do·*ve* eel *ban*·ko·mat pyoo vee·*chee*·no
I'd like to exchange money.	Vorrei cambiare denaro.	vo·*ray* kam·*bya*·re de·*na*·ro
Can I have smaller notes?	Mi può dare banconote più piccole?	mee pwo *da*·re ban·ko·*no*·te pyoo *pee*·ko·le

Paying the Bill

Q How much is this?	Quanto costa questo? *kwan*·to *kos*·ta *kwe*·sto
A It's free.	È gratuito. e gra·too·*ee*·to
A It's ... euros.	È ... euro. e ... e·*oo*·ro
Can you write down the price?	Può scrivere il prezzo? pwo *skree*·ve·re eel *pre*·tso
Do you accept credit/ debit cards?	Accettate la carta di credito/debito? a·che·*ta*·te la *kar*·ta dee *kre*·dee·to/*de*·bee·to

Do you accept travellers cheques?	Accettate gli assegni di viaggio? a·che·*ta*·te lyee a·*se*·nyee dee *vya*·jo
I'd like a receipt, please.	Vorrei una ricevuta, per favore. vo·*ray oo*·na ree·che·*voo*·ta per fa·*vo*·re
I'd like a refund, please.	Vorrei un rimborso, per favore. vo·*ray* oon reem·*bor*·so per fa·*vo*·re
I'd like my change, please.	Vorrei il mio resto, per favore. vo·*ray* eel *mee*·o *res*·to per fa·*vo*·re
There's a mistake in the bill.	C'è un errore nel conto. che oon e·*ro*·re nel *kon*·to
I don't want to pay the full price.	Non voglio pagare il prezzo intero. non *vo*·lyo pa·*ga*·re eel *pre*·tso een·*te*·ro
Do I need to pay upfront?	Devo pagare in anticipo? *de*·vo pa·*ga*·re ee·nan·*tee*·chee·po

Banking

What time does the bank open?	A che ora apre la banca? a ke *o*·ra *a*·pre la *ban*·ka
Do you change money here?	Si cambiano i soldi qui? see *kam*·bya·no ee *sol*·dee kwee
Where can I ...?	Dove posso ...? *do*·ve *po*·so ...

I'd like to ...	Vorrei ...	*vo·ray ...*
arrange a transfer	trasferire soldi	tras·fe·*ree*·re *sol*·dee
cash a cheque	riscuotere un assegno	ree·*skwo*·te·re oo·na·*se*·nyo
change a travellers cheque	cambiare un assegno di viaggio	kam·*bya*·re oo·na·*se*·nyo dee vee·*a*·jo
change money	cambiare denaro	kam·*bya*·re de·*na*·ro
get a cash advance	prelevare con carta di credito	pre·le·*va*·re kon *kar*·ta dee *kre*·dee·to
get change for this note	cambiare questa banconota	kam·*bya*·re *kwe*·sta ban·ko·*no*·ta
withdraw money	fare un prelievo	*fa*·re oon pre·*lye*·vo

Where's the nearest automatic teller machine?
Dov'è il Bancomat più vicino?
do·*ve* eel *ban*·ko·mat pyoo vee·*chee*·no

Where's the nearest foreign exchange office?
Dov'è il cambio più vicino?
do·*ve* eel *kam*·byo pyoo vee·*chee*·no

What's the commission?
Quant'è la commissione?
kwan·*te* la ko·mee·*syo*·ne

What's the exchange rate?
Quant'è il cambio?
kwan·*te* eel *kam*·byo

The automatic teller machine took my card.
Il Bancomat ha trattenuto la mia carta di credito.
eel *ban*·ko·mat a tra·te·*noo*·to la *mee*·a *kar*·ta dee *kre*·dee·to

LISTEN FOR

Il Suo passaporto.	eel *soo*·o pa·sa·*por*·to	Your passport.
Vuole firmare o usare il suo PIN?	*vwo*·le feer·*ma*·re o oo·*sa*·re eel *soo*·o peen	Do you want to sign or use your PIN?
Può firmare qui, per favore?	pwo feer·*ma*·re kwee per fa·*vo*·re	Please sign here.
C'è un problema con il Suo conto.	che oon pro·*ble*·ma ko·*neel* *soo*·o *kon*·to	There's a problem with your account.
Non possiamo farlo.	non po·*sya*·mo *far*·lo	We can't do that.

I've forgotten my PIN.	Ho dimenticato il mio codice PIN. o dee·men·tee·*ka*·to eel *mee*·o *ko*·dee·che peen
Can I use my credit card to withdraw money?	Si può usare la carta di credito per fare prelievi? see pwo oo·*za*·re la *kar*·ta dee *kre*·dee·to per *fa*·re pre·*lye*·vee
Can I have smaller notes?	Mi può dare banconote più piccole? mee pwo *da*·re ban·ko·*no*·te pyoo *pee*·ko·le
Has my money arrived yet?	È arrivato il mio denaro? e a·ree·*va*·to eel *mee*·o de·*na*·ro
How long will it take to arrive?	Quanto tempo ci vorrà per il trasferimento? *kwan*·to *tem*·po chee vo·*ra* per eel tras·fe·ree·*men*·to

Business

KEY PHRASES

I'm attending a conference.	Sono qui per una conferenza.	*so*·no kwee per *oo*·na kon·fe·*ren*·tsa
I have an appointment with ...	Ho un appuntamento con ...	o oon· a·poon·ta·*men*·to kon ...
Can I have your business card?	Potrei avere il suo biglietto da visita?	po·*tray* a·*ve*·re eel *soo*·o bee·*lye*·to da *vee*·zee·ta

Where's the conference/ meeting?
Dov'è la conferenza/ riunione?
do·*ve* la kon·fe·*ren*·tsa/ ree·oo·*nyo*·ne

I'm attending a ...
Sono qui per ...
so·no kwee per ...

conference	una conferenza	*oo*·na kon·fe·*ren*·tsa
course	un corso	oon *kor*·so
meeting	una riunione	*oo*·na ree·oo·*nyo*·ne
trade fair	una fiera commerciale	*oo*·na *fye*·ra ko·mer·*cha*·le

I'm here with my company.
Sono qui con la mia azienda.
so·no kwee kon la *mee*·a a·*dzyen*·da

I'm here with my colleague.	Sono qui con il/la mio/a collega. **m/f** *so*·no kwee kon eel/la *mee*·o/a ko·*le*·ga
Q Can I have your business card?	Potrei avere il suo biglietto da visita? po·*tray* a·*ve*·re eel *soo*·o bee·*lye*·to da *vee*·zee·ta
A Here's my business card.	Ecco il mio biglietto da visita. *e*·ko eel *mee*·o bee·*lye*·to da *vee*·zee·ta
I have an appointment with ...	Ho un appuntamento con ... o oo·na·poon·ta·*men*·to kon ...
I'm expecting a call.	Aspetto una telefonata. a·*spe*·to *oo*·na te·le·fo·*na*·ta
I need a computer.	Ho bisogno di un computer. o bee·*zo*·nyo dee oon kom·*pyoo*·ter
I need a connection to the internet.	Ho bisogno di una connessione Internet. o bee·*zo*·nyo dee *oo*·na ko·ne·*syo*·ne *een*·ter·net
I need an interpreter.	Ho bisogno di un/un'interprete. **m/f** o bee·*zo*·nyo dee oo·neen·*ter*·pre·te

CULTURE TIP

Business Etiquette

Italian business culture is formal and hierarchical. First names aren't used between executives and subordinates, and using the right titles (see p106) may help you clinch that deal. Business isn't usually discussed over a meal. As a visitor you'll be expected to be *in orario* een o·*ra*·ryo (on time), but don't get touchy about being kept waiting.

Sightseeing

KEY PHRASES

I'd like a guide.	Vorrei una guida.	vo·*ray* oo·na *gwee*·da
Can I take a photograph?	Posso fare una foto?	*po*·so *fa*·re *oo*·na *fo*·to
When's the museum open?	Quando è aperto il museo?	*kwan*·do e a·*per*·to eel moo·*ze*·o

I'd like a/an ... Vorrei ... vo·*ray* ...

audio set	un auricolare	oo·now·ree·ko·*la*·re
guide (person)	una guida	*oo*·na *gwee*·da
guidebook in English	una guida in inglese	*oo*·na *gwee*·da ee·neen·*gle*·ze
local map	una cartina della zona	*oo*·na kar·*tee*·na *de*·la *dzo*·na

Do you have information on ... sights? Avete delle informazioni su posti ...? a·*ve*·te *de*·le een·for·ma·*tsyo*·nee soo *pos*·tee ...

architectural	architettonici	ar·kee·te·*to*·nee·chee
historical	storici	*sto*·ree·chee
local	locali	lo·*ka*·lee
natural	di bellezza naturale	dee be·*le*·tsa na·too·*ra*·le

I'd like to see ...	Vorrei vedere ... vo·*ray* ve·*de*·re ...
I'd like to hire a local guide.	Vorrei ingaggiare una guida del posto. vo·*ray* een·ga·*ja*·re *oo*·na *gwee*·da del *po*·sto
What's that?	Cos'è? ko·*ze*
How old is it?	Quanti anni ha? *kwan*·tee *a*·nee a
Could you take a photograph of me?	Può farmi una foto? pwo *far*·mee *oo*·na *fo*·to
Can I take a photograph (of you)?	Posso fare una foto (di Lei/tu)? **pol/inf** *po*·so *fa*·re *oo*·na *fo*·to (dee lay/too)

Getting In

What time does it open/close?	A che ora apre/chiude? a ke *o*·ra *a*·pre/*kyoo*·de
What's the admission charge?	Quant'è il prezzo d'ingresso? kwan·*te* eel *pre*·tso deen·*gre*·so
Is there a discount for ...?	C'è uno sconto per ...? che *oo*·no *skon*·to per ...

children	bambini	bam·*bee*·nee
families	famiglie	fa·*mee*·lye
groups	gruppi	*groo*·pee
older people	persone anziane	per·*so*·ne an·*tsya*·ne
students	studenti	stoo·*den*·tee

Tours

Can you recommend a tour?	Può consigliare una gita turistica? pwo kon·see·*lya*·re *oo*·na *jee*·ta too·*ree*·stee·ka
When's the next tour?	A che ora parte la prossima gita? a ke *o*·ra *par*·te la *pro*·see·ma *jee*·ta
When's the next day trip?	A che ora parte la prossima escursione in giornata? a ke *o*·ra *par*·te la *pro*·see·ma es·koor·*syo*·ne een jor·*na*·ta
When's the next excursion?	A che ora parte la prossima escursione? a ke *o*·ra *par*·te la *pro*·see·ma es·koor·*syo*·ne
Is accommodation included?	È incluso l'alloggio? e een·*kloo*·zo la·*lo*·jo
Is food included?	È incluso il vitto? e een·*kloo*·zo eel *vee*·to
Is transport included?	È incluso il trasporto? e een·*kloo*·zo eel tras·*por*·to
Are there organised walking tours?	Ci sono visite guidate a piedi? chee so·no *vee*·zee·te gwee·*da*·te a *pye*·dee
I'd like to do cooking/ language classes.	Vorrei fare un corso di cucina/lingua. vo·*ray fa*·re oon *kor*·so dee koo·*chee*·na/*leen*·gwa
The guide has paid.	La guida ha pagato. la *gwee*·da a pa·*ga*·to

How long is the tour?	Quanto dura la gita? *kwan*·to *doo*·ra la *jee*·ta
What time should we be back?	A che ora dovremmo ritornare? a ke *o*·ra dov·*re*·mo ree·tor·*na*·re
I've lost my group.	Ho perso il mio gruppo. o *per*·so eel *mee*·o *groo*·po

Museums & Galleries

When's the gallery open?	Quando è aperta la galleria? *kwan*·do e a·*per*·ta la ga·le·*ree*·a
When's the museum open?	Quando è aperto il museo? *kwan*·do e a·*per*·to eel moo·*ze*·o
What do you think of ...?	Cosa ne pensa/pensi di ...? **pol/inf** *ko*·za ne *pen*·sa/*pen*·see dee ...
It's a/an (futurist art) exhibition.	Cosa ne pensa/pensi di ...? **pol/inf** *ko*·za ne *pen*·sa/*pen*·see dee ...

Quanto dura la gita?

kwan·to *doo*·ra la *jee*·ta

How long is the tour?

LANGUAGE TIP

Irregular Plurals

Italian has some irregular plural forms – here are some examples:

il dio m sg	eel *dee*·o	the god
i dei m pl	ee day	the gods
la ala f sg	la *a*·la	the wing
le ali f pl	le *a*·lee	the wings

Some words even change gender in the plural:

il labbro m sg	eel *la*·bro	the lip
le labbra f pl	le *la*·bra	the lips

See also **plurals** in the **grammar** chapter (p23).

Q **What kind of art are you interested in?**
Che tipo di arte Le/ti interessa? pol/inf
ke *tee*·po dee *ar*·te le/tee een·te·*re*·sa

A **I'm interested in ... art/architecture.**
Mi interessa l'arte/ l'architettura ...
mee een·te·*re*·sa *lar*·te/ lar·kee·te·*too*·ra ...

baroque	barocca	ba·*ro*·ka
Byzantine	bizantina	bee·dzan·*tee*·na
modernist	modernista	mo·der·*nee*·sta
Renaissance	rinascimentale	ree·na·shee·men·*ta*·le
Romanesque	romanica	ro·*ma*·nee·ka

LOOK FOR

Gabinetti	ga·bee·*ne*·tee	Toilets
Ingresso Gratuito	een·*gre*·so gra·*too*·ee·to	Free Admission
Messa in Corso	*me*·sa een *kor*·so	Service in Progress
Non Calpestare l'Erba	non kal·pe·*sta*·re *ler*·ba	Keep Off the Grass
Non Entrare	no·nen·*tra*·re	No Entry
Proibito	pro·ee·*bee*·to	Prohibited
Servizi Pubblici	ser·*vee*·tsee *poo*·blee·chee	Public Toilets
Uscita di Sicurezza	oo·*shee*·ta dee see·koo·*re*·tsa	Emergency Exit
Vietato	vye·*ta*·to	Prohibited
Vietato Consumare Cibi o Bevande	vye·*ta*·to kon·soo·*ma*·re *chee*·bee o be·*van*·de	No Eating or Drinking Allowed
Vietato Fotografare	vye·*ta*·to fo·to·gra·*fa*·re	Do Not Take Photographs
Vietato Toccare	vye·*ta*·to to·*ka*·re	Do Not Touch

Senior & Disabled Travellers

KEY PHRASES

I need assistance.	Ho bisogno di assistenza.	o bee·*zo*·nyo dee a·sees·*ten*·tsa
Is there wheelchair access?	C'è un'entrata per sedie a rotelle?	che oo·nen·*tra*·ta per *se*·dye a ro·*te*·le
Are there toilets for the disabled?	Ci sono gabinetti per disabili?	chee so·no ga·bee·*ne*·tee per dee·*za*·bee·lee

I'm disabled.	Sono disabile. *so*·no dee·*za*·bee·le
I need assistance.	Ho bisogno di assistenza. o bee·*zo*·nyo dee a·sees·*ten*·tsa
Are guide dogs permitted?	Sono ammessi i cani guida? *so*·no a·*me*·see ee *ka*·nee *gwee*·da
Is there wheelchair access?	C'è un'entrata per sedie a rotelle? che oo·nen·*tra*·ta per *se*·dye a ro·*te*·le
How many steps are there?	Quanti gradini ci sono? *kwan*·tee gra·*dee*·nee chee *so*·no
How wide is the entrance?	Quant'è larga l'entrata? kwan·*te lar*·ga len·*tra*·ta
Is there a lift?	C'è un ascensore? che oo·na·shen·*so*·re

LOOK FOR

Riservato ai Disabili	ree·ser·*va*·to ai dee·*za*·bee·lee	Reserved for People with a Disability

Is there somewhere I can sit down?	C'è un posto dove sedersi? che oon *pos*·to *do*·ve se·*der*·see
Are there toilets for the disabled?	Ci sono gabinetti per disabili? chee *so*·no ga·bee·*ne*·tee per dee·*za*·bee·lee
Are there rails in the bathroom?	Ci sono corrimani nel bagno? chee *so*·no ko·ree·*ma*·nee nel *ba*·nyo
Are there parking spaces for the disabled?	Ci sono parcheggi per disabili? chee *so*·no par·*ke*·jee per dee·*za*·bee·lee
Could you call me a taxi for the disabled?	Può chiamarmi un tassì per i disabili? pwo kya·*mar*·mee oon ta·*see* per ee dee·*za*·bee·lee
Could you help me cross the street?	Può aiutarmi ad attraversare la strada? pwo a·yoo·*tar*·mee a·da·tra·*ver*·*sa*·re la *stra*·da
crutches	stampelle **f pl** stam·*pe*·le
ramp	rampa **f** *ram*·pa
walking frame	deambulatore **m** de·am·boo·la·*to*·re
walking stick	bastone **m** ba·*sto*·ne

Travel with Children

KEY PHRASES

Are children allowed?	I bambini sono ammessi?	ee bam·*bee*·nee *so*·no a·*me*·see
Is there a child discount?	C'è uno sconto per bambini?	che *oo*·no *skon*·to per bam·*bee*·nee
Is there a baby change room?	C'è un bagno con fasciatoio?	che oon *ba*·nyo kon fa·sha·*to*·yo

Is there a/an ...? C'è ...? che ...

baby change room	un bagno con fasciatoio	oon *ba*·nyo kon fa·sha·*to*·yo
(English-speaking) babysitter	un/una babysitter (che parli inglese) m/f	oon/*oo*·na be·bee·*see*·ter (ke *par*·lee een·*gle*·ze)
child discount	uno sconto per bambini	*oo*·no *skon*·to per bam·*bee*·nee
child-minding service	un servizio di babysitter	oon ser·*vee*·tsyo dee be·bee·*see*·ter
children's menu	un menù per bambini	oon me·*noo* per bam·*bee*·nee
family discount	uno sconto per famiglia	*oo*·no *skon*·to per fa·*mee*·lya
playground nearby	un parco giochi da queste parti	oon *par*·ko *jo*·kee da *kwe*·ste *par*·tee

I need a ...	Ho bisogno di ... o bee·*zo*·nyo dee ...

child seat	un seggiolino per bambini	oon se·jo·*lee*·no per bam·*bee*·nee
cot	una culla	*oo*·na *koo*·la
potty	un vasino	oon va·*zee*·no
stroller	un passeggino	oon pa·se·*jee*·no

Do you sell ...?	Vendete ...? ven·*de*·te ...

baby wipes	salviettine detergenti per bambini	sal·vye·*tee*·ne de·ter·*jen*·tee per bam·*bee*·nee
disposable nappies/ diapers	pannolini usa-e-getta	pa·no·*lee*·nee *oo*·sa·e·*je*·ta
milk formula	latte in polvere	*la*·te een *pol*·ve·re
painkillers for infants	anti-dolorifici per bambini	an·tee·do·lo·*ree*·fee·chee per bam·*bee*·nee

Do you mind if I breastfeed (him/her) here?	Le dispiace se allatto il/la bimbo/a qui? **m/f** le dees·*pya*·che se a·*la*·to eel/la *beem*·bo/a kwee
Are children allowed?	I bambini sono ammessi? ee bam·*bee*·nee *so*·no a·*me*·see
Is this suitable for (two)-year-old children?	Questo è adatto per bambini di (due) anni? *kwe*·sto e a·*da*·to per bam·*bee*·nee dee (*doo*·e) *a*·nee

If your child is sick, see **health** (p150).

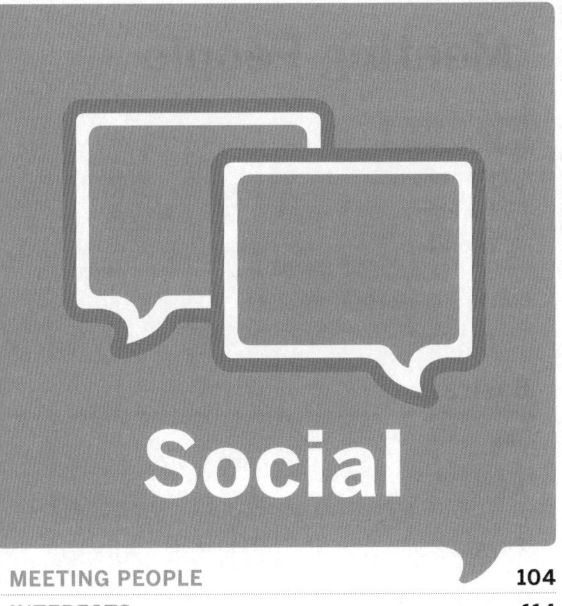

MEETING PEOPLE 104

INTERESTS 114

FEELINGS & OPINIONS 118

GOING OUT 122

ROMANCE 128

BELIEFS & CULTURE 133

SPORTS 135

OUTDOORS 140

Meeting People

KEY PHRASES

My name is ...	Mi chiamo ...	mee *kya*·mo ...
I'm from ...	Vengo ...	*ven*·go ...
I work in ...	Lavoro nel campo de ...	la·*vo*·ro nel *kam*·po de ...
I'm ... years old.	Ho ... anni.	o ... *a*·nee
And you?	E Lei/tu? **pol/inf**	e lay/too

Basics

Yes.	Sì. see
No.	No. no
Please.	Per favore. per fa·*vo*·re
Thank you (very much).	Grazie (mille). *gra*·tsye (*mee*·le)
You're welcome.	Prego. *pre*·go
Sorry.	Mi dispiace. mee dees·*pya*·che
Excuse me. (for attention/apology)	Mi scusi. **pol** mee *skoo*·zee Scusami. **inf** *skoo*·za·mee
Excuse me. (if going past)	Permesso. per·*me*·so

Greetings

Although *ciao* chow is a common greeting, it's best not to use it when addressing strangers. Also note that in Italy the word *buonasera* bwo·na·*se*·ra (good evening) may be heard any time from early afternoon onwards.

Hello.	Buongiorno./ bwon·*jor*·no/ Salve. **pol** *sal*·ve
Hi.	Ciao. **inf** chow
Good day/morning/ afternoon.	Buongiorno. bwon·*jor*·no
Good evening.	Buonasera. bwo·na·*se*·ra
Good night.	Buonanotte. bwo·na·*no*·te
See you.	Ci vediamo. chee ve·*dya*·mo
See you later.	A più tardi. a pyoo *tar*·dee
Goodbye.	Arrivederci. **pol** a·ree·ve·*der*·chee
Bye.	Ciao. **inf** chow
Q **How are you?**	Come sta? **sg pol** *ko*·me sta Come stai? **sg inf** *ko*·me stai Come state? **pl pol&inf** *ko*·me *sta*·te
A **Fine.**	Bene. *be*·ne
A **And you?**	E Lei/tu? **pol/inf** e lay/too

Q What's your name?	Come si chiama? **pol** *ko*·me see *kya*·ma Come ti chiami? **inf** *ko*·me tee *kya*·mee
A My name is ...	Mi chiamo ... mee *kya*·mo ...
I'm pleased to meet you.	Piacere. pya·*che*·re
I'd like to introduce you to ...	Le/Ti presento ... **pol/inf** le/tee pre·*zen*·to ...

✂	**This is ...**	Questo/Questa è... **m/f**	*kwe*·sto/*kwes*·ta e ...

Titles & Addressing People

Italians will greatly appreciate your efforts to try to speak their language and you'll leave an even better impression if you use the correct titles and forms of address. So when in Rome ...

Mr/Sir	Signore see·*nyo*·re
Mrs/Madam	Signora see·*nyo*·ra
Miss/Ms	Signorina see·nyo·*ree*·na
Doctor (anyone with a university degree)	Dottore/Dottoressa **m/f** do·*to*·re/do·to·*re*·sa
Professor (high-school or university lecturer)	Professore/ Professoressa **m/f** pro·fe·*so*·re/ pro·fe·so·*re*·sa
Director or Manager (anybody that runs anything)	Direttore/Direttrice **m/f** dee·re·*to*·re/dee·re·*tree*·che

LANGUAGE TIP

Addressing People

Italian has two forms for the singular 'you'. With family, friends, children or peers use the informal form *tu* too. When addressing strangers, older people, or people you've just met, use the polite form *Lei* lay. When your newly made friends feel it's time to start using the informal form, they might suggest:

Let's use the 'tu' form.	Diamoci del tu.	*dya*·mo·chee del too

See also **personal pronouns** in the **grammar** chapter (p21).

Making Conversation

Do you live here?	Lei è di qui? **pol** lay e dee kwee Tu sei di qui? **inf** too say dee kwee
Where are you going?	Dove va/vai? **pol/inf** *do*·ve va/vai
What are you doing?	Che fa/fai? **pol/inf** ke fa/fai
That's (beautiful), isn't it!	È (bello/a), no? **m/f** e (*be*·lo/a) no
How long are you here for?	Quanto tempo si fermerà? **pol** *kwan*·to *tem*·po see fer·me·*ra* Quanto tempo ti fermerai? **inf** *kwan*·to *tem*·po tee fer·me·*rai*
Q **Are you here on holiday?**	È/Sei qui in vacanza? **pol/inf** e/say kwee een va·*kan*·tsa
A **I'm here for a holiday.**	Sono qui in vacanza. *so*·no kwee een va·*kan*·tsa

A I'm here on business.	Sono qui per affari. *so*·no kwee per a·*fa*·ree
A I'm here to study.	Sono qui per motivi di studio. *so*·no kwee per mo·*tee*·vee dee *stoo*·dyo

Nationalities

Q Where are you from?	Da dove viene/vieni? **pol/inf** da *do*·ve *vye*·ne/*vye*·nee
A I'm from ...	Vengo ... *ven*·go ...

Australia	dall'Australia	dal·ow·*stra*·lya
Canada	dal Canada	dal *ka*·na·da
England	dall'Inghilterra	da·leen·geel·*te*·ra
New Zealand	dalla Nuova Zelanda	*da*·la *nwo*·va ze·*lan*·da
the USA	dagli Stati Uniti	*da*·lyee *sta*·tee oo·*nee*·tee

For more countries, see the **dictionary**.

Age

Q How old are you?	Quanti anni ha/hai? **pol/inf** *kwan*·tee *a*·nee a/ai
A I'm ... years old.	Ho ... anni. o ... *a*·nee
Q How old is your son?	Quanti anni ha Suo/tuo figlio? **pol/inf** *kwan*·tee *a*·nee a *soo*·o/*too*·o *fee*·lyo

Q How old is your daughter?	Quanti anni ha Sua/tua figlia? **pol/inf** *kwan*·tee *a*·nee a *soo*·a/*too*·a *fee*·lya
A He/She is ... years old.	Ha ... anni. a ... *a*·nee

For your age, see **numbers & amounts** (p32).

Occupations & Studies

Q What's your occupation?	Che lavoro fa/fai? **pol/inf** ke la·*vo*·ro fa/fai
A I'm a manual worker.	Sono manovale. *so*·no ma·no·*va*·le
A I'm an office worker.	Sono impiegato/a. **m/f** *so*·no eem·pye·*ga*·to/a
A I'm a tradesperson.	Sono operaio/a. **m/f** *so*·no o·pe·*ra*·yo/a
A I work in administration.	Lavoro nel campo dell'amministrazione. la·*vo*·ro nel *kam*·po de·la·mee·nee·stra·*tsyo*·ne
A I'm retired.	Sono pensionato/a. **m/f** *so*·no pen·syo·*na*·to/a
A I'm unemployed.	Sono disoccupato/a. **m/f** *so*·no dee·zo·koo·*pa*·to/a
A I'm self-employed.	Lavoro in proprio. la·*vo*·ro een *pro*·pryo

CULTURE TIP

Conversation Do's & Don'ts

Italians are great communicators, so you shouldn't have too much trouble striking up a conversation. Talking about the Mafia, Mussolini or the Vatican, however, could see the conversation come to a premature halt. Try topics such as Italian architecture, films, food and soccer.

Q What are you studying?	Cosa studia/studi? **pol/inf** *ko*·za *stoo*·dya/*stoo*·dee
A I'm studying arts/humanities.	Sto studiando lettere. sto stoo·*dyan*·do *le*·te·re
A I'm studying business.	Sto studiando commercio. sto stoo·*dyan*·do ko·*mer*·cho
A I'm studying engineering.	Sto studiando ingegneria. sto stoo·*dyan*·do een·je·nye·*ree*·a

For more occupations and studies, see the **dictionary**.

Family

Q Do you have (children)?	Ha/Hai (bambini)? **pol/inf** a/ai (bam·*bee*·nee)
A I have (a partner).	Ho (un/una compagno/a). **m/f** o (oon/*oo*·na kom·*pa*·nyo/a)
Q Do you live with (your family)?	Abita con (la Sua famiglia)? **pol** *a*·bee·ta kon (la *soo*·a fa·*mee*·lya) Abiti con (la tua famiglia)? **inf** *a*·bee·tee kon (la *too*·a fa·*mee*·lya)
A I live with (my parents).	Abito con (i miei genitori). *a*·bee·to kon (ee myay je·nee·*to*·ree)

CULTURE TIP

Well-Wishing

An Italian will typically wish you good luck with the expression *In bocca al lupo!* een *bo*·ka·*loo*·po, which is literally translated as 'In the mouth of the wolf!'. Make sure your answer is *Crepi!* *kre*·pee (literally 'Die!'), to ward off bad luck.

LISTEN FOR

Figuriamoci!	fee·goo·*rya*·mo·chee	Yeah, right!
Incredibile!	een·kre·*dee*·bee·le	Unbelievable!
Non è vero!	non e *ve*·ro	That's not true!
Scherzi!	*sker*·tsee	You're kidding!
Taci!	*ta*·chee	Shut up!

Q **Are you married?**	È sposato/a? **m/f pol** e spo·*za*·to/a Sei sposato/a? **m/f inf** say spo·*za*·to/a
A **I live with someone.**	Convivo. kon·*vee*·vo
A **I'm ...**	Sono ... *so*·no ...

married	sposato/a **m/f**	spo·*za*·to/a
separated	separato/a **m/f**	se·pa·*ra*·to/a
single (man)	celibe	*che*·lee·be
single (woman)	nubile	*noo*·bee·le

For more kinship terms, see the **dictionary**.

Talking with Children

What's your name?	Come ti chiami? *ko*·me tee *kya*·mee
How old are you?	Quanti anni hai? *kwan*·tee *a*·nee ai
What grade are you in?	Quale classe fai? *kwa*·le *kla*·se fai

CULTURE TIP

Body Language

Italians are emotionally demonstrative, so expect to see lots of cheek-kissing among acquaintances, embraces between good friends and lingering handshakes. Both men and women may walk along arm-in-arm. Pushing and shoving in busy places is not considered rude.

Be aware that respectful behaviour is expected in churches. Women should ideally cover their heads and avoid exposing too much flesh – wearing shorts or skimpy tops is considered disrespectful.

Do you like school?	Ti piace la scuola? tee *pya*·che la *skwo*·la
Do you like sport?	Ti piace lo sport? tee *pya*·che lo sport
What do you do after school?	Cosa fai dopo la scuola? *ko*·za fai *do*·po la *skwo*·la
Do you learn English?	Stai imparando l'inglese? stai eem·pa·*ran*·do leen·*gle*·ze
Do you have a pet at home?	Hai un animale domestico a casa? ai oon a·nee·*ma*·le do·*mes*·tee·ko a *ka*·za

Farewells

Q **What's your ...?**	Qual'è il Suo/tuo ...? **pol/inf** kwa·*le* eel *soo*·o/*too*·o ...
A **Here's my (email) address.**	Ecco il mio indirizzo (di email). *e*·ko eel *mee*·o een·dee·*ree*·tso (dee e·mayl)

LISTEN FOR

Assolutamente no!	a·so·loo·ta·*men*·te no	No way!
Forse.	*for*·se	Maybe.
Non c'è problema.	non che pro·*ble*·ma	No problem.
Sto bene.	sto *be*·ne	I'm OK.

Here's my mobile number.	Ecco il mio numero di cellulare. e·ko eel *mee*·o *noo*·me·ro dee che·loo·*la*·re
If you ever visit (England), come and visit us.	Caso mai venissi in (Inghilterra), vieni a trovarci. *ka*·zo mai ve·*nee*·see een (leen·geel·*te*·ra) *vye*·ne a tro·*var*·chee
If you ever visit (England), you can stay with me.	Caso mai venissi in (Inghilterra), puoi stare da me. *ka*·zo mai ve·*nee*·see een (leen·geel·*te*·ra) pwoy *sta*·re da me
It's been great meeting you.	È stato veramente un piacere conoscerti. e *sta*·to ve·ra·*men*·te oon pya·*che*·re ko·*no*·sher·tee
Are you on Facebook?	Lei è su Facebook? **pol** lay e soo *fays*·book Sei su Facebook? **inf** say soo *fays*·book
Keep in touch!	Teniamoci in contatto! te·*nya*·mo·chee een kon·*ta*·to

For more on addresses, see **directions** (p55).

Interests

KEY PHRASES

What do you do in your spare time?	Cosa fai nel tuo tempo libero?	*ko*·za fai nel *too*·o *tem*·po *lee*·be·ro
Do you like ...?	Ti piace/ piacciono ...? **sg/pl**	tee *pya*·che/ *pya*·cho·no ...
I (don't) like ...	(Non) Mi piace/ piacciono ... **sg/pl**	(non) mee *pya*·che/ *pya*·cho·no ...

Common Interests

What do you do in your spare time?	Cosa fai nel tuo tempo libero? *ko*·za fai nel *too*·o *tem*·po *lee*·be·ro
Q **Do you like ...?**	Ti piace/piacciono ...? **sg/pl** tee *pya*·che/*pya*·cho·no ...
A **I (don't) like ...**	(Non) Mi piace/ piacciono ... **sg/pl** (non) mee *pya*·che/ *pya*·cho·no ...

art	l'arte **sg**	*lar*·te
card games	i giochi di carte **pl**	ee *jo*·kee dee *kar*·te
cooking	cucinare **sg**	koo·chee·*na*·re
travelling	viaggiare **sg**	vee·a·*ja*·re

For more hobbies and sporting interests, see **sports** (p135) and the **dictionary**.

Music

Do you like to ...?	Ti piace ...?	tee *pya*·che ...
dance	ballare	ba·*la*·re
go to concerts	andare ai concerti	an·*da*·re ai kon·*cher*·tee
listen to music	ascoltare la musica	as·kol·*ta*·re la *moo*·zee·ka
play an instrument	suonare uno strumento	swo·*na*·re *oo*·no stroo·*men*·to
sing	cantare	kan·*ta*·re

What bands do you like? Quali gruppi ti piacciono? *kwa*·lee *groo*·pee tee *pya*·cho·no

What music do you like? Quale tipo di musica ti piace? *kwa*·le *tee*·po dee *moo*·zee·ka tee *pya*·che

... music musica ... *moo*·zee·ka ...

classical	classica	*kla*·see·ka
electronic	elettronica	e·le·*tro*·nee·ka
traditional	tradizionale	tra·dee·tsyo·*na*·le
world	etnica	*et*·nee·ka

Planning to go to a concert? See **buying tickets** (p41), and **going out** (p122).

LANGUAGE TIP

Likes & Dislikes

In Italian, to say you like something, use the expression *mi piace* mee *pya*·che (lit: me it-pleases). For plural, use *mi piacciono* mee *pya*·cho·no (lit: me they-please). To say 'no', just add *non* non: *non mi piace* non mee *pya*·che (lit: not me it-pleases).

I like this band.	Mi piace questo gruppo.	mee *pya*·che *kwe*·sto *groo*·po
I like soap operas.	Mi piacciono le telenovelle.	mee *pya*·cho·no le te·le·no·*ve*·le
I don't like to sing.	Non mi piace cantare.	non mee *pya*·che kan·*ta*·re

Cinema & Theatre

I feel like going to a ...
Ho voglia d'andare a ...
o *vo*·lya dan·*da*·re a ...

ballet	un balletto	oon ba·*le*·to
comedy	una commedia comica	*oo*·na ko·*me*·dya *ko*·mee·ka
film	vedere un film	ve·*de*·re oon feelm
play	teatro	te·*a*·tro

What's showing at the cinema/theatre tonight?
Cosa danno al cinema/teatro stasera?
ko·za *da*·no al *chee*·ne·ma/te·*a*·tro sta·*se*·ra

Is it in English/Italian?
È in inglese/italiano?
e een een·*gle*·ze/ee·ta·*lya*·no

Does it have subtitles?
Ci sono i sottotitoli?
chee *so*·no ee so·to·*tee*·to·lee

Have you seen ...?	Hai visto ...? ai *vee*·sto ...
Who's in it?	Chi sono i protagonisti? kee *so*·no ee pro·ta·go·*nee*·stee
Q **Did you like (the film)?**	Ti è piaciuto (il film)? tee e pya·*choo*·to (eel feelm)
A **I thought it was excellent.**	L'ho trovato/a ottimo/a. **m/f** lo tro·*va*·to/a o·tee·mo/a
A **I thought it was long.**	L'ho trovato/a lungo/a. **m/f** lo tro·*va*·to/a *loon*·go/a
A **I thought it was OK.**	L'ho trovato/a passabile. **m/f** lo tro·*va*·to/a pa·*sa*·bee·le
I (don't) like ...	(Non) Mi piacciono ... (non) mee *pya*·cho·no ...

action movies	i film d'azione	ee feelm da·*tsyo*·ne
animated films	i film animati	ee feelm a·nee·*ma*·tee
black comedy	i film tragicomici	ee feelm tra·jee·*ko*·mee·chee
comedies	le commedie comiche	le ko·*me*·dye *ko*·mee·ke
documentaries	i documentari	ee do·koo·men·*ta*·ree
drama	i film drammatici	ee feelm dra·*ma*·tee·chee
horror movies	i film d'orrore	ee feelm do·*ro*·re
period dramas	i drammi d'ambiente	ee *dra*·mee dam·*byen*·te
sci-fi	i film di fantascienza	ee feelm dee fan·ta·*shen*·tsa
short films	i film corti	ee feelm *kor*·tee
thrillers	i gialli	ee *ja*·lee
war movies	i film di guerra	ee feelm dee *gwe*·ra

Feelings & Opinions

KEY PHRASES

Are you ...?	È/Sei ...? **pol/inf** Ha/Hai ...? **pol/inf**	e/say ... a/ai ...
I'm (not) ...	(Non) Sono ... (Non) Ho ...	(non) *so*·no ... (non) o ...
What did you think of it?	Che cosa ne pensi?	ke *ko*·za ne *pen*·see
I thought it was OK.	Pensavo che fosse passabile.	pen·*sa*·vo ke *fo*·se pa·*sa*·bee·le
How do people feel about ...?	Cosa pensa la gente di ...?	*ko*·za *pen*·sa la *jen*·te dee ...

Feelings

Feelings are described with nouns or adjectives: nouns use 'have' (eg 'I have hunger') and adjectives use 'be' (as in English).

Q Are you (sad)?	È/Sei (triste)? **pol/inf** e/say (*tree*·ste)
A I'm (worried).	Sono (preoccupato/a). **m/f** *so*·no (pre·o·koo·*pa*·to/a)
A I'm not (happy).	Non sono (felice). non *so*·no (fe·*lee*·che)
Q Are you (sleepy)?	Ha/Hai (sonno)? **pol/inf** a/ai (*so*·no)
A I'm (cold).	Ho (freddo). o (*fre*·do)
A I'm not (hungry).	Non ho (fame). non o (*fa*·me)

I'm a little (sad).	Sono un po' (triste). *so*·no oon po (*tree*·ste)
I'm very (content).	Sono molto (contento/a). **m/f** *so*·no *mol*·to (kon·*ten*·to/a)
I feel (extremely lucky).	Mi sento (fortunatissimo/a). **m/f** mee *sen*·to (for·too·na·*tee*·see·mo/a)

If you're not feeling well, see **health** (p150).

Opinions

Q **Did you like it?**	Ti è piaciuto/a? **m/f** tee e pya·*choo*·to/a
Q **What did you think of it?**	Che cosa ne pensi? ke *ko*·za ne *pen*·see
A **I thought it was ...**	Pensavo che fosse ... pen·*sa*·vo ke *fo*·se ...
A **It's ...**	È ... e ...

boring	noioso/a **m/f**	no·*yo*·zo/a
great	ottimo/a **m/f**	o·tee·mo/a
interesting	interessante	een·te·re·*san*·te
OK	passabile	pa·*sa*·bee·le
weird	strano/a **m/f**	*stra*·no/a

Politics & Social Issues

Italians don't shy away from discussing political and social issues and might be interested in knowing your opinion on all kinds of topics. Even *il campionato* eel kam·pyo·*na*·to (football/soccer) takes on the dimensions of a serious political issue.

Q **Who do you vote for?**	Per chi vota Lei? **pol** per kee *vo*·ta lay Per chi voti? **inf** per kee *vo*·tee	
A **I support the ... party.**	Sono per il partito ... *so*·no per eel par·*tee*·to ...	

communist	comunista	ko·moo·*nee*·sta
conservative	conservatore	kon·ser·va·*to*·re
green	verde	*ver*·de
labour	laburista	la·boo·*ree*·sta
liberal	liberale	lee·be·*ra*·le
socialist	socialista	so·cha·*lee*·sta

Are you against ... ?	È/Sei contro ...? **pol/inf** e/say *kon*·tro ..
Are you in favour of ...?	È/Sei a favore di ...? **pol/inf** e/say a fa·*vo*·re dee ...
Q **Do you agree with it?**	È/Sei d'accordo con ...? **pol/inf** e/say da·*kor*·do kon ...
A **I (don't) agree with ...**	(Non) Sono d'accordo con ... (non) *so*·no da·*kor*·do kon ...
How do people feel about (the) ...?	Cosa pensa la gente di ...? *ko*·za *pen*·sa la *jen*·te dee ...

economy	economia	e·ko·no·*mee*·a
health care	servizi sanitari	ser·*vee*·tsee sa·nee·*ta*·ree
immigration	immigrazione	ee·mee·gra·*tsyo*·ne
organised crime	criminalità organizzata	kree·mee·na·lee·*ta* or·ga·nee·*dza*·ta
war in ...	guerra in ...	*gwe*·ra een ...

The Environment

Is there a/an (environmental) problem here?	C'è un problema (ambientale) qui? che oon pro·*ble*·ma (am·byen·*ta*·le) kwee
Where can I recycle this?	Dove lo posso riciclare? *do*·ve lo *po*·so ree·chee·*kla*·re
Is this a protected forest?	È una foresta protetta questa? e *oo*·na fo·*res*·ta pro·*te*·ta *kwe*·sta
Is this a protected park?	È un parco protetto questo? e oon *par*·ko pro·*te*·to *kwe*·sto
Is this a protected species?	È una specie protetta questa? e *oo*·na *spe*·che pro·*te*·ta *kwe*·sta
climate change	cambiamento **m** del clima kam·bya·*men*·to del *klee*·ma
pollution	inquinamento **m** een·kwee·na·*men*·to
recycling programme	programma **m** di riciclaggio pro·*gra*·ma dee ree·chee·*kla*·jo
the environment	ambiente **m** am·*byen*·te

Going Out

KEY PHRASES

What's on tonight?	Che c'è in programma stasera?	ke che een pro·*gra*·ma sta·*se*·ra
Where are the clubs?	Dove sono dei clubs?	*do*·ve *so*·no day kloobs
Would you like to go for a coffee?	Vuoi/Volete andare a prendere un caffè? **sg/pl**	vwoy/vo·*le*·te an·*da*·re a *pren*·de·re oon ka·*fe*
What time shall we meet?	A che ora ci vediamo?	a ke *o*·ra chee ve·*dya*·mo
Where will we meet?	Dove ci vediamo?	*do*·ve chee ve·*dya*·mo

Where to Go

What's there to do in the evenings?	Cosa si fa di sera? *ko*·za see fa dee *se*·ra
What's on ...?	Che c'è in programma ...? ke che een pro·*gra*·ma ...

locally	in zona	een *dzo*·na
this weekend	questo finesettimana	*kwe*·sto fee·ne·se·tee·*ma*·na
today	oggi	*o*·jee
tonight	stasera	sta·*se*·ra

Where are the ...?	Dove sono ...? *do*·ve *so*·no ...

bars	dei locali	day lo·*ka*·lee
cafes	dei bar	day bar
clubs	dei clubs	day kloobs
gay venues	dei locali gay	day lo·*ka*·lee ge
places to eat	posti in cui mangiare	*pos*·tee *een* *koo*·ee man·*ja*·re

Is there a local entertainment guide?	C'è una guida agli spettacoli in questa città? che *oo*·na *gwee*·da *a*·lyee spe·*ta*·ko·lee een *kwe*·sta chee·*ta*
What's the cover charge?	Quant'è l'ingresso? kwan·*te* leen·*gre*·so
I feel like going to a/the ...	Ho voglia d'andare ... o *vo*·lya dan·*da*·re ...

bar	a un locale	a oon lo·*ka*·le
coffee bar	a un caffè	a oon ka·*fe*
concert	a un concerto	a oon kon·*cher*·to
movies	al cinema	al *chee*·nee·ma
nightclub	in un locale notturno	een oon lo·*ka*·le no·*toor*·no
party	a una festa	a *oo*·na *fes*·ta
restaurant	in un ristorante	een oon rees·to·*ran*·te
theatre	al teatro	al te·*a*·tro

For more on bars, drinks and partying, see **eating out** (p173).

Invitations

What are you doing right now?	Cosa fai/fate proprio adesso? **sg/pl** *ko*·za fai/*fa*·te *pro*·pryo a·*de*·so
What are you doing this evening?	Cosa fai/fate stasera? **sg/pl** *ko*·za fai/*fa*·te sta·*se*·ra
What are you doing this weekend?	Cosa fai/fate questo fine settimana? **sg/pl** *ko*·za fai/*fa*·te *kwe*·sto *fee*·ne se·tee·*ma*·na
Would you like to go (for a) ...?	Vuoi/Volete andare a ...? **sg/pl** vwoy/vo·*le*·te an·*da*·re a ...

Facciamo una festa.
fa·*chya*·mo *oo*·na *fes*·ta
We're having a party.

CULTURE TIP

Night Spots

bar m bar – like a snack bar which also sells hot drinks and alcohol
birreria f bee·re·*ree*·a – has a pub-like atmosphere but specialises in beer
discoteca m dees·ko·*te*·ka – the most commonly frequented night spot for the under-30 age group
locale m **notturno** lo·*ka*·le no·*toor*·no – generic term for every type of night spot
nite m nait – a more elegant nightclub
osteria f os·te·*ree*·a – a sit-down eating place where people have wine with their meal

I feel like going (for a) ... Ho voglia d'andare a ...
o *vo*·lya dan·*da*·re a ...

coffee	prendere un caffè	*pren*·de·re oon ka·*fe*
dancing	ballare	ba·*la*·re
drink	bere qualcosa	*be*·re kwal·*ko*·za
meal	mangiare qualcosa	man·*ja*·re kwal·*ko*·za
walk	fare una passeggiata	*fa*·re *oo*·na pa·se·*ja*·ta

My round. Offro io.
o·fro *ee*·o

Do you know a good restaurant? Conosci/Conoscete un buon ristorante? **sg/pl**
ko·*no*·shee/ko·*no*·she·te oon bwon rees·to·*ran*·te

Do you want to come to a (jazz) concert with me? Vuoi/Volete venire a un concerto (di jazz)? **sg/pl**
vwoy/vo·*le*·te ve·*nee*·re a oon kon·*cher*·to (dee jaz)

We're having a party.	Facciamo una festa. fa·*chya*·mo *oo*·na *fes*·ta
You should come.	Dovresti/Dovreste venire. **sg/pl** dov·*res*·tee/dov·*res*·te ve·*nee*·re

Responding to Invitations

Yes, I'd love to.	Sì, mi piacerebbe. see mee pya·che·*re*·be
Where shall we go?	Dove andiamo? *do*·ve an·*dya*·mo
No, I'm afraid I can't.	No, temo di no. no *te*·mo dee no
What about tomorrow?	Domani che ne dici/dite? **sg/pl** do·*ma*·nee ke ne *dee*·chee/*dee*·te

Arranging to Meet

Q **What time shall we meet?**	A che ora ci vediamo? a ke *o*·ra chee ve·*dya*·mo
A **Let's meet at (eight) o'clock.**	Incontriamoci alle (otto). een·kon·*trya*·mo·chee *a*·le (*o*·to)
Q **Where will we meet?**	Dove ci vediamo? *do*·ve chee ve·*dya*·mo
A **Let's meet at the entrance.**	Incontriamoci all'entrata. een·kon·*trya*·mo·chee a·len·*tra*·ta

I'll pick you up.	Ti/Vi vengo a prendere. sg/pl tee/vee *ven*·go a *pren*·de·re
If I'm not there by (nine), don't wait for me.	Se non ci sono entro le (nove), non aspettarmi. se non chee *so*·no *en*·tro le (*no*·ve) non as·pe·*tar*·mee
I'll see you then.	Ci vediamo allora. chee ve·*dya*·mo a·*lo*·ra
I'm looking forward to it.	Non vedo l'ora. non *ve*·do *lo*·ra
Sorry I'm late.	Scusa, sono in ritardo. *skoo*·za *so*·no een ree·*tar*·do

Drugs

I don't take drugs.	Non mi drogo. non mee *dro*·go
I have ... occasionally.	Prendo ... ogni tanto. *pren*·do ... *o*·nyee *tan*·to
Do you want to have a smoke?	Lo vuoi uno spinello? lo vwoy *oo*·no spee·*ne*·lo
Do you have a light?	Hai d'accendere? ai da·*chen*·de·re

If the police are talking to you about drugs, see **police** (p148), for useful phrases.

Romance

KEY PHRASES

Would you like to do something?	Vuoi fare qualcosa?	vwoy *fa*·re kwal·*ko*·za
I love you.	Ti amo.	tee *a*·mo
Leave me alone!	Lasciami in pace!	*la*·sha·mee een *pa*·che

Asking Someone Out

Q **Would you like to do something (tonight)?**	Vuoi fare qualcosa (stasera)? vwoy *fa*·re kwal·*ko*·za (sta·*se*·ra)
A **Yes, I'd love to.**	Sì, mi piacerebbe molto. see mee pya·che·*re*·be *mol*·to
A **No, I'm afraid I can't.**	No, temo di no. no *te*·mo dee no

Pick-Up Lines

Would you like a drink?	Prendi qualcosa da bere? *pren*·dee kwal·*ko*·za da *be*·re
Do you have a light?	Hai d'accendere? ai da·*chen*·de·re
Can I dance with you?	Posso ballare con te? *po*·so ba·*la*·re kon te

Shall we get some fresh air?	Andiamo a prendere un po' d'aria fresca? an·*dya*·mo a *pren*·de·re oon po *da*·rya *fres*·ka
Can I sit here?	Posso sedermi qui? *po*·so se·*der*·mee kwee
Can I take you home?	Posso accompagnarti a casa? *po*·so a·kom·pa·*nyar*·tee a *ka*·za

Rejections

I'm here with my boyfriend.	Sono qui con il mio ragazzo. *so*·no kwee kon eel *mee*·o ra·*ga*·tso
I'm here with my girlfriend.	Sono qui con la mia ragazza. *so*·no kwee kon la *mee*·a ra·*ga*·tsa
Excuse me, I have to go now.	Scusa, adesso devo andare. *skoo*·za a·*de*·so *de*·vo an·*da*·re
I'm sorry, but I don't feel like it.	Mi dispiace ma non ne ho voglia. mee dees·*pya*·che ma non ne o *vo*·lya
I'm not interested.	Non mi interessa. non mee een·te·*re*·sa
Leave me alone!	Lasciami in pace! *la*·sha·mee een *pa*·che
Don't touch me!	Non mi toccare! non mee to·*ka*·re
Let me through!	Lasciami passare! *la*·sha·mee pa·*sa*·re

LANGUAGE TIP

Masculine & Feminine

Throughout this book we have used the abbreviations m and f to indicate whether a word is masculine or feminine. Where a word has both a masculine and a feminine form, the feminine ending is added after a slash, eg *bello/a* m/f *be*·lo/a (beautiful). See also **gender** in the **grammar** chapter (p19).

Getting Closer

You're very nice.	Sei molto simpatico/a. m/f say *mol*·to seem·*pa*·tee·ko/a
You're great.	Sei fantastico/a. m/f say fan·*tas*·tee·ko/a
Can I kiss you?	Ti posso baciare? tee *po*·so ba·*cha*·re
Will you take me home?	Mi porti a casa? mee *por*·tee a *ka*·za
Do you want to come inside for a while?	Vuoi entrare per un po'? vwoy en·*tra*·re per oon po

Sex

I want to make love to you.	Voglio fare l'amore con te. *vo*·lyo *fa*·re la·*mo*·re kon te
Do you have a condom?	Hai un preservativo? ai oon pre·ser·va·*tee*·vo
I won't do it without protection.	Non lo farò senza protezione. non lo fa·*ro sen*·tsa pro·te·*tsyo*·ne
I think we should stop now.	Penso che dovremmo fermarci adesso. *pen*·so ke dov·*re*·mo fer·*mar*·chee a·*de*·so

Let's go to bed!	Andiamo a letto! an·*dya*·mo a *le*·to
Kiss me.	Baciami. *ba*·cha·mee
I want you.	Ti desidero. tee de·*see*·de·ro
Touch me here.	Toccami qui. *to*·ka·mee kwee
Q **Do you like this?**	Ti piace questo? tee *pya*·che *kwe*·sto
A **I (don't) like that.**	(Non) Mi piace quello. (non) mee *pya*·che *kwe*·lo
That was amazing.	È stato stupendo. e *sta*·to stoo·*pen*·do
Can I stay over?	Posso restare la notte? *po*·so res·*ta*·re la *no*·te
When can I see you again?	Quando possiamo rivederci? *kwan*·do po·*sya*·mo ree·ve·*der*·chee

Love

I'm in love with you.	Sono innamorato/a di te. m/f *so*·no ee·na·mo·*ra*·to/a dee te
Q **Do you love me?**	Mi ami? mee *a*·mee
A **I love you.**	Ti amo. tee *a*·mo

LANGUAGE TIP

Double Entendres

Be mindful of the word *finocchio* fee·*no*·kyo, which means both 'fennel' and 'queer' (homosexual). Likewise, keep in mind that *uccello* oo·*che*·lo can mean either 'bird' or 'dick'.

LISTEN FOR

amore mio	a·*mo*·re *mee*·o	my love
caro/a mio/a m/f	*ka*·ro/a *mee*·o/a	my darling
gioia mia	*jo*·ya *mee*·a	my joy
tesoro mio	te·*zo*·ro *mee*·o	my treasure

I think we're good together.	Penso che stiamo bene insieme. *pen*·so ke *stya*·mo *be*·ne een·*sye*·me

Problems

Are you seeing someone else?	Frequenti qualcun'altro/a? m/f fre·*kwen*·tee kwal·koo·*nal*·tro/a
He's just a friend.	È solo un amico. e *so*·lo oo·na·*mee*·ko
She's just a friend.	È solo un'amica. e *so*·lo oo·na·*mee*·ka
I don't think it's working out.	Non credo che stia funzionando fra noi due. non *kre*·do ke *stee*·a foon·tsyo·*nan*·do fra noy *doo*·e
We'll work it out.	Troveremo una soluzione. tro·ve·*re*·mo *oo*·na so·loo·*tsyo*·ne
I never want to see you again.	Non voglio vederti mai più. non *vo*·lyo ve·*der*·tee mai pyoo
I want to stay friends.	Voglio che restiamo amici. *vo*·lyo ke res·*tya*·mo a·*mee*·chee

Beliefs & Culture

KEY PHRASES

What's your religion?	Di che religione è Lei? **pol** Di che religione sei tu? **inf**	dee ke re·lee·*jo*·ne e lay dee ke re·lee·*jo*·ne say too
I'm (not) ...	(Non) Sono ...	(non) *so*·no ...
I'm sorry, it's against my beliefs.	Mi dispiace, non è permesso dalla mia fede.	mee dees·*pya*·che non e per·*me*·so *da*·la *mee*·a *fe*·de

Religion

Q **What's your religion?**
Di che religione è Lei? **pol**
dee ke re·lee·*jo*·ne e lay
Di che religione sei tu? **inf**
dee ke re·lee·*jo*·ne say too

A **I (don't) believe in God.**
(Non) Credo in Dio.
(non) *kre*·do een *dee*·o

A **I'm (not) ...**
(Non) Sono ...
(non) *so*·no ...

agnostic	agnostico/a **m/f**	a·nyos·*tee*·ko/a
atheist	ateo/a **m/f**	*a*·te·o/a
practising	praticante	pra·tee·*kan*·te
religious	religioso/a **m/f**	re·lee·*jo*·zo/a

Where can I pray?
Dove posso pregare?
do·ve *po*·so pre·*ga*·re

I'd like to go to (the) ...	Vorrei andare ... vo·*ray* an·*da*·re ...

church	alla chiesa	*a*·la *kye*·za
mosque	alla moschea	*a*·la mos·*ke*·a
synagogue	alla sinagoga	*a*·la see·na·*go*·ga
temple	al tempio	*a*·la *tem*·pyo

For religions, see the **dictionary**.

Cultural Differences

Is this a local custom?	È una tradizione locale? e *oo*·na tra·dee·*tsyo*·ne lo·*ka*·le
I'm not used to this.	Non ci sono abituato/a. **m/f** non chee *so*·no a·bee·*twa*·to/a
I'll try it.	Lo proverò. lo pro·ve·*ro*
I didn't mean to do/say anything wrong.	Non volevo dire/fare qualcosa di sbagliato. non vo·*le*·vo *dee*·re/*fa*·re kwal·*ko*·za dee sba·*lya*·to
I'm sorry, it's against my beliefs.	Mi dispiace, non è permesso dalla mia fede. mee dees·*pya*·che non e per·*me*·so *da*·la *mee*·a *fe*·de
I'm sorry, it's against my culture.	Mi dispiace, non è permesso dalla mia cultura. mee dees·*pya*·che non e per·*me*·so *da*·la *mee*·a kool·*too*·ra

Sports

KEY PHRASES

Which sport do you play?	Quale sport pratichi?	*kwa*·le sport *pra*·tee·kee
Who's your favourite team?	Qual'è la tua squadra preferita?	kwa·*le* la *too*·a *skwa*·dra pre·fe·*ree*·ta
What's the score?	Qual'è il punteggio?	kwa·*le* eel poon·*te*·jo

Sporting Interests

Q **Do you like (sport)?**	Ti piace (lo sport)? tee *pya*·che (lo sport)
A **Yes, very much.**	Sì, moltissimo. see mol·*tee*·see·mo
A **Not really.**	Non molto. non *mol*·to
A **I like watching it.**	Mi piace assistere. mee *pya*·che a·*see*·ste·re
A **I follow (cycling).**	Seguo (il ciclismo). *se*·gwo (eel cheek·*leez*·mo)
Q **Which sport do you play?**	Quale sport pratichi? *kwa*·le sport *pra*·tee·kee
A **I play (football/soccer).**	Pratico (il calcio). *pra*·tee·ko (eel *kal*·cho)

For more sports, see the **dictionary**.

Who's your favourite sportsman?	Chi è il tuo sportivo preferito? kee e eel *too*·o spor·*tee*·vo pre·fe·*ree*·to
Who's your favourite sportswoman?	Chi è la tua sportiva preferita? kee e la *too*·a spor·*tee*·va pre·fe·*ree*·ta
Who's your favourite team?	Qual'è la tua squadra preferita? kwa·*le* la *too*·a *skwa*·dra pre·fe·*ree*·ta

Going to a Game

Would you like to go to a game?	Ti piacerebbe andare ad una partita? tee pya·che·*re*·be an·*da*·re a·*doo*·na par·*tee*·ta
Who are you supporting?	Per chi fai il tifo? per kee fai eel *tee*·fo
Who's playing?	Chi gioca? kee *jo*·ka
Who's winning?	Chi vince? kee *veen*·che
How much time is left?	Quanto tempo manca? *kwan*·to *tem*·po *man*·ka
Q **What's the score?**	Qual'è il punteggio? kwa·*le* eel poon·*te*·jo
A **It's a draw.**	Hanno pareggiato. *a*·no pa·re·*ja*·to
That was a bad/great game!	Che partita brutta/ fantastica! ke par·*tee*·ta *broo*·ta/ fan·*tas*·tee·ka

LISTEN FOR

Che passaggio!	ke pa·*sa*·jo	What a pass!
Che calcio!	ke *kal*·cho	What a kick!
Che colpo!	ke *kol*·po	What a hit!

Playing Sport

Q **Do you want to play?**	Vuoi giocare? *vwoy jo·ka·re*
A **Yes, that'd be great.**	Sì, sarebbe bello. *see sa·re·be be·lo*
A **I'm sorry, I can't.**	Mi dispiace, non posso. *mee dees·pya·che non po·so*
Can I join in?	Posso giocare anch'io? *po·so jo·ka·re an·kee·o*
Where's the nearest gym?	Dov'è la palestra più vicina? *do·ve la pa·le·stra pyoo vee·chee·na*
Where's the nearest swimming pool?	Dov'è la piscina più vicina? *do·ve la pee·shee·na pyoo vee·chee·na*
Where's the nearest tennis court?	Dov'è il campo da tennis più vicino? *do·ve eel kam·po da te·nees pyoo vee·chee·no*
What's the charge per ...?	Qual'è il prezzo richiesto ...? *kwa·le eel pre·tso ree·kye·sto ...*

day	per la giornata	per la jor·*na*·ta
game	per una partita	per *oo*·na par·*tee*·ta
hour	all'ora	a·*lo*·ra
visit	a visita	a *vee*·see·ta

LISTEN FOR

Passala a me!	*pa*·sa·la a me	Kick/Pass it to me!
Punto a me/te.	*poon*·to a me/te	My/Your point.
Era fuori.	e·ra *fwo*·ree	That was out.
Giochi bene.	*jo*·kee *be*·ne	You're a good player.
Imbroglione/a! m/f	eem·bro·*lyo*·ne/a	Cheat!
Grazie della partita.	*gra*·tsye *de*·la par·*tee*·ta	Thanks for the game.

Can I hire a court?	Posso noleggiare un campo? *po*·so no·le·*ja*·re oon *kam*·po
Can I hire a ball?	Posso noleggiare una palla? *po*·so no·le·*ja*·re *oo*·na *pa*·la
Can I hire a racquet?	Posso noleggiare una racchetta? *po*·so no·le·*ja*·re *oo*·na ra·*ke*·ta
Do I have to be a member to attend?	È necessario essere soci? e ne·che·*sa*·ryo *e*·se·re *so*·chee
Is there a women-only session?	Ci sono i corsi per sole donne? chee *so*·no ee *kor*·see per *so*·le *do*·ne
Where are the changing rooms?	Dove sono gli spogliatoi? *do*·ve *so*·no lyee spo·lya·*to*·ee

Football/Soccer

Who plays for (Sampdoria)?	Chi gioca per (la Sampdoria)? kee *jo*·ka per (la samp·do·*ree*·a)

LISTEN FOR

allenatore/ allenatrice m/f	a·le·na·*to*·re/ a·le·na·*tree*·che	coach
angolo m	*an*·go·lo	corner
cannoniere m	ka·no·*nye*·re	goal-scorer
calciatore/ calciatrice m/f	kal·cha·*to*·re/ kal·cha·*tree*·che	football/soccer player
cartellino giallo/rosso m	kar·te·*lee*·no *ja*·lo/*ro*·so	yellow/red card
fallo m	*fa*·lo	foul
fuorigioco m	fwo·ree·*jo*·ko	offside
giocatore/ giocatrice m/f	jo·ka·*to*·re/ jo·ka·*tree*·che	player
pallone m	pa·*lo*·ne	ball
porta f	*por*·ta	goal (place)
portiere m&f	por·*tye*·re	goalkeeper
rigore m	ree·*go*·re	penalty (kick)
serie f	*se*·rye	league
tifosi m pl	tee·*fo*·zee	fans/supporters

He's a great (player).	È un bravo (giocatore). *e oon bra·vo (jo·ka·to·re)*
Which team is at the top of the league?	Quale squadra è in testa alla classifica? *kwa·le skwa·dra e een tes·ta a·la kla·see·fee·ka*
What a terrible team!	Che squadra schifosa! *ke skwa·dra skee·fo·za*
Come on boys!	Forza ragazzi! *for·tsa ra·ga·tsee*

Outdoors

KEY PHRASES

Where can I buy supplies?	Dove posso comprare delle provviste?	*do*·ve *po*·so kom·*pra*·re *de*·le pro·*vee*·ste
Do we need a guide?	Occorre una guida?	o·*ko*·re *oo*·na *gwee*·da
Is it safe?	È sicuro?	e see·*koo*·ro
I'm lost.	Mi sono perso/a. **m/f**	mee *so*·no *per*·so/a
What's the weather like?	Che tempo fa?	ke *tem*·po fa

Hiking

Where can I ...? Dove posso ...? *do*·ve *po*·so ...

buy supplies	comprare delle provviste	kom·*pra*·re *de*·le pro·*vee*·ste
find out about hiking trails	informarmi sulle piste per l'escursionismo a piedi	een·for·*mar*·mee soo·le *pee*·ste per les·koor·syo·*neez*·mo a *pye*·dee
get a map	trovare una carta	tro·*va*·re *oo*·na *kar*·ta
hire hiking gear	noleggiare l'attrezzatura per l'escursionismo a piedi	no·le·*ja*·re la·tre·tsa·*too*·ra per les·koor·syo·*neez*·mo a *pye*·dee

Do we need to take food?	Dobbiamo portare del cibo? do·*bya*·mo por·*ta*·re del *chee*·bo
Do we need to take water?	Dobbiamo portare dell'acqua? do·*bya*·mo por·*ta*·re de·*la*·kwa
How high is the climb?	Quant'è alta la salita? kwan·*te al*·ta la sa·*lee*·ta
How long is the hike?	Quant'è lunga l'escursione? kwan·*te loon*·ga les·koor·*syo*·ne
How long is the trail?	Quant'è lungo il sentiero? kwan·*te loon*·go eel sen·*tye*·ro
Is the track (well-)marked?	La pista è (ben) segnata? la *pee*·sta e (ben) se·*nya*·ta
Is the track open?	La pista è aperta? la *pee*·sta e a·*per*·ta
Is the track scenic?	La pista è panoramica? la *pee*·sta e pa·no·*ra*·mee·ka
Which is the easiest route?	Qual'è il percorso più facile? kwa·*le* eel per·*kor*·so pyoo *fa*·chee·le
Which is the most interesting route?	Qual'è il percorso più interessante? kwa·*le* eel per·*kor*·so pyoo een·te·re·*san*·te
Where's the nearest village?	Dov'è il villaggio più vicino? do·*ve* eel vee·*la*·jo pyoo vee·*chee*·no
Do we need a guide?	Occorre una guida? o·*ko*·re *oo*·na *gwee*·da
I'm lost.	Mi sono perso/a. **m/f** mee *so*·no *per*·so/a

Are there guided treks?	Ci sono delle escursioni guidate? chee *so*·no *de*·le es·koor·*syo*·nee gwee·*da*·te
Is it safe?	È sicuro? e see·*koo*·ro
Is there a hut there?	C'è un rifugio là? che oon re·*foo*·jo la
When does it get dark?	Quando fa buio? *kwan*·do fa *boo*·yo
Does this path go to (Ginostra)?	Questo sentiero va verso (Ginostra)? *kwe*·sto sen·*tye*·ro va *ver*·so (jee·*nos*·tra)
Can we go through here?	Possiamo passare da qui? po·*sya*·mo pa·*sa*·re da kwee
Is the water OK to drink?	Si può bere l'acqua? see pwo *be*·re *la*·kwa

At the Beach

Where's the best beach?	Dov'è la spiaggia migliore? do·*ve* la *spya*·ja mee·*lyo*·re
Where's the nearest beach?	Dov'è la spiaggia più vicina? do·*ve* la *spya*·ja pyoo vee·*chee*·na
Is it safe to dive here?	Si può fare i tuffi senza pericolo? see pwo *fa*·re ee *too*·fee *sen*·tsa pe·*ree*·ko·lo
Is it safe to swim here?	Si può nuotare senza pericolo? see pwo nwo·*ta*·re *sen*·tsa pe·*ree*·ko·lo

LOOK FOR

Vietato Nuotare	vye·*ta*·to noo·o·*ta*·re	No Swimming

What time is high tide?	A che ora è l'alta marea? a ke *o*·ra e *lal*·ta ma·*re*·a
What time is low tide?	A che ora è la bassa marea? a ke *o*·ra e la *ba*·sa ma·*re*·a
How much for a deckchair?	Quanto costa una sedia a sdraio? *kwan*·to *ko*·sta *oo*·na *se*·dya a *zdra*·yo
How much for an umbrella?	Quanto costa un ombrello? *kwan*·to *ko*·sta oo·nom·*bre*·lo

Weather

Q **What's the weather like?**	Che tempo fa? ke *tem*·po fa
A **It's cloudy.**	È nuvoloso. e noo·vo·*lo*·zo
A **It's windy.**	Tira vento. *tee*·ra *ven*·to
A **It's cold.**	Fa freddo. fa *fre*·do
A **It's hot.**	Fa caldo. fa *kal*·do
A **It's raining.**	Piove. *pyo*·ve
A **It's snowing.**	Nevica. ne·*vee*·ka

È pericoloso!	e pe·ree·ko·*lo*·zo	It's dangerous!
Fa attenzione al risucchio!	fa a·ten·*tsyo*·ne al ree·*soo*·kyo	Be careful of the undertow!

What's the weather forecast? Cosa dicono le previsioni del tempo? *ko*·za *dee*·ko·no le pre·vee·*zyo*·nee del *tem*·po

Flora & Fauna

What (kind of) ... is that? Che (tipo di) ... è quello? ke (*tee*·po dee) ... e *kwe*·lo

animal	animale	a·nee·*ma*·le
bird	uccello	oo·*che*·lo
plant	pianta	*pyan*·ta
tree	albero	*al*·be·ro

Is it ...? È ...? e ...

common	comune	ko·*moo*·ne
dangerous	pericoloso/a **m/f**	pe·ree·ko·*lo*·zo/a
poisonous	velenoso/a **m/f**	ve·le·*no*·zo/a
protected	protetto/a **m/f**	pro·*te*·to/a

For geographical and agricultural terms, and names of animals and plants, see the **dictionary**.

Safe Travel

EMERGENCIES 146
POLICE 148
HEALTH 150

Emergencies

KEY PHRASES

Help!	Aiuto!	a·*yoo*·to
There's been an accident.	C'è stato un incidente.	che *sta*·to oon een·chee·*den*·te
It's an emergency!	È un'emergenza!	e oo·ne·mer·*jen*·tsa

Help!	Aiuto! a·*yoo*·to
Stop!	Fermi! *fer*·mee
Go away!	Vai via! vai *vee*·a
Thief!	Ladro! *la*·dro
Fire!	Al fuoco! al *fwo*·ko
Watch out!	Attenzione! a·ten·*tsyo*·ne
Call the police!	Chiami la polizia! *kya*·mee la po·lee·*tsee*·a
Call a doctor!	Chiami un medico! *kya*·mee oon *me*·dee·ko
Call an ambulance!	Chiami un'ambulanza! *kya*·mee o·nam·boo·*lan*·tsa
It's an emergency!	È un'emergenza! e oo·ne·mer·*jen*·tsa

LISTEN FOR

Cristo!	*kree*·sto	Christ!
Dio!	*dee*·o	God!
Gesù!	je·*soo*	Jesus!
Madonna!	ma·*do*·na	Goodness!
Maledizione!	ma·le·dee·*tsyo*·ne	Damn!
Merda!	*mer*·da	Shit!

There's been an accident.	C'è stato un incidente. che *sta*·to oon een·chee·*den*·te
Can you help me, please?	Mi può aiutare, per favore? mee pwo a·yoo·*ta*·re per fa·*vo*·re
I have to use the telephone.	Devo fare una telefonata. *de*·vo *fa*·re *oo*·na te·le·fo·*na*·ta
I'm lost.	Mi sono perso/a. **m/f** mee *so*·no *per*·so/a
Do you have a first-aid kit?	Avete una cassetta di pronto soccorso? a·*ve*·te *oo*·na ka·*se*·ta dee *pron*·to so·*kor*·so
Where are the toilets?	Dove sono i gabinetti? *do*·ve *so*·no ee ga·bee·*ne*·tee

Police

KEY PHRASES

Where's the police station?	Dov'è il posto di polizia?	do·*ve* eel *pos*·to dee po·lee·*tsee*·a
I want to contact my embassy.	Vorrei contattare la mia ambasciata.	vo·*ray* kon·ta·*ta*·re la *mee*·a am·ba·*sha*·ta
My bag was stolen.	Mi hanno rubato la mia borsa.	mee *a*·no roo·*ba*·to la *mee*·a *bor*·sa

Where's the police station?	Dov'è il posto di polizia? do·*ve* eel *pos*·to dee po·lee·*tsee*·a
I want to report an offence.	Voglio fare una denuncia. *vo*·lyo *fa*·re *oo*·na de·*noon*·cha
I have insurance.	Ho l'assicurazione. o la·see·koo·ra·*tsyo*·ne
(My bag) was stolen.	Mi hanno rubato (la mia borsa). mee *a*·no roo·*ba*·to (la *mee*·a *bor*·sa)
I've lost (my wallet).	Ho perso (il mio portafoglio). o *per*·so (eel *mee*·o por·ta·*fo*·lyo)
I've been raped.	Sono stato/a violentato/a. **m/f** *so*·no *sta*·to/a vyo·len·*ta*·to/a

I want to contact my embassy.	Vorrei contattare la mia ambasciata. vo·*ray* kon·ta·*ta*·re la *mee*·a am·ba·*sha*·ta
Can I have a lawyer (who speaks English)?	Posso avere un avvocato (che parli inglese)? *po*·so a·*ve*·re oo·na·vo·*ka*·to (ke *par*·lee een·*gle*·ze)
Can I have a copy, please?	Potrei avere una copia, per favore? po·*tray* a·*ve*·re *oo*·na *ko*·pya per fa·*vo*·re
I have a prescription for this drug.	Ho una ricetta per questa medicina. o *oo*·na re·*che*·ta per *kwe*·sta me·dee·*chee*·na
What am I accused of?	Di che cosa sono stato/a accusato/a? **m/f** dee ke *ko*·za *so*·no *sta*·to/a a·koo·*za*·to/a
I didn't realise I was doing anything wrong.	Non sapevo che facessi qualcosa di male. non sa·*pe*·vo ke fa·*che*·see kwal·*ko*·za dee *ma*·le

CULTURE TIP

Cop Shops

In Italy, both the *polizia* po·lee·*tsee*·a (civilian police) and the *carabinieri* ka·ra·bee·*nye*·ree (administered by the Ministry of Defence) investigate crimes, but the *posto di polizia pos*·to dee po·lee·*tsee*·a (civilian police station) or the *questura* kwes·*too*·ra (police headquarters) is where to go to report a theft. Nevertheless, if you happen to be closer to the *carabinieri,* they'll redirect you from their *caserma* ka·*ser*·ma (barracks) if necessary.

Health

KEY PHRASES

Where's the nearest hospital?	Dov'è l'ospedale più vicino?	do·*ve* los·pe·*da*·le pyoo vee·*chee*·no
I'm sick.	Mi sento male.	mee *sen*·to *ma*·le
I need a doctor.	Ho bisogno di un medico.	o bee·*zo*·nyo dee oon *me*·dee·ko
I'm on medication for ...	Prendo la medicina per ...	*pren*·do la me·dee·*chee*·na per ...
I'm allergic to ...	Sono allergico/a ... **m/f**	*so*·no a·*ler*·jee·ko/a ...

Where's the nearest ...? Dov'è ... più vicino/a? **m/f**
do·*ve* ... pyoo vee·*chee*·no/a

(night) chemist	la farmacia **f** (di turno)	la far·ma·*chee*·a (dee *toor*·no)
dentist	il/la dentista **m/f**	eel/la den·*tee*·sta
doctor	il medico **m**	eel *me*·dee·ko
hospital	l'ospedale **m**	los·pe·*da*·le
optometrist	l'ottico **m**	*lo*·tee·ko

I need a doctor (who speaks English). Ho bisogno di un medico (che parli inglese).
o bee·*zo*·nyo dee oon *me*·dee·ko (ke *par*·lee een·*gle*·ze)

Could I see a female doctor? Posso vedere una dottoressa?
po·so ve·*de*·re *oo*·na do·to·*re*·sa

LISTEN FOR

Dove Le fa male?	*do*·ve le fa *ma*·le	Where does it hurt?
Ha la febbre?	a la *fe*·bre	Do you have a temperature?
Da quanto (tempo) è che si sente così?	da *kwan*·to (*tem*·po) e ke see *sen*·te ko·*zee*	How long have you been like this?
Si è mai sentito/a così prima? m/f	see e mai sen·*tee*·to/a ko·*zee pree*·ma	Have you had this before?

Can the doctor come here?	Può venire qui il medico? pwo ve·*nee*·re kwee eel *me*·dee·ko
I've been vaccinated for hepatitis A/B/C.	Sono stato/a vaccinato/a per l'epatite A/B/C. m/f *so*·no *sta*·to/a va·chee·*na*·to/a per le·pa·*tee*·te a/bee/chee
I've been vaccinated for tetanus.	Sono stato/a vaccinato/a per il tetano. m/f *so*·no *sta*·to/a va·chee·*na*·to/a per eel *te*·ta·no
I've been vaccinated for typhoid.	Sono stato/a vaccinato/a per il tifo. m/f *so*·no *sta*·to/a va·chee·*na*·to/a per eel *tee*·fo
I need new contact lenses.	Ho bisogno di nuove lenti a contatto. o bee·*zo*·nyo dee *nwo*·ve *len*·tee a kon·*ta*·to

I need new glasses.	Ho bisogno di nuovi occhiali. o bee·*zo*·nyo dee *nwo*·vee o·*kya*·lee
I've run out of my medication.	Ho finito la mia medicina. o fee·*nee*·to la *mee*·a me·dee·*chee*·na
Can I have a receipt for my insurance?	Potrebbe darmi una ricevuta per l'assicurazione? po·*tre*·be *dar*·mee *oo*·na ree·che·*voo*·ta per la·see·koo·ra·*tsyo*·ne

Symptoms & Conditions

I'm sick.	Mi sento male. mee *sen*·to *ma*·le
It hurts here.	Mi fa male qui. mee fa *ma*·le kwee
I've been injured.	Sono stato/a ferito/a. **m/f** *so*·no *sta*·to/a fe·*ree*·to/a
I've been vomiting.	Ho vomitato alcune volte. o vo·mee·*ta*·to al·*koo*·ne *vol*·te
I can't sleep.	Non riesco a dormire. non *ryes*·ko a dor·*mee*·re

LISTEN FOR

È allergico/a a qualcosa? m/f	e a·*ler*·jee·ko/a a kwal·*ko*·za	Are you allergic to anything?
Sta prendendo medicine?	sta pren·*den*·do me·dee·*chee*·ne	Are you on medication?
Beve?	*be*·ve	Do you drink?
Fuma?	*foo*·ma	Do you smoke?
Si droga?	see *dro*·ga	Do you take drugs?

I have an infection.	Ho un'infezione. o oon een·fe·*tsyo*·ne
I have a rash.	Ho uno sfogo. o *oo*·no *sfo*·go
I feel weak.	Mi sento debole. mee *sen*·to *de*·bo·le
I feel ...	Ho ... o ...

dizzy	il capogiro	eel ka·po·*gee*·ro
hot and cold	vampate di calore	vam·*pa*·te dee ka·*lo*·re
nauseous	la nausea	la *now*·ze·a
shivery	i brividi	ee *bree*·vee·dee

I have a ...	Ho ... o ...

cold	un raffreddore	oon ra·fre·*do*·re
fever	la febbre	la *fe*·bre
headache	mal di testa	mal dee *tes*·ta
heart condition	un problema cardiaco	oon pro·*ble*·ma kar·*dee*·a·ko
migraine	un'emicrania	oo·ne·mee·*kra*·nya

I'm asthmatic.	Sono asmatico/a. **m/f** *so*·no az·*ma*·tee·ko/a
I'm diabetic.	Sono diabetico/a. **m/f** *so*·no dee·a·*be*·tee·ko/a
I'm epileptic.	Sono epilettico/a. **m/f** *so*·no e·pee·*le*·tee·ko/a
I've (recently) had ...	Ho avuto ... (di recente). o a·*voo*·to ... (dee re·*chen*·te)

I'm on medication for ...	Prendo la medicina per ... *pren*·do la me·dee·*chee*·na per ...

For more symptoms and conditions, see the **dictionary**.

Women's Health

I'm pregnant.	Sono incinta. *so*·no een·*cheen*·ta
I need a pregnancy test.	Ho bisogno di un test di gravidanza. o bee·*zo*·nyo dee oon test dee gra·vee·*dan*·tsa
I'm on the Pill.	Prendo la pillola. *pren*·do la *pee*·lo·la
I have period pain.	Ho dolori mestruali. o do·*lo*·ree mes·*trwa*·lee

LISTEN FOR

Prende contraccettivi?	*pren*·de kon·tra·che·*tee*·vee	Are you using contraception?
Ha avuto rapporti non protetti?	a a·*voo*·to ra·*por*·tee non pro·*te*·tee	Have you had unprotected sex?
Ha le mestruazioni?	a le mes·troo·a·*tsyo*·nee	Are you menstruating?
È incinta?	e een·*cheen*·ta	Are you pregnant?
Quand'è l'ultima volta che Le sono venute le mestruazioni?	kwan·*de* *lool*·tee·ma *vol*·ta ke le *so*·no ve·*noo*·te le mes·troo·a·*tsyo*·nee	When did you last have your period?
È incinta.	e een·*cheen*·ta	You're pregnant.

I haven't had my period for (two) weeks.	Sono (due) settimane che non mi vengono le mestruazioni. *so*·no (*doo*·e) se·tee·*ma*·ne ke non mee *ven*·go·no le mes·troo·a·*tsyo*·nee
I've noticed a lump/ swelling here.	Ho notato un nodulo/gonfiore qui. o no·*ta*·to oon *no*·doo·lo/ gon·*fyo*·re kwee
I need contraception.	Ho bisogno di contraccettivi. o bee·*zo*·nyo dee kon·tra·che·*tee*·vee
I need the morning-after pill.	Ho bisogno della pillola del mattino dopo. o bee·*zo*·nyo *de*·la *pee*·lo·la del ma·*tee*·no *do*·po

Allergies

I have a skin allergy.	Ho un'allergia alla pelle. o oo·na·ler·*jee*·a *a*·la *pe*·le
I'm allergic to ...	Sono allergico/a ... **m/f** *so*·no a·*ler*·jee·ko/a ...

antibiotics	agli antibiotici	*a*·lyee an·tee·bee·*o*·tee·chee
anti-inflammatories	agli antinfiammatori	*a*·lyee an·teen·fya·ma·*to*·ree
bees	alle api	*a*·le *a*·pee
sulphur-based drugs	agli medicinali a base di zolfo	*a*·lyee me·dee·chee·*na*·lee a *ba*·ze dee *dzol*·fo

For food-related allergies, see **vegetarian & special meals** (p181).

Parts of the Body

My (stomach) hurts.	Mi fa male (lo stomaco). mee fa *ma*·le (lo *sto*·ma·ko)
I can't move (my ankle).	Non riesco a muovere (la caviglia). non *ryes*·ko a *mwo*·ve·re (la ka·*vee*·lya)
I have a cramp (in my foot).	Ho crampi (al piede). o *kram*·pee (al *pye*·de)
(My throat) is swollen.	(La gola) è gonfia. (la *go*·la) e *gon*·fya

Chemist

I need something for (diarrhoea).	Ho bisogno di qualcosa per (la diarrea). o bee·*zo*·nyo dee kwal·*ko*·za per (la dee·a·*re*·a)
Do I need a prescription for (antihistamines)?	C'è bisogno di una ricetta per (gli antistaminici)? che bee·*zo*·nyo dee *oo*·na re·*che*·ta per (lyee an·tee·sta·*mee*·nee·chee)

LISTEN FOR

Questo l'ha mai preso?	*kwe*·sto la mai *pre*·so	Have you taken this before?
Deve completare il ciclo.	*de*·ve kom·ple·*ta*·re eel *cheek*·lo	You must complete the course.
Due volte al giorno (con i pasti).	*doo*·e *vol*·te al *jor*·no (kon ee *pas*·tee)	Twice a day (with food).

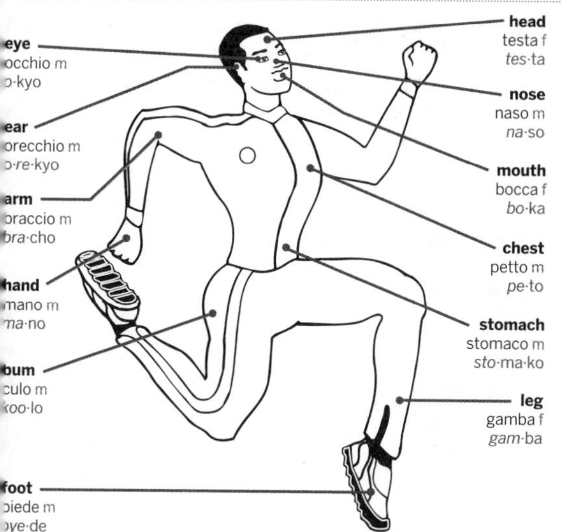

How many times a day?	Quante volte al giorno? *kwan*·te *vol*·te al *jor*·no
Will it make me drowsy?	Mi farà dormire? mee fa·*ra* dor·*mee*·re

For pharmaceutical items, see the **dictionary**.

Dentist

I have a broken tooth.	Ho un dente rotto. o oon *den*·te *ro*·to
I have a cavity.	Ho una cavità. o *oo*·na ka·vee·*ta*

SAFE TRAVEL HEALTH

LISTEN FOR

Apra bene la bocca.	*a*·pra *be*·ne la *bo*·ka	Open wide.
Morda questo.	*mor*·da *kwe*·sto	Bite down on this.
Sciacqui!	*sha*·kwee	Rinse!

I have a toothache.	Ho mal di denti. o mal dee *den*·tee
I need an anaesthetic.	Ho bisogno di un anestetico. o bee·*zo*·nyo dee oo·na·nes·*te*·tee·ko
I need a filling.	Ho bisogno di un'otturazione. o bee·*zo*·nyo dee oo·no·too·ra·*tsyo*·ne
I need a crown.	Ho bisogno di una corona. o bee·*zo*·nyo dee *oo*·na ko·*ro*·na
I've lost a filling.	Ho perso un'otturazione. o *per*·so oo·no·too·ra·*tsyo*·ne
My dentures are broken.	La mia dentiera è rotta. la *mee*·a den·*tye*·ra e *ro*·ta
My gums hurt.	Mi fanno male le gengive. mee *fa*·no *ma*·le le jen·*jee*·ve
My orthodontic braces broke.	Mi si è rotto l'apparecchio. mee see e *ro*·to la·pa·*re*·kyo
My orthodontic braces fell off.	Mi è caduto l'apparecchio. mee e ka·*doo*·to la·pa·*re*·kyo
I don't want it extracted.	Non voglio che mi venga tolto. non *vo*·lyo ke mee *ven*·ga *tol*·to

EATING OUT	160
SELF-CATERING	176
VEGETARIAN & SPECIAL MEALS	181

Eating Out

KEY PHRASES

Can you recommend a restaurant?	Potrebbe consigliare un ristorante?	po·*tre*·be kon·see·*lya*·re oon rees·to·*ran*·te
A table for two people, please.	Un tavolo per due persone, per favore.	oon *ta*·vo·lo per *doo*·e per·*so*·ne per fa·*vo*·re
Can I see the menu, please?	Vorrei il menù, per favore.	vo·*ray* eel me·*noo* per fa·*vo*·re
I'd like a beer, please.	Vorrei una birra, per favore.	vo·*ray oo*·na *bee*·ra per fa·*vo*·re
Please bring the bill.	Mi porta il conto, per favore?	mee *por*·ta eel *kon*·to per fa·*vo*·re

Basics

breakfast	prima colazione **f** *pree*·ma ko·la·*tsyo*·ne
lunch	pranzo **m** *pran*·dzo
dinner	cena **f** *che*·na
afternoon snack	merenda **f** me·*ren*·da
snack	spuntino **m** spoon·*tee*·no

Eateries

bar/caffè m bar/ka·*fe* – serves drinks and offers light meals, eg bread rolls and snacks

osteria/trattoria f os·te·*ree*·a/tra·to·*ree*·a – provides simple food and some local specialities

paninoteca f pa·nee·no·*te*·ka – serves delicious sandwiches made with cheese and cold meats

pizzeria f pee·tse·*ree*·a – specialises in pizza and *calzoni* kal·*tso*·nee (a folded pizza dish), usually prepared in a wood-fired oven

ristorante m ree·sto·*ran*·te – a more sophisticated eatery, with a higher standard of service, a more expensive menu and a decent wine list

tavola f **calda** *ta*·vo·la *kal*·da – a buffet offering local specialities, pizza, roasted meats and salads

set menu	menu m turistico me·*noo* too·*ree*·stee·ko
daily special	piatto m del giorno *pya*·to del *jor*·no
eat	mangiare man·*ja*·re
drink	bere *be*·re
Enjoy the meal!	Buon appetito! bwon a·pe·*tee*·to

Finding a Place to Eat

Can you recommend a cafe?	Potrebbe consigliare un bar? po·*tre*·be kon·see·*lya*·re oon bar

Can you recommend a restaurant?
Potrebbe consigliare un ristorante?
po·*tre*·be kon·see·*lya*·re oon rees·to·*ran*·te

Where would you go for (a) ...?
Dove andrebbe per ...?
do·ve an·*dre*·be per ...

business lunch	un pranzo d'affari	oon *pran*·dzo da·*fa*·ree
celebration	una celebrazione	*oo*·na che·le·bra·*tsyo*·ne
cheap meal	un pasto economico	oon *pas*·to e·ko·*no*·mee·ko
local specialities	le specialità locali	le spe·cha·lee·*ta* lo·*ka*·lee

I'd like to reserve a table for (eight) o'clock.
Vorrei prenotare un tavolo per le (otto).
vo·*ray* pre·no·*ta*·re oon *ta*·vo·lo per le (*o*·to)

I'd like to reserve a table for (two) people.
Vorrei prenotare un tavolo per (due) persone.
vo·*ray* pre·no·*ta*·re oon *ta*·vo·lo per (*doo*·e) per·*so*·ne

For two, please.	Per due, per favore.	per *doo*·e per fa·*vo*·re

Are you still serving food?
Servite ancora da mangiare?
ser·*vee*·te an·*ko*·ra da man·*ja*·re

How long is the wait?
Quanto si deve aspettare?
kwan·to see *de*·ve as·pe·*ta*·re

LISTEN FOR

È al completo.	e al kom·*ple*·to	We're fully booked.
Non abbiamo tavoli.	non a·*bya*·mo *ta*·vo·lee	We have no tables.
Siamo chiusi.	*sya*·mo *kyoo*·zee	We're closed.

At the Restaurant

I'd like ..., please.
Vorrei ..., per favore.
vo·*ray* ... per fa·*vo*·re

a table for (four)	un tavolo per (quattro)	oon *ta*·vo·lo per (*kwa*·tro)
the drink list	la lista delle bevande	la *lee*·sta *de*·le be·*van*·de
the menu	il menù	eel me·*noo*

Menu, please.	Il menù, per favore.	eel me·*noo* per fa·*vo*·re

Do you have a menu in English?
Avete un menù in inglese?
a·*ve*·te oon me·*noo* een een·*gle*·ze

Do you have children's meals?
Avete pasti per bambini?
a·*ve*·te *pas*·tee per bam·*bee*·nee

We're just having drinks.	Prendiamo solo da bere. pren·*dya*·mo *so*·lo da *be*·re

Just drinks.	Solo da bere, grazie.	*so*·lo da *be*·re *gra*·tsye

What would you recommend?	Cosa mi consiglia? *ko*·za mee kon·*see*·lya
I'll have what they're having.	Vorrei quello che stanno mangiando loro. vo·*ray kwe*·lo ke *sta*·no man·*jan*·do *lo*·ro
I'd like a local speciality.	Vorrei una specialità di questa regione. vo·*ray oo*·na spe·cha·lee·*ta* dee *kwe*·sta re·*jo*·ne
What's in that dish?	Quali ingredienti ci sono in questo piatto? *kwa*·li een·gre·*dyen*·tee chee *so*·no een *kwe*·sto *pya*·to
Does it take long to prepare?	Ci vuole molto per prepararlo? chee *vwo*·le *mol*·to per pre·pa·*rar*·lo

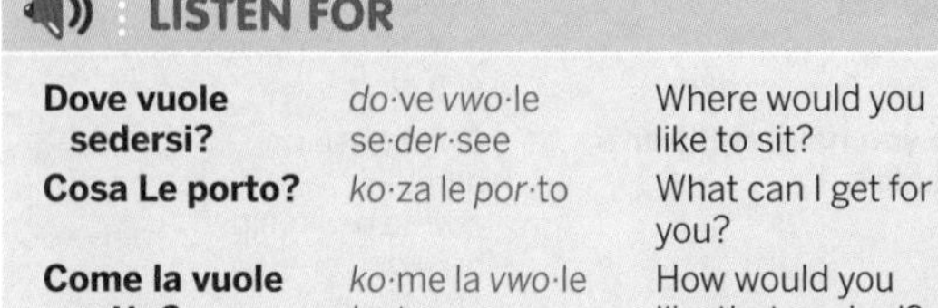

LISTEN FOR

Dove vuole sedersi?	*do*·ve *vwo*·le se·*der*·see	Where would you like to sit?
Cosa Le porto?	*ko*·za le *por*·to	What can I get for you?
Come la vuole cotta?	*ko*·me la *vwo*·le *ko*·ta	How would you like that cooked?
Ecco!	*e*·ko	Here you go!

Eating Out

Can I see the menu, please?

Posso vedere il menù, per favore?
po·so ve·*de*·re eel me·*noo* per fa·*vo*·re

What would you recommend for ...?

Cosa mi consiglia ...?
ko·za mee kon·*see*·lya ...

the main course
per il secondo piatto
per eel se·*kon*·do *pya*·to

dessert
per dolci
per *dol*·chee

drinks
da bere
da *be*·re

Can you bring me some ..., please?

Mi porta ..., per favore?
mee *por*·ta ... per fa·*vo*·re

I'd like the bill, please.

Vorrei il conto, per favore.
vo·*ray* eel *kon*·to per fa·*vo*·re

Requests

Please bring a glass.	Mi porta un bicchiere, per favore? mee *por*·ta oon bee·*kye*·re per fa·*vo*·re
Is there (any Parmesan cheese)?	C'è (del parmigiano)? che (del par·mee·*ja*·no)
I'd like it ...	Lo/La vorrei ... **m/f** lo/la vo·*ray* ...
I don't want it ...	Non lo/la voglio ... **m/f** non lo/la *vo*·lyo ...

boiled	bollito/a **m/f**	bo·*lee*·to/a
broiled	cotto/a **m/f** a fuoco vivo	*ko*·to/a a *fwo*·ko *vee*·vo
deep-fried	fritto/a **m/f** in abbondante olio	*free*·to/a een a·bon·*dan*·te o·lyo
fried	fritto/a **m/f**	*free*·to/a
grilled	(cotto/a) **m/f** ai ferri	(*ko*·to/a) ai *fe*·ree
medium	non troppo cotto/a **m/f**	non *tro*·po *ko*·to/a
rare	al sangue	al *san*·gwe
re-heated	riscaldato/a **m/f**	rees·kal·*da*·to/a
steamed	cotto/a **m/f** a vapore	*ko*·to/a a va·*po*·re
well-done	ben cotto/a **m/f**	ben *ko*·to/a
with the dressing on the side	con il condimento a parte	kon eel kon·dee·*men*·to a *par*·te

For other specific meal requests, see **vegetarian & special meals** (p181).

LOOK FOR

Antipasti	an·tee·*pas*·tee	Appetisers
Zuppe	*tsoo*·pe	Soups
Primi (Piatti)	*pree*·mee (*pya*·tee)	Entrees
Insalate	een·sa·*la*·te	Salads
Contorni	kon·*tor*·nee	Side Dishes
Pasti Leggeri	*pas*·tee le·*je*·ree	Light Meals
Secondi (Piatti)	se·*kon*·dee (*pya*·tee)	Main Courses
Dolci	*dol*·chee	Desserts
Bevande	be·*van*·de	Drinks
Aperitivi	a·pe·ree·*tee*·vee	Aperitifs
Bibite	*bee*·bee·te	Soft Drinks
Liquori	lee·*kwo*·ree	Spirits
Birre	*bee*·re	Beers
Vini della Casa	*vee*·nee *de*·la *ka*·za	House Wines
Vini Locali	*vee*·nee lo·*ka*·lee	Local Wines
Vini Frizzanti	*vee*·nee free·*tsan*·tee	Sparkling Wines
Vini Bianchi	*vee*·nee *byan*·kee	White Wines
Vini Rossi	*vee*·nee *ro*·see	Red Wines
Vini Rosati	*vee*·nee ro·*za*·tee	Roses
Vini da Dessert	*vee*·nee da de·*sert*	Dessert Wines
Digestivi	dee·jes·*tee*·vee	Digestifs

For more words you might see on a menu, see the **menu decoder** (p184), and the **dictionary**.

LOOK FOR

Donne	*do*·ne	Women
Gabinetti	ga·bee·*ne*·tee	Toilets
Prenotato	pre·no·*ta*·to	Booked
Riservato	ree·ser·*va*·to	Reserved
Uomini	*wo*·mee·nee	Men

Compliments & Complaints

I didn't order this.	Questo non l'ho ordinato. *kwe*·sto non lo or·dee·*na*·to
That was delicious!	Era squisito! *e*·ra skwee·*zee*·to
My compliments to the chef.	Complimenti al cuoco! kom·plee·*men*·tee al *kwo*·ko
I'm full.	Sono sazio/a. **m/f** *so*·no *sa*·tsyo/a
I love this dish.	Vado matto/a per questo piatto. **m/f** *va*·do *ma*·to/a per *kwe*·sto *pya*·to
I love the local cuisine.	Vado matto/a per la cucina locale. **m/f** *va*·do *ma*·to/a per la koo·*chee*·na lo·*ka*·le
This is ...	Questo/a è ... **m/f** *kwe*·sto/a e ...

cold	freddo/a **m/f**	*fre*·do/a
(too) hot	(troppo) caldo/a **m/f**	(*tro*·po) *kal*·do/a
spicy	piccante	pee·*kan*·te
superb	delizioso/a **m/f**	de·lee·*tsyo*·zo/a

Paying the Bill

Is the cover charge included in the bill?	Il coperto è compreso nel conto? eel ko·*per*·to e kom·*pre*·zo nel *kon*·to
Is the service included in the bill?	Il servizio è compreso nel conto? eel ser·*vee*·tsyo e kom·*pre*·zo nel *kon*·to
Please bring the bill.	Mi porta il conto, per favore? mee *por*·ta eel *kon*·to per fa·*vo*·re

Bill, please.	Il conto, per favore.	eel *kon*·to per fa·*vo*·re

There's a mistake in the bill.	C'è un errore nel conto. che oo·ne·*ro*·re nel *kon*·to

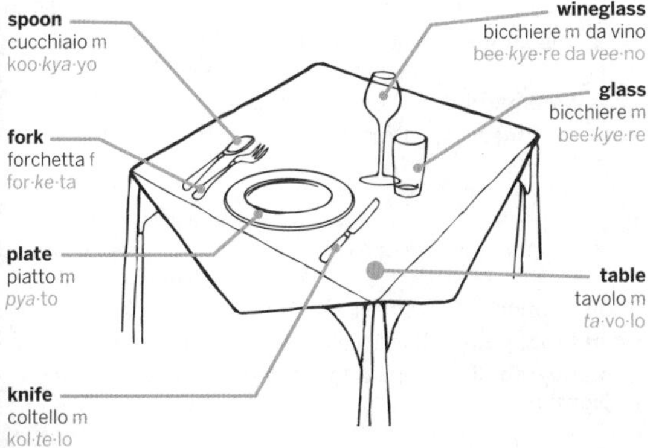

 LOOK FOR

Pasta comes in all shapes and sizes from the standard *spaghetti* spa·*ge*·tee to potato *gnocchi* *nyo*·kee and bow-shaped *farfalle* far·*fa*·le. Note that *alla/al* *a*·la/al means 'in the style of'.

aglio e olio	*a*·lyo e *o*·lyo	oil, garlic and sometimes chilli
al ragù	al ra·*goo*	meat, vegetables, lemon peel and nutmeg
all'amatriciana	a·la·ma·tree·*cha*·na	pig's cheek, lard, white wine, tomato, chilli and sheep's cheese
alla carbonara	*a*·la kar·bo·*na*·ra	bacon, butter, eggs and sheep's cheese
alla partenopea	*a*·la par·te·no·*pe*·a	mozzarella, olives, tomato, bread crust, capers, anchovies, basil, oil, chilli and salt
alla pescatora	*a*·la pes·ka·*to*·ra	fish, tomato and sweet herbs
alla pommarola	*a*·la po·ma·*ro*·la	tomato
alla puttanesca	*a*·la poo·ta·*nes*·ka	garlic, anchovies, black olives, capers, tomato, oil and chilli
cacio e pepe	*ka*·cho e *pe*·pe	black pepper and sheep's cheese
con il tonno	kon eel *to*·no	with tuna
con le vongole	kon le *von*·go·le	with clams
con tartufo di Norcia	kon tar·*too*·fo dee *nor*·cha	with Norcia truffles

Nonalcoholic Drinks

almond milk	orzata **f** or·*dza*·ta
bitter cola	chinotto **m** kee·*no*·to
fruit juice (bottled)	succo **m** di frutta *soo*·ko dee *froo*·ta
fruit juice (fresh)	spremuta **f** spre·*moo*·ta
lemonade	limonata **f** lee·mo·*na*·ta
orangeade	aranciata **f** a·ran·*cha*·ta
soft drink	bibita **f** *bee*·bee·ta
(cup of) tea/coffee	(un) tè/caffè (oon) te/ka·*fe*
with milk	con latte kon *la*·te
without sugar	senza zucchero *sen*·tsa *tsoo*·ke·ro
... water	acqua ... *a*·kwa ...

boiled	bollita	bo·*lee*·ta
mineral	minerale	mee·ne·*ra*·le
sparkling	frizzante	free·*tsan*·te
still	naturale	na·too·*ra*·le

 LOOK FOR

Italians often drink their coffee standing up at the bar. Simply ask for a *caffè* ka·*fe* and you'll get an *espresso* es·*pre*·so, but don't order a *latte* *la*·te unless you want a glass of milk. Make sure you don't ask for coffee with milk in the afternoon.

caffè m **alla valdostana**	ka·*fe* *a*·la val·dos·*ta*·na	with grappa, lemon peel and spices
caffè m **americano**	ka·*fe* a·me·ree·*ka*·no	long and black
caffè m **corretto**	ka·*fe* ko·*re*·to	with a dash of liqueur
caffè m **doppio**	ka·*fe* *do*·pyo	long, strong and black
caffè m **macchiato**	ka·*fe* ma·*kya*·to	strong coffee with a drop of milk
caffè m **ristretto**	ka·*fe* ree·*stre*·to	superstrong black coffee
caffellatte m	ka·fe·*la*·te	coffee with milk
cappuccino m	ka·poo·*chee*·no	coffee with milk, served with a lot of froth and sprinkled with cocoa
espresso m	es·*pre*·so	short black coffee
ristretto m	ree·*stre*·to	very short black coffee

Alcoholic Drinks

draught beer	birra f a la spina *bee*·ra a la *spee*·na
a shot of ...	un sorso di ... oon *sor*·so dee ...

a bottle of ... wine	una bottiglia di vino ... *oo*·na bo·*tee*·lya dee *vee*·no ...
a glass of ... wine	un bicchiere di vino ... oon bee·*kye*·re dee *vee*·no ...

dessert	da dessert	da de·*sert*
red	rosso	*ro*·so
rose	rosato	ro·*za*·to
sparkling	spumante	spoo·*man*·te
white	bianco	*byan*·ko

a ... of beer	... di birra ... dee *bee*·ra

bottle	una bottiglia	*oo*·na bo·*tee*·lya
glass	un bicchiere	oon bee·*kye*·re
jug	una caraffa	*oo*·na ka·*ra*·fa
pint	una pinta	*oo*·na *peen*·ta

In the Bar

I'll have (a glass of red wine).	Prendo (un bicchiere di vino rosso). *pren*·do (oon bee·*kye*·re dee *vee*·no *ro*·so)
I'd like a beer, please.	Vorrei una birra, per favore. vo·*ray oo*·na *bee*·ra per fa·*vo*·re
Same again, please.	Un altro, per favore. oon *al*·tro per fa·*vo*·re
No ice, thanks.	Senza ghiaccio, grazie. *sen*·tsa *gya*·cho *gra*·tsye
Straight, please.	Liscio, per favore. *lee*·sho per fa·*vo*·re

LANGUAGE TIP

Tongue Twisters

The sing-song music of the Italian language lends itself beautifully to tongue twisters or *scioglilingue* sho·lyee·*leen*·gwe. Try to impress Italian acquaintances by casually slipping out one of these:

O schiavo con lo schiaccianoci che cosa schiacci? Schiaccio sei noci del vecchio noce con lo schiaccianoci.
o *skya*·vo kon lo skya·cha·*no*·chee ke *ko*·za *skya*·chee *skya*·cho say *no*·chee del *ve*·kyo *no*·che kon lo skya·cha·*no*·chee
Oh, slave with the nutcracker what are you cracking? I am cracking six nuts from the old walnut tree with the nutcracker.

Orrore, orrore, un ramarro verde su un muro marrone!
o·*ro*·re o·*ro*·re oon ra·*ma*·ro *ver*·de soo oon *moo*·ro ma·*ro*·ne
Horror, horror, a green lizard on a brown wall!

Trentatre Trentini entrarono a Trento, tutti e trentatre trotterelando.
tren·ta·*tre* tren·*tee*·nee en·*tra*·ro·no a *tren*·to *too*·tee e tren·ta·*tre* tro·te·re·*lan*·do
Thirty-three Trentonians came into Trento, all thirty-three trotting.

I'll buy you a drink.	Ti offro da bere. tee *of*·ro da *be*·re
What would you like?	Cosa prendi? *ko*·za *pren*·dee
It's my round.	Offro io. *of*·ro *ee*·o

You can get the next one.	La prossima la paghi tu. la *pro*·see·ma la *pa*·gee too
How much alcohol does this contain?	Quanto alcool contiene? *kwan*·to *al*·kol kon·*tye*·ne
Do you serve meals here?	Servite da mangiare qui? ser·*vee*·te da man·*ja*·re kwee

Drinking Up

Cheers!	Salute! sa·*loo*·te
Thanks, but I don't feel like it.	Grazie, ma non mi va. *gra*·tsye ma non mee va
No thanks, I'm driving.	No, grazie, devo guidare. no *gra*·tsye *de*·vo gwee·*da*·re
I don't drink alcohol.	Non bevo. non *be*·vo
This is hitting the spot.	Ci voleva proprio! chee vo·*le*·va *pro*·pryo
I'm feeling drunk.	Mi sento un po' ubriaco/a. **m/f** mee *sen*·to oon po oo·bree·*a*·ko/a
I think I've had one too many.	Penso d'aver bevuto troppo. *pen*·so da·*ver* be·*voo*·to *tro*·po
I'm pissed.	Ho la ciucca. o la *choo*·ka
Can you call a taxi for me?	Mi puoi chiamare un tassì? mee pwoy kya·*ma*·re oon ta·*see*
I don't think you should drive.	È meglio che non guidi. e *me*·lyo ke non *gwee*·dee

Self-Catering

KEY PHRASES

What's the local speciality?	Qual'è la specialità di questa regione?	kwa·*le* la spe·cha·lee·*ta* dee *kwe*·sta re·*jo*·ne
Where can I find the ... section?	Dove posso trovare il reparto ...?	*do*·ve *po*·so tro·*va*·re eel re·*par*·to ...
I'd like ...	Vorrei ...	vo·*ray* ...

Buying Food

What's the local speciality?	Qual'è la specialità di questa regione? kwa·*le* la spe·cha·lee·*ta* dee *kwe*·sta re·*jo*·ne
Can I taste it?	Lo/La posso assaggiare? **m/f** lo/la *po*·so a·sa·*ja*·re

 **LISTEN FOR**

Cosa desidera?	*ko*·za de·*see*·de·ra	What would you like?
E poi?	e poy	Anything else?
È (una gorgonzola).	e (*oo*·na gor·gon·*dzo*·la)	That's (a gorgonzola).
Non ne ho.	non ne ho	I don't have any.
Sono (cinque euro).	*so*·no (*cheen*·kwe e·*oo*·ro)	That's (five euros).

How much is (a kilo of cheese)?	Quanto costa (un chilo di formaggio)? *kwan*·to *kos*·ta (oon *kee*·lo dee for·*ma*·jo)
Do you have anything cheaper?	Avete qualcosa di meno costoso? a·*ve*·te kwal·*ko*·za dee *me*·no kos·*to*·zo
Do you have other kinds?	Avete altri tipi? a·*ve*·te *al*·tree *tee*·pee
Can I have a bag, please?	Posso avere un sacchetto, per favore? *po*·so a·*ve*·re oon sa·*ke*·to per fa·*vo*·re
I'd like ...	Vorrei ... vo·*ray* ...

100 grams	un etto	oo·*ne*·to
200 grams	due etti	*doo*·e e·tee
a kilo	un chilo	oon *kee*·lo
(two) kilos	(due) chili	(*doo*·e) *kee*·lee
a bottle	una bottiglia	*oo*·na bo·*tee*·lya
a dozen	una dozzina	*oo*·na do·*dzee*·na
a jar	un barattolo	oon ba·*ra*·to·lo
a packet	un sacchetto	oon sa·*ke*·to
a piece	un pezzo	oon *pe*·tso
(three) pieces	(tre) pezzi	(tre) *pe*·tsee
a slice	una fetta	*oo*·na *fe*·ta
(six) slices	(sei) fette	(say) *fe*·te
a tin	una scatola	*oo*·na *ska*·to·la
some ...	alcuni/e ... **m/f**	al·*koo*·nee/ al·*koo*·ne ...
that one	quello/a **m/f**	*kwe*·lo/a
this one	questo/a **m/f**	*kwe*·sto/a

LOOK FOR

alimentari m	a·lee·men·*ta*·ree	grocery store
caseificio m	ka·ze·ee·*fee*·cho	creamery
enoteca f	e·no·*te*·ka	wine shop
formaggeria f	for·ma·je·*ree*·a	cheese shop (also sells other dairy products)
macelleria f	ma·che·le·*ree*·a	butcher
mercato m	mer·*ka*·to	market
pasticceria f	pas·tee·che·*ree*·a	cake shop
pastificio m	pas·tee·*fee*·cho	specialist pasta shop
pescheria f	pes·ke·*ree*·a	fish shop
polleria f	po·le·*ree*·a	poultry shop
salumeria f	sa·loo·me·*ree*·a	delicatessen
tabacchi m	ta·*ba*·kee	tobacconist
torrefazione f	to·re·fa·*tsyo*·ne	coffee roasting house

Enough.	Basta, grazie. *bas*·ta *gra*·tsye
A bit more.	Un po' di più. oon po dee pyoo
Less.	(Di) Meno. (dee) *me*·no

For food items, see the **menu decoder** (p184), and the **dictionary**.

Where can I find the ... section?	Dove posso trovare il reparto ...? *do*·ve *po*·so tro·*va*·re eel re·*par*·to ...

dairy	dei latticini	day la·tee·*chee*·nee
frozen goods	dei surgelati	day soor·je·*la*·tee
fruit and vegetable	della frutta e verdura	*de*·la *froo*·ta e ver·*doo*·ra
health-food	dei cibi macrobiotici	day *chee*·bee ma·kro·bee·o·tee·chee
meat	della carne	*de*·la *kar*·ne
poultry	del pollame	del po·*la*·me

Lo/La posso assaggiare? m/f
lo/la *po*·so a·sa·*ja*·re
Can I taste it?

Cooking

Could I please borrow (a corkscrew)?	Posso prendere in prestito (un cavatappi), per favore? *po*·so *pren*·de·re een *pres*·tee·to (oon ka·va·*ta*·pee) per fa·*vo*·re
Where's (a saucepan)?	Dov'è (un tegame)? do·*ve* (oon te·*ga*·me)
cooked	cotto/a **m/f** *ko*·to/a
dried	secco/a **m/f** *se*·ko/a
fresh	fresco/a **m/f** *fres*·ko/a
frozen	congelato/a **m/f** kon·je·*la*·to/a
raw	crudo/a **m/f** *kroo*·do/a
smoked	affumicato/a **m/f** a·foo·mee·*ka*·to/a

For more cooking implements, see the **dictionary**.

Vegetarian & Special Meals

KEY PHRASES

Do you have vegetarian food?	Avete piatti vegetariani?	a·*ve*·te *pya*·tee ve·je·ta·*rya*·nee
Could you prepare a meal without ...?	Potreste preparare un pasto senza ...?	po·*tres*·te pre·pa·*ra*·re oon *pas*·to *sen*·tsa ...
I'm allergic to ...	Sono allergico/a a ... m/f	*so*·no a·*ler*·jee·ko/a a ...

Special Diets & Allergies

Is there a vegetarian restaurant near here?	C'è un ristorante vegetariano qui vicino? che oon rees·to·*ran*·te ve·je·ta·*rya*·no kwee vee·*chee*·no
Is there a halal restaurant near here?	C'è un ristorante halal qui vicino? che oon rees·to·*ran*·te a·*lal* kwee vee·*chee*·no
Is there a kosher restaurant near here?	C'è un ristorante kasher qui vicino? che oon rees·to·*ran*·te *ka*·sher kwee vee·*chee*·no
I'm vegan.	Sono vegetaliano/a. m/f *so*·no ve·je·ta·*lya*·no/a

I'm on a special diet.	Seguo una dieta speciale. *se*·gwo *oo*·na *dye*·ta spe·*cha*·le
I don't eat (fish).	Non mangio (pesce). non *man*·jo (*pe*·she)
I'm allergic to ...	Sono allergico/a ... **m/f** *so*·no a·*ler*·jee·ko/a ...

dairy produce	ai latticini	ai la·tee·*chee*·nee
eggs	alle uova	*a*·le *wo*·va
fish	al pesce	al *pe*·she
gelatin	alla gelatina	*a*·la je·la·*tee*·na
gluten	al glutine	al *gloo*·tee·ne
honey	al miele	al *mye*·le
nuts	alle noci	*a*·le *no*·chee
peanuts	alle arachidi	*a*·le a·*ra*·kee·dee
seafood	ai frutti di mare	ai *froo*·tee dee *ma*·re
shellfish	ai crostacei	ai kros·*ta*·che·ee

Ordering Food

Do you have (vegetarian) food?	Avete piatti (vegetariani)? a·*ve*·te *pya*·tee (ve·je·ta·*rya*·nee)

Controllo con il cuoco.	kon·*tro*·lo kon eel *kwo*·ko	I'll check with the cook.
Può mangiare ...?	pwo man·*ja*·re ...	Can you eat ...?
Tutto contiene (la carne).	*too*·to kon·*tye*·ne (la *kar*·ne)	It all has (meat) in it.

Is it cooked with (oil)?	È cotto con (olio)? e *ko*·to kon (*o*·lyo)	
Is this ...?	È ...? e ...	

cholesterol-free	senza colesterolo	*sen*·tsa ko·le·ste·*ro*·lo
decaffeinated	decaffeinato/a **m/f**	de·ka·fey·*na*·to/a
free of animal produce	senza prodotti animali	*sen*·tsa pro·*do*·tee a·nee·*ma*·lee
free-range	ruspante	roos·*pan*·te
genetically modified	geneticamente modificato/a **m/f**	je·ne·tee·ka·*men*·te mo·dee·fee·*ka*·to/a
gluten-free	senza glutine	*sen*·tsa *gloo*·tee·ne
organic	biologico/a **m/f**	bee·o·*lo*·jee·ko/a
salt-free	senza sale	*sen*·tsa *sa*·le

Could you prepare a meal without ...?	Potreste preparare un pasto senza ...? po·*tres*·te pre·pa·*ra*·re oon *pas*·to *sen*·tsa ...

butter	burro	*boo*·ro
eggs	uova	*wo*·va
meat/fish stock	brodo di carne/pesce	*bro*·do dee *kar*·ne/*pe*·she
poultry	pollame	po·*la*·me
red meat	carne rossa	*kar*·ne *ro*·sa

Menu DECODER

Il Lessico Culinario

This miniguide to Italian cuisine is designed to help you navigate menus. Italian nouns, and adjectives affected by gender, have their gender indicated by ⓜ and/or ⓕ. If it's a plural noun, you'll also see pl.

~ A ~

abbacchio ⓜ a·*ba*·kyo young lamb
— alla cacciatora *a*·la ka·cha·*to*·ra lamb casserole with spices, white wine & anchovies
— a scottadito a·sko·ta·*dee*·to lamb cutlets fried in oil
acciughe ⓕ pl a·*choo*·ge anchovies (often preserved in salt)
aceto ⓜ a·*che*·to vinegar
acqua ⓕ *a*·kwa water
— bollita bo·*lee*·ta boiled water
— calda *kal*·da hot water
— del rubinetto del roo·bee·*ne*·to tap water
— minerale mee·ne·*ra*·le mineral water
— non gassata non ga·*sa*·ta still water
acquacotta ⓕ a·kwa·*ko*·ta soup prepared with tomato, peppers, celery, eggs, artichokes or mushrooms
acquapazza ⓕ a·kwa·*pa*·tsa 'crazy water' – a type of fish soup
aglio ⓜ *a*·lyo garlic
— e olio ⓜ e *o*·lyo garlic & olive oil pasta sauce
agnello ⓜ a·*nye*·lo lamb
— ai funghi ai *foon*·gee with mushrooms
— al forno al *for*·no with garlic & sometimes potatoes
— da latte da *la*·te very young milk-fed lamb
agnolini ⓜ pl a·nyo·*lee*·nee round pasta stuffed with stewed beef, eggs, cheese & other ingredients
agnolotti ⓜ pl **ripieni** a·nyo·*lo*·tee ree·*pye*·nee pasta stuffed with meat, herbs, eggs & parmesan
agro, all' *ag*·ro, al with oil & lemon dressing
albicocca ⓕ al·bee·*ko*·ka apricot
alborella ⓕ al·bo·*re*·la common freshwater fish
alici ⓕ pl a·*lee*·chee anchovies
— a crudo a *kroo*·do raw, marinated in oil & spices
al dente al *den*·te 'to the tooth' – describes cooked pasta & rice that are still slightly hard
all'/alla ... al/*a*·la ... in the style of ...
alloro ⓜ a·*lo*·ro bay leaf
al sangue al *san*·gwe rare (cooked)
amaretti ⓜ pl a·ma·*re*·tee almond biscuits (macaroons)

amatriciana a·ma·tree·*cha*·na spicy sauce with salami, tomato, capsicums & cheese
ananas ⓜ *a*·na·nas pineapple
anatra ⓕ *a*·na·tra duck
— al sale al *sa*·le roast duck cooked in a crust of salt
angiulottus ⓜ an·joo·*lo*·toos stuffed square pasta served with meat sauce or tomato sauce
anguilla ⓕ an·*gwee*·la eel
anice ⓜ *a*·nee·che aniseed
annoglia ⓕ a·*no*·lya dry-cured pork sausage with chilli
anolini ⓜ pl a·no·*lee*·nee stuffed round pasta with braised beef, cheese, parmesan, egg & breadcrumbs
aragosta ⓕ a·ra·*go*·sta lobster • crayfish
arancia ⓕ a·*ran*·cha orange
arancia, all' a·*ran*·cha, al sprinkled or baked with orange juice
arancini ⓜ pl a·ran·*chee*·nee riceballs stuffed with a meat mixture
aranzada ⓕ a·ran·*tsa*·da almond nougat
arborio ⓜ ar·*bo*·ryo short-grain rice used for risotto
aringa ⓕ a·*reen*·ga herring
arista ⓕ a·*ree*·sta loin (generally pork)
— alla fiorentina *a*·la fyo·ren·*tee*·na baked with spices
aromi ⓜ pl a·*ro*·mee herbs
arrabbiata, all' a·ra·*bya*·ta, al 'angry-style' – with spicy sauce
arrosticini ⓜ a·ros·tee·*chee*·nee skewered & roasted meat (often lamb)
arrosto/a ⓜ/ⓕ a·*ro*·sto/a roasted
— alla griglia *a*·la *gree*·lya barbecued
artigianale ar·tee·ja·*na*·le home-made
asiago ⓜ a·*zya*·go hard white cheese
asparagi ⓜ pl as·*pa*·ra·jee asparagus
aspro/a ⓜ/ⓕ *as*·pro/a sour

~ B ~

babà ⓜ ba·*ba* dessert containing sultanas
baccalà ⓜ ba·ka·*la* dried salted cod
— alla pizzaiola *a*·la pee·tsa·*yo*·la with a tomato sauce
— mantecato man·te·*ka*·to mixed to a puree
baci ⓜ pl *ba*·chee 'kisses' – type of chocolate • type of pastry or biscuit
bagnetto ⓜ **verde** ba·*nye*·to *ver*·de parsley & garlic sauce
barbabietola ⓕ bar·ba·*bye*·to·la beetroot
basilico ⓜ ba·*zee*·lee·ko basil
batsoà ⓜ bat·so·*a* boned, boiled & fried pig's trotters
battuto ⓜ ba·*too*·to soup or meat seasoning prepared with lard & vegetables
bavetta ⓕ ba·*ve*·ta long, thick pasta
bel paese ⓜ bel pa·*e*·ze soft, creamy cheese
besciamella ⓕ be·sha·*me*·la bechamel sauce
bescó'cc ⓜ bes·*koch* almond biscuits soaked in **grappa**
bianchetti ⓜ pl byan·*ke*·tee whitebait fried in oil
bianco ⓜ **d'uovo** *byan*·ko *dwo*·vo egg white
bigné ⓜ bee·*nye* cream puff
bigoli ⓜ pl *bee*·go·lee thick, wholemeal flour spaghetti
bisció'la ⓕ bee·*sho*·la cake with nuts, dried figs & raisins
biscotti ⓜ pl bees·*ko*·tee biscuits
biscó'cc ⓜ bees·*koch* see **bescó'cc**
bisi ⓜ pl *bee*·zee peas
bistecca ⓕ bees·*te*·ka steak
— alla fiorentina *a*·la fyo·ren·*tee*·na tasty, thick loin steak with its bone
bitto ⓜ *bee*·to cow's milk cheese
blanc manger ⓜ blank *man*·je dessert with milk, sugar & vanilla

bocconcini Ⓜ pl bo·kon·*chee*·nee tiny portions of **mozzarella**
boghe Ⓕ pl **in scabescio** *bo*·ge een ska·*be*·sho marinated, floured fish, browned in oil
bollito bo·*lee*·to boiled
bollito (Bú'i) Ⓜ bo·*lee*·to (boo·*ee*) mixed boiled meat with various sauces
bomba Ⓕ **di riso** bom·*ba* dee *ree*·zo baked rice with stewed pigeon, eggs, mushrooms, truffles & sausage
bombas Ⓜ *bom*·bas stewed veal meatballs
bonèt Ⓜ bo·*net* baked pudding of macaroons, cocoa, coffee, **marsala** & rum
bostrengo Ⓜ bos·*tren*·go cake prepared with boiled rice, chocolate, sugar, spices & pine nuts
boudin Ⓜ boo·*deen* blood sausage
bra Ⓜ bra mild cheese
braciola Ⓕ bra·*cho*·la chop • cutlet
braciolone Ⓜ **napoletano** bra·cho·*lo*·ne na·po·le·*ta*·no steak rolled & filled with bacon, **provolone** & other ingredients
branzi Ⓜ pl *bran*·dzee soft table cheese
branzino Ⓜ bran·*dzee*·no sea bass
brasato Ⓜ bra·*za*·to beef marinated in red wine & spices, then stewed
brioche Ⓜ bree·*osh* breakfast pastry
brochat Ⓜ bro·*shat* sweet, thick cream made with milk, wine & sugar & eaten with rye bread
brodetto Ⓜ **di pesce** *bro*·de·to dee *pe*·she fish soup
brodo Ⓜ *bro*·do broth
brôs Ⓜ broos creamy paste made by fermenting older cheese with herbs, spices & grappa
bruschetta Ⓕ broos·*ke*·ta stale bread sliced, toasted, rubbed with garlic & flavoured with salt, pepper & olive oil
bruscitt Ⓜ broo·*sheet* beef pieces cooked with red wine & served with polenta or mashed potatoes
brutti ma buoni Ⓜ pl *broo*·tee ma *bwo*·nee 'ugly but good' – hazelnut macaroons
bucatini Ⓜ pl boo·ka·*tee*·nee long hollow tubes of pasta
buccellato Ⓜ **di Lucca** boo·che·*la*·to dee *loo*·ka traditional ring-shaped cake
budino Ⓜ boo·*dee*·no milk-based pudding
bugie Ⓕ pl boo·*jee*·e 'lies' – small ribbons of sweet pastry covered with icing sugar
burro Ⓜ *boo*·ro butter
burtléina Ⓕ boort·*lay*·na little omelette prepared with water, flour, lard & onion, served with salami
busecca Ⓕ boo·*ze*·ka tripe
bussolà Ⓜ **vicentino** boo·so·*la* vee·chen·*tee*·no sponge cake-based dessert

~ C ~

caciotta Ⓕ ka·*cho*·ta semi-soft mild cheese
cacciucco Ⓜ **(alla livornese)** ka·*choo*·ko (a·la lee·vor·*ne*·ze) fish soup with at least five kinds of fish
cacio Ⓜ *ka*·cho cheese (in general) • a creamy cheese
caciocavallo Ⓜ ka·cho·ka·*va*·lo hard cow's milk cheese from southern Italy
cacioricotta Ⓕ ka·cho·ree·*ko*·ta small round cheese made from cow/sheep/goat's milk curd
caciuni Ⓜ pl ka·*choo*·nee big ravioli or puff pastry filled with egg yolks, cheeses, sugar & lemon peel
caffè Ⓜ ka·*fe* coffee (see also box on p172)
calamari Ⓜ pl ka·la·*ma*·ree calamari • squid

calhiettes ⓜ **tradizionali** ka·*lyet* tra·dee·tsyo·*na*·lee mixture of raw, grated potatoes, left-over meat, minced lard, onion, flour & eggs mixed & boiled, normally used to prepare dumplings & omelettes
calzone ⓜ kal·*tso*·ne fried or baked flat bread made with two thin sheets of pasta stuffed with any number of ingredients
canederli ⓜ pl ka·*ne*·der·lee big dumplings made with stale bread, speck & other ingredients such as liver, cheese, spinach or dried prunes
cannaroni ⓜ pl ka·na·*ro*·nee large pasta tubes
cannella ⓕ ka·*ne*·la cinnamon
cannelloni ⓜ pl ka·ne·*lo*·nee tubes of pasta stuffed with spinach, minced roast veal, ham, eggs, parmesan & spices
cannoli ⓜ pl **(ripieni)** ka·*no*·lee (ree·*pye*·nee) sweet pastry tubes filled with a mixture of sugar, candied fruit, sweet ricotta & other ingredients
cantarelli ⓜ pl kan·ta·*re*·lee chanterelle mushrooms
cantucci ⓜ pl kan·*too*·chee crunchy, hard biscuits made with aniseed & almonds
capasante ⓕ pl ka·pa·*san*·te scallops
capocollo ⓜ ka·po·*ko*·lo dry-cured pork sausage washed with red wine
caponata ⓕ ka·po·*na*·ta starter prepared with vegetables cooked in oil & vinegar – served with olives, anchovies & capers
capelli ⓜ pl **d'angelo** ka·*pe*·lee *dan*·je·lo 'angel's hair' – long, thin strands of pasta
cappellacci ⓜ pl **di zucca** ka·pe·*la*·chee dee *tsoo*·ka small pasta, filled with pumpkin & parmesan
cappelletti ⓜ pl ka·pe·*le*·tee similar to **tortellini**, only larger
cappello ⓜ **da prete** ka·*pe*·lo da *pre*·te boiled lower part of the pig's trotter, served with **salsa verde** or mustard
capperi ⓜ pl *ka*·pe·ree capers
cappon ⓜ **magro** ka·*pon ma*·gro salad with vegetables, fish & shellfish, dressed with a rich green sauce
capra ⓕ *ka*·pra goat • goat's cheese
caprese ⓜ ka·*pre*·ze salad with tomato, basil & **mozzarella**
capretto ⓜ ka·*pre*·to kid (goat)
caprino ⓜ ka·*pree*·no tart goat cheese often mixed at the table into a paste
carbonada ⓕ kar·bo·*na*·da diced, salted beef cooked in red wine
carbonara kar·bo·*na*·ra pasta sauce with egg, cheese & pancetta
carciofi ⓜ pl kar·*cho*·fee artichokes
cardoncelli ⓜ pl kar·don·*che*·lee type of mushroom, similar to oyster mushrooms
carnaroli ⓜ pl kar·na·*ro*·lee short-grain rice used for **risotto**
carne ⓕ *kar*·ne meat
— equina e·*kwee*·na horse meat
— suina *swee*·na pork
— trita/tritata *tree*·ta/tree·*ta*·ta mince meat
carota ⓕ ka·*ro*·ta carrot
carpa ⓕ *kar*·pa carp
carpaccio ⓜ kar·*pa*·cho very thin slices of raw meat
carpione ⓜ kar·*pyo*·ne fried fish preserved in a marinade of oil & spices
carta ⓕ **da musica** *kar*·ta da *moo*·zee·ka thin & very crunchy bread
cartoccio ⓜ kar·*to*·cho cooking method – fish, chicken or game are tightly wrapped in tinfoil & baked
cascà ⓕ **di carloforte** kas·*ka* dee kar·lo·*for*·te couscous with vegetables, minced meat & spices

C

câsonséi ⓜ pl ka·zon·*say* rectangles of pasta usually stuffed with parmesan, vegetables & sausage
cassata ⓕ ka·*sa*·ta ice cream or sponge cake stuffed with sweet ricotta, vanilla, chocolate, pistachios, candied fruit & liqueur
cassola ⓕ ka·*so*·la fish-soup with tomato sauce & herbs
casoncelli ⓜ pl ka·zon·*che*·lee pasta stuffed with meat & (depending on the region) spinach, eggs, raisins, almond biscuits, breadcrumbs or cheese
castagnaccio ⓜ ka·sta·*nya*·cho cake made with chestnut flour & sprinkled with pine nuts & rosemary
castagne ⓕ pl ka·*sta*·nye chestnuts
castelmagno ⓜ ka·stel·*ma*·nyo nutty blue cheese
casunzei ⓜ pl ka·zoon·*say* kind of ravioli stuffed with pumpkin or spinach, ham & cinnamon – served with smoked **ricotta**
caulada ⓕ kow·*la*·da cabbage-based soup with meat, mint & garlic
cavallucci ⓜ pl ka·va·*loo*·chee white sweets made with candied orange, nuts & spices
cavatelli ⓜ pl ka·va·*te*·lee small, round home-made pasta – often served with tomato sauce, oil & rocket
cavolo ⓜ *ka*·vo·lo cabbage
cavolfiore ⓜ ka·vol·*fyo*·re cauliflower
cazzimperio ⓜ ka·tseem·*pe*·ree·o fresh & crunchy vegetables dunked into a tasty sauce
cazzmar ⓜ *kats*·mar sliced sausage containing lamb's entrails, liver & giblets
cecenielli ⓜ pl che·che·*nye*·lee very small fish that can be fried or put on pizzas
ceci ⓜ pl *che*·chee chickpeas
cefalo ⓜ *che*·fa·lo mullet
cervello ⓜ cher·*ve*·lo brain
cervo ⓜ *cher*·vo venison
chenella ⓕ ke·*ne*·la meatballs (sometimes fishballs)
chinulille ⓕ pl kee·noo·*lee*·le ravioli stuffed with sugar, ricotta, egg yolks, fried lemon & orange peel
chiodino ⓜ kyo·*dee*·no honey-coloured fungus – mushroom that must be cooked
ciabatta ⓕ cha·*ba*·ta crisp, flat & long bread
cialzons ⓜ pl chal·*tsons* ravioli stuffed with ricotta, spinach, sultanas, chocolate & sometimes chicken & herbs
ciambelle ⓕ pl **al mosto** cham·*be*·le al *mos*·to ring-shaped cakes made with grape must
ciammotta ⓕ cha·*mo*·ta mixed-vegetable fry
cianfotta ⓕ chan·*fo*·ta stew with vegetables, garlic & basil
ciaudedda ⓕ chow·*de*·da vegetable stew with artichokes, onions & potatoes
ciavarro ⓜ cha·*va*·ro spring soup made with cereals & legumes
cibuddau ⓜ chee·boo·*da*·oo onion-based dish
cicala ⓕ chee·*ka*·la crustacean
ciccioli ⓜ pl *chee*·cho·lee tasty pieces of crispy fat
ciceri ⓜ pl **e tria** ⓕ *chee*·che·ree e *tree*·a dish of boiled chickpeas & pasta, served with onions
cicirata ⓕ chee·chee·*ra*·ta small, sweet balls fried & covered with honey
ciliegia ⓕ chee·*lye*·ja cherry
cima ⓕ *chee*·ma breast, normally veal
cime ⓕ pl **di rapa** *chee*·me dee *ra*·pa turnip tops
cioccolato ⓜ cho·ko·*la*·to chocolate
— fondente fon·*den*·te cooking chocolate

cipollata ⓕ chee·po·*la*·ta dish with pork, spare ribs, stale bread & a lot of white onion
cipolle ⓕ pl chee·*po*·le onions
— ripiene ree·*pye*·ne stuffed half onions
— selvatiche sel·*va*·tee·ke wild onions
coccois ⓜ ko·*ko*·ees flat bread made with salty cheese & crackling
cocomero ⓜ ko·*ko*·me·ro watermelon
coda ⓕ *ko*·da tail • angler fish
cognà ⓜ ko·*nya* apple, pear, fig & grape sauce
coietas ⓜ pl ko·*ye*·tas roulades made with savoy cabbage & meat sauce
colombo/a ⓜ/ⓕ ko·*lom*·bo/a dove • pigeon • type of cake
conchiglie ⓕ pl kon·*kee*·lye pasta shells
condimento ⓜ kon·dee·*men*·to dressing
confetti ⓜ pl kon·*fe*·tee sugar-coated almonds
coniglio ⓜ ko·*nee*·lyo rabbit
conserva ⓕ kon·*ser*·va preserve
— di pomodoro dee po·mo·*do*·ro traditional tomato sauce
cornetto ⓜ kor·*ne*·to breakfast pastry
coscia ⓕ *ko*·sha leg • haunch
costata ⓕ kos·*ta*·ta beef steak (rib)
— alla napoletana *a*·la na·po·le·*ta*·na with oil, tomato sauce, oregano, garlic & white wine
— di manzo alla pizzaiola dee *man*·dzo *a*·la pee·tsa·*yo*·la with garlic, oil, tomatoes & oregano
costine ⓕ pl kos·*tee*·ne ribs
— di maiale dee ma·*ya*·le pork spare ribs grilled on stone
costoletta ⓕ kos·to·*le*·ta veal cutlet
cotechinata ⓕ ko·te·kee·*na*·ta roulade of pig rind stuffed with garlic, parsley & lard cooked with tomato sauce
cotechino ⓜ ko·te·*kee*·no boiled pork sausage
— in galera een ga·*le*·ra 'in prison' – meatloaf stuffed with a boiled **cotechino**
cotoletta ⓕ ko·to·*le*·ta (veal) cutlet usually breaded & fried
— alla bolognese *a*·la bo·lo·*nye*·ze breaded veal cutlet sauteed with butter & baked with cured ham & fresh parmesan
— alla milanese *a*·la mee·la·*ne*·ze veal loin steak breaded & fried in butter
cotto/a ⓜ/ⓕ *ko*·to/a cooked
ben — ben well done
non troppo — non *tro*·po medium rare
poco — *po*·ko rare
cozze ⓕ pl *ko*·tse mussels
crema ⓕ **inglese** *kre*·ma een·*gle*·ze custard
cren ⓜ kren horseradish
crescenza ⓕ kre·*shen*·tsa fresh, soft cheese (see **stracchino**)
crespella ⓕ kres·*pe*·la thin fritter
crespelle ⓕ pl **bagnate** kres·*pe*·le ba·*nya*·te pasta with savoury filling served in chicken stock
crocchette ⓕ pl kro·*ke*·te croquettes of mashed potatoes & various ingredients
crostacei ⓜ pl kro·*sta*·chay crustaceans
crostata ⓕ kro·*sta*·ta fruit tart • crust
crostini ⓜ pl kro·*stee*·nee slices of bread toasted with savoury toppings
crostoi ⓜ pl kro·*stoy* little fritters with sweet or savoury fillings
crostoli ⓜ pl *kro*·sto·lee fried sweet pastry with icing sugar • small flat bread
crucetta ⓕ kroo·*che*·ta sweet made with figs stuffed with nuts & arranged as a cross
crudo/a ⓜ/ⓕ *kroo*·do/a raw

crumiri ⓜ pl *kroo*·mee·ree type of dry biscuits
crusca ⓕ *kroos*·ka bran
culatello ⓜ **(di Busseto)** koo·la·*te*·lo (dee boo·*se*·to) ham made of salted & spiced pig's rump
culingiones ⓜ pl koo·leen·*jo*·nes kind of **ravioli** stuffed with potatoes or chard, sheep's cheese, garlic & mint
cupeta ⓕ koo·*pe*·ta nougat stuffed between two wafers
cuscus ⓜ *koos*·koos couscous
cutturiddi ⓜ pl koo·too·*ree*·dee lamb stew with chilli, tomatoes, small onions & celery

~ D ~

di/d' ... dee/d ... from ...
datteri ⓜ pl *da*·te·ree dates (fruit)
— di mare dee *ma*·re type of mussel
della casa *de*·la *ka*·za 'of the house' – house speciality
diavola, alla *dya*·vo·la, *a*·la spicy dish
diavolicchio ⓜ dya·vo·*lee*·kyo dynamite chilli
ditali(ni) ⓜ pl dee·*ta*·lee/ dee·ta·*lee*·nee small bits of pasta often used in soups
dolce *dol*·che dessert • sweet • soft
dolcelatte ⓜ dol·che·*la*·te soft mild blue cheese
dolcetti ⓜ pl **di pasta di mandorle** dol·*che*·tee dee *pas*·ta dee *man*·dor·le traditional sweets made with marzipan, sugar & egg whites

~ E ~

erbazzone ⓜ er·ba·*tso*·ne baked pasta stuffed with spinach, lard, spices, parmesan, eggs & parsley
— dolce *dol*·che sweet baked shortcrust pastry filled with boiled & chopped chards mixed with **ricotta**, sugar & almonds
erbe ⓕ pl *er*·be herbs

~ F ~

fagiano ⓜ fa·*ja*·no pheasant
fagioli ⓜ pl fa·*jo*·lee beans (usually dried)
fagiolini ⓜ pl fa·jo·*lee*·nee green beans
false salsicce ⓕ pl *fal*·se sal·*see*·che 'false sausages' – sausages made with lard & potatoes & coloured with beet
farcito ⓜ far·*chee*·to stuffed food
farfalle ⓕ pl far·*fa*·le butterfly-shaped pasta
farina ⓕ fa·*ree*·na flour
farinata ⓕ fa·ree·*na*·ta thin, flat bread made from chickpea flour
farro ⓜ *fa*·ro spelt (an ancient grain)
fasoi ⓜ pl **col muset** fa·*zoy* kol myoo·*zet* dish with dried beans, sausage, pork rind & spices
fatto/a ⓜ/ⓕ *fa*·to/a made
— a mano a *ma*·no made by hand
— in casa een *ka*·za home-made • made on the premises
favata ⓕ fa·*va*·ta rustic dish of broad beans, lard, pork, sausages, tomatoes & herbs
fave ⓕ pl *fa*·ve broad beans
fegato ⓜ *fe*·ga·to liver
felino ⓜ fe·*lee*·no type of salami
ferri, ai *fe*·ree, ai grilled on an open fire
fesa ⓕ *fe*·za veal (term used in northern Italy)
fetta ⓕ *fe*·ta slice (of meat/cheese)
fettuccine ⓕ pl fe·too·*chee*·ne long ribbon-shaped pasta
— alla romana *a*·la ro·*ma*·na 'Roman-style' – served with meat sauce, mushrooms & sheep's cheese
fiadoni ⓜ pl **alla trentina** fya·*do*·nee a·la tren·*tee*·na little sweets stuffed with almonds, honey, cinnamon & rum

fiandolein ⓜ fyan·do·*layn* 'egg flip' made with yolks, milk, sugar & lemon peel
fico ⓜ *fee*·ko fig
filoncino ⓜ fee·lon·*chee*·no breadstick
finanziera ⓕ fee·nan·*tsye*·ra sweetbreads, mushrooms & chicken livers in a creamy sauce
finocchio ⓜ fee·*no*·kyo fennel
fior di latte ⓜ fyor dee *la*·te fresh & very soft cheese • a **gelato** flavour
fiori ⓜ pl *fyo*·ree flowers – some are commonly eaten (eg zucchini flowers)
— di zucca farciti dee *tsoo*·ka far·*chee*·tee stuffed, fried zucchini or squash flowers
focaccia ⓕ fo·*ka*·cha flat bread often filled or topped with cheese, ham, vegetables & other ingredients
foglia ⓕ **d'alloro** *fo*·lya da·*lo*·ro bay leaf
fondo ⓜ *fon*·do stock
fondua ⓕ fon·*doo*·a **fontina** cheese melted with butter & eggs & topped with thin slices of truffle
fontina ⓕ fon·*tee*·na sweet & creamy cheese, similar to Gruyère
formaggio ⓜ for·*ma*·jo cheese
forno, al *for*·no, al cooked in an oven
fragole ⓕ pl *fra*·go·le strawberries
freddo/a ⓜ/ⓕ *fre*·do/a cold
fresco/a ⓜ/ⓕ *fres*·ko/a fresh
fregola ⓕ *fre*·go·la type of couscous
fregnacce ⓕ pl fre·*nya*·che thin rolled pancakes stuffed with meat
frisceu ⓜ free·*she*·oo fritters with lettuce, whitebait, zucchini, liver, brain, dried cod, pumpkin etc
frisedde ⓜ free·*ze*·de big ring-shaped cakes, boiled, baked then served with tomatoes, oil, salt & oregano
fritole ⓕ pl *free*·to·le fritters containing sultanas, pine nuts, candied lemon & liqueur
frittata ⓕ free·*ta*·ta thick omelette slice, served hot or cold
frittatensuppe ⓕ pl free·ta·ten·*soo*·pe thin omelettes cut into strips & served with meat stock
frittatine ⓕ pl **di farina al miele di fichi** free·ta·*tee*·ne dee fa·*ree*·na al *mye*·le dee *fee*·kee pancakes folded & stuffed with fig honey
frittelle ⓕ pl free·*te*·le fritters
frittelloni ⓜ pl free·te·*lo*·nee boiled spinach **tortellini** sauteed with butter, sultanas & cheese, then fried in lard
fritto/a ⓜ/ⓕ *free*·to/a fried
frito ⓜ **misto** *free*·to *mees*·to a mixture of various ingredients, depending on the region & time of year, fried in olive oil (some versions contain offal)
— abruzzese a·broo·*tse*·ze diced artichokes & boiled fennel, breaded & fried
frumento ⓜ froo·*men*·to wheat
frutta ⓕ *froo*·ta fruit
— secca *se*·ka dried fruit
frutti ⓜ pl **di mare** *froo*·tee dee *ma*·re seafood
fugazza ⓕ foo·*ga*·tsa rich, sweet pastry
funghi ⓜ pl *foon*·gee mushrooms
fusilli ⓜ pl foo·*zee*·lee corkscrew-shaped pasta

~ G ~

galani ⓜ pl ga·*la*·nee layered strips of fried pastry sprinkled with icing sugar
gallina ⓕ ga·*lee*·na chicken • hen
gambero ⓜ *gam*·be·ro prawn • shrimp
gamberoni ⓜ pl gam·be·*ro*·nee prawns
gambon ⓜ gam·*bon* pig's leg, boned, pressed & matured
garagoli ⓜ pl ga·*ra*·go·lee shellfish similar to periwinkles

garganelli ⓜ pl gar·ga·*ne*·lee short pasta served with various sauces
gattò ⓜ **di patate e salsiccia** ga·*to* dee pa·*ta*·te e sal·*see*·cha baked meatloaf made with mashed potato, eggs, ham & cheeses
gelato ⓜ je·*la*·to ice cream
genovese, alla je·no·*ve*·ze, *a*·la sauce including olive oil, garlic & herbs
gerstensuppe ⓜ ger·sten·*soo*·pe barley soup with onions, parsley, spices & speck
gianduiotto ⓜ jyan·doo·*yo*·to hazelnut chocolate
giardiniera ⓕ jar·dee·*nye*·ra pickled vegetables
girello ⓜ jee·*re*·lo round cut of meat
gnocchi ⓜ pl *nyo*·kee small (most commonly potato) dumplings
gnocchetti ⓜ pl nyo·*ke*·tee small shell-shaped pasta
gnocco ⓜ **di pane (al prosciutto)** *nyo*·ko dee *pa*·ne (al pro·*shoo*·to) pieces of bread fried in a mixture of butter, eggs, milk & ham
goregone ⓜ go·re·*go*·ne freshwater lake fish
gorgonzola ⓕ gor·gon·*dzo*·la spicy, sweet, creamy blue-vein cow's milk cheese
grana ⓕ **(padano)** *gra*·na (pa·*da*·no) hard cheese, also refers to cheeses such as **parmigiano**
granchio ⓜ *gran*·kyo crab
granita ⓕ gra·*nee*·ta finely crushed flavoured ice
granseola ⓕ gran·se·o·la spider crab
grano ⓜ *gra*·no wheat
gran(o)turco ⓜ gran(·o)·*toor*·ko maize
grappa ⓕ *gra*·pa distilled grape must
grissini ⓜ pl gree·*see*·nee breadsticks
guanciale ⓜ gwan·*cha*·le cheek, usually pig's
gubana ⓕ goo·*ba*·na sweet pastry

~ I ~

impanada ⓕ eem·pa·*na*·da savoury tart stuffed with vegetables & many kinds of meat & fish
impepata ⓕ **di cozze** eem·pe·*pa*·ta dee *ko*·tse fish-based dish prepared with mussels & lemon
infarinata ⓕ een·fa·ree·*na*·ta polenta as a soup, or fried in strips, with various meat & vegetable combinations
insalata ⓕ een·sa·*la*·ta salad
— caprese ka·*pre*·ze with mozzarella, tomato & basil
— di carne cruda dee *kar*·ne *kroo*·da with raw minced meat
involtini ⓜ pl een·vol·*tee*·nee stuffed rolls of meat or fish
— di carne dee *kar*·ne small veal slices, rolled up, stuffed, pierced on kebabs & baked or grilled
— siciliani see·chee·*lya*·nee meat rolled in breadcrumbs, stuffed with egg, ham & cheese

~ J ~

jota ⓕ *yo*·ta soup with beans, milk, & polenta • soup with beans, potatoes, sauerkraut & smoked pork rinds

~ L ~

laganelle ⓕ pl **e fagioli** la·ga·*ne*·le e fa·*jo*·lee sheets of pasta served in a bean soup
lamponi ⓜ pl lam·*po*·nee raspberries
lasagne ⓕ pl la·*za*·nye flat sheets of egg pasta
— alla bolognese *a*·la bo·lo·*nye*·ze baked lasagne with meat sauce, bechamel & parmesan
lattuga ⓕ la·*too*·ga lettuce
lavarelli ⓜ pl la·va·*re*·lee fresh water whitefish
lecca-lecca ⓕ *le*·ka *le*·ka lollipop

nticchie ⓕ pl len·*tee*·kye lentils
pre ⓜ *lep*·re hare
sso/a ⓜ/ⓕ *le*·so/a boiled
scio/a ⓜ/ⓕ *lee*·sho/a smooth – escribes pasta with a smooth urface
aneddè ⓜ pl lya·ne·*de* noodles with hickpeas or rabbit sauce
evito ⓜ *lye*·vee·to yeast
mone ⓜ lee·*mo*·ne lemon
ngua ⓕ *leen*·gwa tongue
nguine ⓕ pl leen·*gwee*·ne long thin bbons of pasta
ccio ⓜ *loo*·cho pike
ganega ⓕ loo·*ga*·ne·ga pork sausage
ganiga di verze ⓕ loo·*ga*·nee·ga ee *ver*·dze cabbage sausage uffed with mince, cheese, eggs & readcrumbs
mache ⓕ pl loo·*ma*·ke snails
ppoli ⓜ pl *loo*·po·lee hops

~ M ~

accaruni ⓜ pl **di casa con ragù** a·ka·*roo*·nee dee *ka*·za kon ra·*goo* nall pasta tubes served with tomato meat sauce
accheroni ⓜ pl ma·ke·*ro*·nee any be pasta
alla chitarra *a*·la kee·*ta*·ra square paghetti, generally served with a eat sauce
con la ricotta kon la ree·*ko*·ta asta served with ricotta, sheep's eese & sometimes also parmesan
agro/a ⓜ/ⓕ *mag*·ro/a thin • lean • eatless
aturo/a ⓜ/ⓕ ma·*too*·ro/a ripe
aiale ⓜ ma·*ya*·le pork
ais ⓜ *ma*·eez maize
alfatti ⓜ pl mal·*fa*·tee dumplings th spinach, eggs & cheese
alloreddus ⓜ pl ma·lo·*re*·doos mplings with saffron in a meat uce
maltagliati ⓜ pl mal·ta·*lya*·tee odd shapes of pasta
mandorle ⓕ pl *man*·dor·le almonds
manteca ⓕ man·*te*·ka fresh cheese rolled in a ball & stuffed with butter
mantecato ⓜ man·te·*ka*·to any ingredients pounded to a paste
manzo ⓜ *man*·dzo beef
maraschino ⓜ ma·ras·*kee*·no cherry liqueur
marcetto ⓜ mar·*che*·to very spicy cheese paste
marille ⓕ pl ma·*ree*·le crazily shaped pasta designed to retain the maximum amount of sauce
marinara, alla ma·ree·*na*·ra, *a*·la dish containing seafood
maritozzi ⓜ pl ma·ree·*to*·tsee small, soft sweet cakes stuffed with pine nuts, sultanas, orange peel & fruit
marrone ⓜ ma·*ro*·ne large chestnut
marsala ⓕ mar·*sa*·la fortified wine
marubini ⓜ pl ma·roo·*bee*·nee pasta stuffed with toasted bread, parmesan, marrow & eggs
mascarpone ⓜ mas·kar·*po*·ne very soft & creamy cheese
maturo/a ⓜ/ⓕ ma·*too*·ro/a ripe
mazzafegato ⓕ pl ma·tsa·*fe*·ga·to matured dry-cured pork sausage, made with minced liver, kidney, tripe & lung
mela ⓕ *me*·la apple
melagrana ⓕ me·la·*gra*·na pomegranate
melanzanata ⓕ **(di Lecce)** me·lan·dza·*na*·ta (dee *le*·che) eggplant pasta sauce • baked eggplant, tomato, onion, basil & sheep's cheese
melanzane ⓕ pl me·lan·*dza*·ne eggplants • aubergines
— ripiene ree·*pye*·ne baked eggplants stuffed with their pulp, eggs, cheese, herbs, spices & bread
— violette vee·o·*le*·te purple eggplant

meringa ⓕ me·*reen*·ga meringue
merlano ⓜ mer·*la*·no whiting
merluzzo ⓜ mer·*loo*·tso cod
mesta ⓕ **e fasoi** ⓜ pl *mes*·ta e fa·*zoy* polenta cooked with beans
miele ⓜ *mye*·le honey
migliaccio ⓜ **'e cigule** ⓕ pl mee·*lya*·cho e chee·*goo*·le baked polenta with pork, sausages, sheep's cheese & pepper
milanese, alla mee·la·*ne*·ze, *a*·la any sauce associated with Milan – normally includes butter
millecosedde ⓜ mee·le·ko·*ze*·de hearty soup with vegetables, legumes & short pasta
minestra ⓕ mee·*ne*·stra soup
— alla pignata *a*·la pee·*nya*·ta with beans, pork & vegetables
— cò i cece ko ee *che*·che with chickpeas & pasta
minestrone ⓜ mee·ne·*stro*·ne trad-itional soup usually including many vegetables & sometimes pasta or rice, bacon cubes & pork rinds
misticanza ⓕ mees·tee·*kan*·tsa salad with mixed greens
misto/a ⓜ/ⓕ *mees*·to/a mixed
mollusco ⓜ mo·*loo*·sko mollusc
montasio ⓜ mon·*ta*·zyo hard cheese
montato/a ⓜ/ⓕ mon·*ta*·to/a whipped
morbido/a ⓜ/ⓕ *mor*·bee·do soft
mortadella ⓕ **(di Bologna)** mor·ta·*de*·la (dee bo·*lo*·nya) salami made with minced pork, lard & black pepper
mostaccioli ⓜ pl mos·ta·*cho*·lee small chocolate-coated biscuits
mozzetta ⓕ mo·*tse*·ta salami made with haunch of mountain-goat or chamois, salted & dried
mozzarella ⓕ mo·tsa·*re*·la soft, fresh white cheese made from cow's milk
— di bufala dee *boo*·fa·la made from buffalo's milk
— in carrozza een ka·*ro*·tsa on slices of bread, battered & fried
'mpanada ⓕ m·pa·*na*·da see **impanada**
'mpepata ⓕ **di cozze** m·pe·*pa*·ta dee *ko*·tse see **impepata di cozze**
muggine ⓜ *moo*·jee·ne mullet

~ N ~

napoletana, alla na·po·le·*ta*·na, *a*·la from or in the style of Naples – usually includes tomatoes & garlic
nasello ⓜ na·*ze*·lo hake
'ndugghia ⓕ n·*doo*·gya dry-cured pork & fennel-seed sausage
nero ⓜ **di seppia/calamaro** *ne*·ro dee *se*·pya/ka·la·*ma*·ro squid/calamari ink
nocciola ⓕ no·*cho*·la hazelnut
noce ⓜ *no*·che nut • walnut
— di cocco dee *ko*·ko coconut
— moscata mos·*ka*·ta nutmeg
norma, alla *nor*·ma, *a*·la pasta sauce with eggplant & tomato
nostrano ⓜ nos·*tra*·no hard cheese local, home-made or domestic produce

~ O ~

oca ⓕ *o*·ka goose
offelle ⓕ pl o·*fe*·le sweet biscuits with mixed dried fruit
olio ⓜ *o*·lyo oil – almost always olive oil
ombrichelli ⓜ pl om·bree·*ke*·lee coarse home-made spaghetti
opinus ⓜ o·*pee*·noos pine-cone-shaped biscuits sprinkled with melted sugar & egg whites
orata ⓕ o·*ra*·ta bream • gilthead
orecchiette ⓕ pl o·re·*kye*·te shell-shaped, hand-made pasta, served with vegetables & olive oil or a rich meat sauce

orzo ⓜ *or*·dzo barley
— e fagioli e fa·*jo*·lee thick barley & bean broth
ossi di morti ⓜ pl *o*·see dee *mor*·tee 'bones of the dead' – very hard crunchy biscuits
ossobuco ⓜ o·so·*boo*·ko veal shanks
— milanese mee·la·*ne*·ze cut into small pieces & cooked with spices
ostriche ⓕ pl *os*·tree·ke oysters

~ P ~

pagnottella ⓕ pa·nyo·*te*·la bread roll
palle ⓕ pl *pa*·le balls
— del nonno del *no*·no 'grandpa's balls' – sweet fried ricotta balls • crinkly pork sausages
— di riso dee *ree*·zo stuffed rice croquettes
palombo ⓜ pa·*lom*·bo dove • pigeon
— alla todina *a*·la to·*dee*·na roasted pigeon
pan ⓜ **biscotto condito** pan bees·*ko*·to kon·*dee*·to toasted bread with oil, tomatoes, herbs
panadas ⓕ pl pa·*na*·das see **pancotto**
pancetta ⓕ pan·*che*·ta salt-cured bacon
pancotto ⓜ pan·*ko*·to soup made with boiled bread, cheese & eggs or fresh tomatoes
pane ⓜ *pa*·ne bread
— a pasta acida a *pas*·ta a·*chee*·da sourdough bread
— all'olio a·*lo*·lyo bread with oil
— aromatico a·ro·*ma*·tee·ko herb or vegetable bread
— carasau ka·ra·*zow* long-lasting bread eaten by shepherds
— casereccio ka·ze·*re*·cho firm, floury loaf
— col mosto kol *mos*·to bread with nuts, anise, almonds, raisins, sugar & must
— di segale dee *se*·ga·le rye bread
— frattau fra·*tow* slices of bread with sheep's cheese, tomato or meat sauce, boiling broth & eggs
— fresa *fre*·za flat, crispy bread
— integrale een·te·*gra*·le wholemeal bread
— pugliese poo·*lye*·ze large, crusty loaf
— salato sa·*la*·to salty bread
— toscano tos·*ka*·no crumbly, unsalted bread
— unto *oon*·to slices of bread toasted with garlic, olive oil, salt & pepper
panelle ⓕ pl pa·*ne*·le fried chickpea fritters
panforte ⓜ **(senese)** pan·*for*·te (se·*ne*·ze) hard cake made with almonds, fruit & spices
panino ⓜ pa·*nee*·no bread roll
paniscia ⓕ **novarese** pa·*nee*·sha no·va·*re*·ze rice-based dish with onion, sausage & soup
panna ⓕ *pa*·na cream
— cotta *ko*·ta thick creamy dessert
panpepato ⓜ pan·pe·*pa*·to sweet, ring-shaped cake
pan ⓜ **speziale** pan spe·*cha*·le bread with honey, nuts, raisins & fruit
panzanella ⓕ pan·tsa·*ne*·la Tuscan bread served with tomato sauce, onion, lettuce, anchovies, basil, olive oil, vinegar & salt
panzerotti ⓜ pl pan·tse·*ro*·tee filled pasta or pastries in a half-moon shape
paparot ⓜ pa·pa·*rot* spinach & corn soup
papassinas ⓜ pl pa·pa·*see*·nas small, sweet cone-shaped cakes
pappa ⓕ *pa*·pa baby food
— col pomodoro kol po·mo·*do*·ro soup made with thin slices of stale bread, tomatoes & spices

P

pappardelle ⓕ pl pa·par·*de*·le wide, flat pasta ribbons
— alla lepre *a*·la *le*·pre with stewed hare, red wine & tomato sauce
parmigiana, alla par·mee·*ja*·na, *a*·la any type of cheesy sauce
parmigiana ⓕ **di melanzane** par·mee·*ja*·na dee me·lan·*dza*·ne fried eggplant layered with eggs, basil, tomato sauce, onion & **mozzarella**
parmigiano ⓜ **(reggiano)** par·mee·*ja*·no (re·*ja*·no) parmesan cheese, often simply called **grana**
parrozzo ⓜ pa·*ro*·tso sweet bread, sometimes chocolate-coated
passatelli ⓜ pl pa·sa·*te*·lee small dumplings made with eggs, parmesan, ox marrow & nutmeg
pasta ⓕ *pas*·ta general name for the numerous types of pasta shapes • dough • pastry (see also p170)
— col bianchetto kol byan·*ke*·to spaghetti with a whitebait, tomato, garlic & chilli sauce
— cresciuta kre·*shoo*·ta anchovy or courgette flower fritters
— e fagioli e fa·*jo*·lee bean soup with pasta
— fresca *fres*·ka freshly made pasta
pastasciutta ⓕ pas·ta·*shoo*·ta dry pasta
pastissada/pastizzada ⓕ pas·tee·*sa*·da/pas·tee·*tsa*·da stew prepared with beef, ox or horse meat & vegetables
patate ⓕ pl pa·*ta*·te potatoes
pecorino ⓜ **(romano)** pe·ko·*ree*·no (ro·*ma*·no) hard & spicy cheese made from ewe's milk
penne ⓕ pl *pe*·ne short & tubular pasta
pepe ⓜ *pe*·pe pepper
peperonata ⓕ pe·pe·ro·*na*·ta capsicum, onion & tomato stew
peperoncini ⓜ pl pe·pe·ron·*chee*·nee hot chilli
peperoni ⓜ pl pe·pe·*ro*·nee peppers • capsicum
— ripieni ree·*pye*·nee stuffed with various fillings
pere ⓕ pl *pe*·ra pears
— imbottite eem·bo·*tee*·te baked stuffed pears
persico ⓜ *per*·see·ko perch
pesca ⓕ *pe*·ska peach
pesce ⓜ *pe*·she fish
pesto ⓜ *pes*·to sauce prepared with fresh basil, pine nuts, olive oil, garlic, cheese & salt
petto ⓜ *pe*·to breast
pettole ⓕ pl *pe*·to·le home-made, long thin ribbons of pasta
piadina ⓕ pya·*dee*·na flat round bread
piccagge ⓕ pl pee·*ka*·je long ribbon pasta served with **pesto** or an artichoke & mushroom sauce
piccata ⓕ pee·*ka*·ta veal with a lemon & **marsala** sauce
picchi pacchiu ⓜ *pee*·kee *pa*·kyoo pasta sauce with tomato & chilli
pici ⓜ pl *pee*·chee fresh pasta, like thick spaghetti
piccione ⓜ pee·*cho*·ne squab • pigeon
picula ⓕ **ad caval** pee·koo·*la* ad ka·*val* horse-meat stew
pinoli ⓜ pl pee·*no*·lee pine nuts
pinza ⓕ **padovana** *peen*·tsa pa·do·*va*·na sweet pastry
pinzimonio ⓜ peen·tsee·*mo*·nyo seasoned virgin olive oil for dipping (see also **cazzimperio**)
pioppparello ⓜ pyo·pa·*re*·lo common flat mushroom
pisarei ⓜ pl **e fasó** ⓜ pl pee·za·*ray* e fa·*zo* small dumplings flavoured with tomato sauce, bacon & boiled beans
piselli ⓜ pl pee·*ze*·lee green peas
pistum ⓜ pees·*toom* sweet & sour dumplings served with pork stock
pitta ⓕ *pee*·ta soft & flat loaf of bread

pitte ⓕ *pee*·te fring-shaped cake
pizza ⓕ *pee*·tsa there are more than 50 kinds, with varying bases & toppings
— a(l) taglio a(l) *ta*·lyo slice of pizza
— dolce di Pasqua *dol*·che dee *pas*·kwa sweet pizza dough with dried fruits
— Margherita mar·ge·*ree*·ta topped with simple ingredients such as oil, tomato, **mozzarella**, basil & oregano
— rustica *roos*·tee·ka topped with various combinations of ham, salami, sausage, egg or cheese
pizzaiola, alla pee·tsa·*yo*·la, *a*·la a tomato & oil sauce
pizzoccheri ⓜ pl pee·*tso*·ke·ree short, buckwheat pasta with cabbage & potatoes
polenta ⓕ po·*len*·ta cornmeal porridge
— al ragù al ra·*goo* served with a meat sauce
— concia *kon*·cha flavoured with a variety of cheeses
— e osei e o·*zay* served with sparrows, thrushes or larks • sponge cake with jam
— pasticciata pas·tee·*cha*·ta baked with meat sauce, mushrooms & cheese
— sulla spianatoria *soo*·la spya·na·*to*·rya with sausages, tomato & sheep's cheese served from a pastry board in the middle of the table
— taragna ta·*ra*·nya originally buckwheat **polenta**
polipo ⓜ *po*·lee·po octopus (also called **polpi**)
pollo ⓜ *po*·lo chicken
— alla diavola *a*·la *dya*·vo·la grilled with red pepper or chilli
— con peperoni e patate al coccio kon pe·pe·*ro*·nee e pa·*ta*·te al *ko*·cho slowly cooked in a terracotta pot with sage, potatoes & capsicum
polpette ⓜ pol·*pe*·te meatballs
polpettine ⓕ pl pol·pe·*tee*·ne small meatballs
— di carne con salsa di pomodoro dee *kar*·ne kon *sal*·sa dee po·mo·*do*·ro in tomato sauce
polpettone ⓜ pol·pe·*to*·ne meatloaf
polpi ⓜ pl *pol*·pee octopus (also called **polipo**)
— alla luciana *a*·la loo·*cha*·na sliced octopus with tomatoes, oil, garlic, parsley & lemon
— in purgatorio een poor·ga·*to*·ryo stewed with tomato, parsley, chilli & garlic
pomodori ⓜ pl po·mo·*do*·ree tomatoes
— secchi *se*·kee sun-dried tomatoes
pomodorini ⓜ pl po·mo·do·*ree*·nee tiny tomatoes • sun-dried tomatoes
pompelmo ⓜ pom·*pel*·mo grapefruit
porchetta ⓕ por·*ke*·ta stuffed suckling pig
porcini ⓜ pl por·*chee*·nee ceps (type of mushrooms)
porco ⓜ *por*·ko pig
potizza ⓕ po·*tee*·tsa soft cake prepared with leavened pastry
prataiolo ⓜ pra·ta·*yo*·lo popular button mushroom
preboggion ⓜ pre·bo·*jon* mixture of wild herbs
prosciutto ⓜ pro·*shoo*·to basic name for many types of thinly-sliced ham
— affumicato a·foo·mee·*ka*·to smoked salami
— San Daniele san da·*nye*·le sweet & delicate ham
provola ⓕ *pro*·vo·la semi-hard cheese made from buffalo & cow's milk
provolone ⓜ pro·vo·*lo*·ne rich medium-hard cheese made from cow's milk
prugna ⓕ *proo*·nya plum

puttanesca, alla poo·ta·*ne*·ska, a·la 'whore's style' – tomato, chilli, anchovies & black-olive pasta sauce

~ Q ~

quaglie Ⓕ pl *kwa*·lye quails
quartirolo Ⓜ kwar·tee·*ro*·lo sweet & delicate soft cheese
quattro formaggi *kwa*·tro for·*ma*·jee pasta sauce with four different cheeses
quattro stagioni *kwa*·tro sta·*jo*·nee pizza with different toppings on each quarter

~ R ~

rabarbaro Ⓜ ra·*bar*·ba·ro rhubarb
radicchio Ⓜ ra·*dee*·kyo chicory
— rosso *ro*·so slightly bitter vegetable with long leaves
rafano Ⓜ **tedesco** *ra*·fa·no te·*des*·ko horseradish
ragù Ⓜ ra·*goo* generally a meat sauce but sometimes vegetarian
— alla bolognese *a*·la bo·lo·*nye*·ze sauce of minced veal & pork
— alla napoletana *a*·la na·po·le·*ta*·na sauce made with chunks of meat, vegetables & red wine
rambasicci Ⓜ pl ram·ba·*zee*·chee stuffed cabbage leaves
rapa Ⓕ *ra*·pa turnip
ravioli Ⓜ pl ra·vee·*o*·lee pasta squares usually stuffed with meat, parmesan cheese & breadcrumbs
— liguri lee·*goo*·ree sometimes filled with ricotta & herbs
raviolini Ⓜ pl ra·vee·o·*lee*·nee small ravioli
ravioloni Ⓜ pl ra·vee·o·*lo*·nee large ravioli
razza Ⓕ *ra*·tsa skate
ri(so) Ⓜ **in cagnon** *ree*(·zo) een *ka*·nyon rice sauteed in garlic, butter, sage & sprinkled with parmesan

ribes Ⓜ **nero** *ree*·bes *ne*·ro blackcurrant
ribes Ⓜ **rosso** *ree*·bes *ro*·so redcurrant
ribollita Ⓕ ree·bo·*lee*·ta reheated & thickened vegetable soup
ricciarelli Ⓜ pl ree·cha·*re*·lee almond biscuits
ricotta Ⓕ ree·*ko*·ta fresh, moist, white cheese
— affumicata a·foo·mee·*ka*·ta smoked
— infornata een·for·*na*·ta oven-baked
rigaglie Ⓕ pl ree·*ga*·lye giblets
rigatoni Ⓜ pl ree·ga·*to*·nee short, fat tubes of pasta
— con la pagliata kon la pa·*lya*·ta served with small intestines of calves
ripieno Ⓜ ree·*pye*·no stuffing
risi Ⓜ pl **e bisi** Ⓜ pl *ree*·zee e *bee*·zee thick rice-based soup with peas
risi Ⓜ pl **e bruscandoli** Ⓜ pl *ree*·zee e broos·*kan*·do·lee bitter hop sprouts cooked in a broth with rice
riso Ⓜ *ree*·zo rice
— al salto al *sal*·to boiled rice sauteed with saffron
— comune ko·*moo*·ne lowest quality, usually used in soups
— fino *fee*·no good quality with large grains
— integrale een·te·*gra*·le brown rice
— semifino se·mee·*fee*·no slightly better quality than **comune**, with larger grains
— superfino soo·per·*fee*·no best-quality rice, used in risotto
risotto Ⓜ ree·*zo*·to rice dish slowly cooked in broth to a creamy consistency
— alla milanese *a*·la mee·la·*ne*·ze with ox marrow, meat stock & saffron
— alla monzese *a*·la mon·*dze*·ze with sausage & saffron or red wine

— alla piemontese a·la pye·mon·te·ze with white wine & truffles (& sometimes tomato sauce)
— alla sbirraglia a·la sbee·ra·lya with chicken breasts
— alla trevisana a·la tre·vee·za·na with sausage or chicken livers
— allo zafferano a·lo dza·fe·ra·no see **risotto alla milanese**
— con filetti di pesce persico kon fee·le·tee dee pe·she per·see·ko with perch fillets
— con le rane kon le ra·ne with frog legs, frog broth & herbs
— nero ne·ro black risotto with chard, onion, cuttlefish & their ink
— polesano po·le·za·no with eel, grey mullet, bass, white wine & fish broth
robiola ⓕ ro·byo·la soft cheese made mainly from cow's milk
romana, alla ro·ma·na, a·la sauce, usually tomato-based
rombo ⓜ rom·bo turbot
rosolata ⓕ ro·zo·la·ta saute
rosbif ⓜ roz·beef roast beef
rospo ⓜ ros·po angler fish
rosumada ⓕ ro·zoo·ma·da egg-nog with red wine
rotolo ⓜ ro·to·lo folded sheet of pasta filled with spinach, ricotta or meat
ruchetta ⓕ roo·ke·ta rocket
rucola ⓕ roo·ko·la rocket
rum-babà ⓜ room ba·ba **babà** sprinkled with rum & sugar
ruta ⓕ roo·ta rue (bitter herb)

~ S ~

sa fregula ⓕ sa fre·goo·la soup with small balls of flour & saffron
sagne chine ⓕ sa·nye kee·ne baked pasta with meatballs, eggs & cheese
salama ⓕ **da sugo ferrarese** sa·la·ma da soo·go fe·ra·re·ze pork sausage
salame ⓕ **di Felino** sa·la·me dee fe·lee·no dry-cured pork sausage
salami ⓜ pl sa·la·mee (pork) sausage
salamino ⓜ sa·la·mee·no small salami
salato/a ⓜ/ⓕ sa·la·to/a salty
sale ⓜ sa·le salt
salmi ⓜ sal·mee marinade with spices & sometimes wine
salmone ⓜ sal·mo·ne salmon
salsa ⓕ sal·sa sauce
— alfredo al·fre·do with butter, cream, parmesan & parsley
— alla checca a·la ke·ka cold sauce with tomatoes, olives, basil, capers & oregano
— alla pizzaiola a·la pee·tsa·yo·la pizza-style sauce
— di cren dee kren with grated radish & apples, onion, broth & white wine
— di pomodoro al tonno e funghi dee po·mo·do·ro al to·no e foon·gee with tuna, mushroom & tomato
— di pomodoro alla siciliana dee po·mo·do·ro a·la see·chee·lya·na with eggplant, anchovies, olives, capers, tomato & garlic
— verde ver·de green sauce with herbs, capers, olives, nuts, anchovies, breadcrumbs, garlic & vinegar
saltimbocca ⓕ sal·teem·bo·ka 'jump into the mouth' – bite-sized
salume ⓜ sa·loo·me salami
sanguinaccio ⓜ san·gwee·na·cho black pudding made with pig's blood, olives & cocoa
saor, in sowr, een sweet & sour, vinegar-based marinade for fish
sarago ⓜ sa·ra·go white bream
sarde ⓕ pl sar·de sardines
— a scapece a ska·pe·che fried sardines
— alla marchigiana a·la mar·kee·ja·na baked, marinated sardines

S

sardele in saor ⓕ pl sar·*de*·le een sowr dish with fried, marinated pilchards
sartù ⓜ **'e riso** ⓜ sar·*too* e *ree*·zo savoury rice dish
sas melicheddas ⓜ pl sas me·lee·*ke*·das marzipan cakes sprinkled with sugar
sausa ⓕ **d'avie** *sow*·sa da·*vee*·e honey, nut & mustard sauce
savoiardi ⓜ pl sa·vo·*yar*·dee lady-finger biscuits
sbrofadej ⓜ zbro·fa·*day* thin pasta
— in brodo een *bro*·do served in broth
scagliuozzoli ⓜ pl ska·lyoo·o·tso·lee fried **polenta** & **provolone**
scaloppine ⓕ pl ska·lo·*pee*·ne thin cutlets, usually veal, pork or turkey
— al marsala al mar·*sa*·la lean veal cutlet with **marsala**
scamorza ⓕ ska·*mor*·tsa soft, white cheese, similar to **mozzarella**, often smoked
scampi ⓜ pl *skam*·pee a small type of lobster
scapece ⓜ ska·*pe*·che vinegar-based marinade usually used for fish
— di Vasto dee *vas*·to dish prepared with sliced & fried fish, preserved in a marinade
scarole ⓜ ska·*ro*·le bitter leafy vegetable
schiaffettuni ⓜ pl **chini** skya·fe·*too*·nee *kee*·nee **maccheroni** with pork & eggs
schmorbraten ⓜ shmor·*bra*·ten veal marinated & cooked in wine & tomato sauce
sciatt ⓜ schat soft, round fritters containing **grappa**
scimú'd ⓜ shee·*mood* salted & spicy skim milk cheese
sciroppo ⓜ shee·*ro*·po syrup
scivateddi ⓜ shee·va·*te*·dee thick spaghetti served with meat sauce & ricotta
scottiglia ⓕ sko·*tee*·lya rich stew with tomatoes & meat
sebadas ⓜ se·*ba*·das large, round & sweet ravioli with cheese & honey
seccia ⓕ **'mbuttunata** se·cha m·boo·too·*na*·ta stuffed cuttlefish stewed with tomato sauce
selvaggina ⓕ sel·va·*jee*·na game
semifreddo ⓜ se·mee·*fre*·do cold, creamy desserts
— al torrone al to·*ro*·ne dessert with milk, vanilla, eggs & nougat
semola ⓕ *se*·mo·la bran • semolina
semolino ⓜ se·mo·*lee*·no semolina
senape ⓕ *se*·na·pe mustard
seno ⓜ *se*·no breast
seppia ⓕ *se*·pya cuttlefish
serpe ⓜ *ser*·pe cake with marzipan, almonds, icing sugar or chocolate
sfogliatelle ⓕ pl sfo·lya·*te*·le cake or pastry stuffed with **ricotta**, cinnamon, candied fruit & vanilla
sformato ⓜ sfor·*ma*·to flan
— di spinaci con cibreo al vinsanto dee spee·*na*·chee kon chee·*bre*·o al veen·*san*·to flan with spinach, served with liver
sgombro ⓜ *sgom*·bro mackerel
sogliola ⓕ *so*·lyo·la sole
sopa ⓕ **còada** *so*·pa ko·*a*·da soup of meat stock, pigeon, cheese & bread
soppressa ⓕ so·*pre*·sa pork sausage
soppressata ⓕ so·pre·*sa*·ta matured raw salami made with minced pig's tongue, lean pork & spices • soft salami made with pork & lard
— molisana mo·lee·*za*·na large pork sausage
sorbetto ⓜ sor·*be*·to sorbet
sott'aceti ⓜ pl so·ta·*che*·tee pickles
sott'olio ⓜ so·*to*·lyo preserved in oil
spaghetti ⓜ pl spa·*ge*·tee ubiquitous long thin strands of pasta
spá'tzle ⓜ *spa*·tsle little dumplings that can be served in broth
speck ⓜ spek type of smoked ham

MENU DECODER

spiedino/spiedo ⓜ spye·*dee*·no/ *spye*·do skewer
spezie ⓕ pl *spe*·tsye spices
spigola ⓕ *spee*·go·la sea bass
spinaci ⓜ pl spee·*na*·chee spinach
sponga(r)da ⓕ spon·*ga(r)*·da sweet pastry with vanilla, egg & sometimes mixed dried fruits
spugnola ⓕ spoo·*nyo*·la morel (sponge-like mushroom)
stecchi ⓜ pl *ste*·kee sticks • kebabs
— alla ligure *a*·la *lee*·goo·re with veal, chicken, sweetbread, eggs, mushrooms, artichokes & spices
stiacciata ⓕ stya·*cha*·ta sweet bun
stinco ⓜ *steen*·ko shank
stoccafisso ⓜ sto·ka·*fee*·so stockfish (small air-dried cod)
— a brandacujun a bran·da·*koo*·yoon creamy dish of potatoes & stockfish
— accomodato a·ko·mo·*da*·to stockfish cooked in a casserole with anchovies or mushrooms
stracchino ⓜ stra·*kee*·no soft & delicate cheese
stracciatella ⓕ stra·cha·*te*·la broth with whipped egg & parmesan
stracotto ⓜ stra·*ko*·to beef stew
stracotto/a ⓜ/ⓕ stra·*ko*·to/a cooked for a long time • overcooked
strangolapreti ⓜ pl stran·go·la·*pre*·tee 'priest throttler' – cheese & egg dumplings, varying from region to region
stravecchio ⓜ stra·*ve*·kyo 'very old' – aged for a long time
stringozzi ⓜ pl streen·*go*·tsee short pasta served with tomato or meat sauce
strinù ⓜ stree·*noo* tasty sausage, usually grilled
stroscia ⓕ **(di Pietrabruna)** *stro*·sha (dee pye·tra·*broo*·na) sweet cake
strozzapreti ⓜ pl stro·tsa·*pre*·tee long strips of pasta • dumplings made with spinach, chard & ricotta
strudel ⓜ *stroo*·del pastry with a stuffing including apples
stufatino ⓜ stoo·fa·*tee*·no lean veal stewed with tomatoes & spices
supa ⓕ **barbetta** *soo*·pa bar·*be*·ta rich meat & vegetable stock
suppa ⓕ *soo*·pa soup
supplì ⓜ soo·*plee* fried rice balls (similar to **crocchettes**)
suricitti ⓜ pl soo·ree·*chee*·tee flavoured polenta dumplings
susamelli ⓜ pl soo·za·*me*·lee 's'-shaped biscuits

~ T ~

tacchino ⓜ ta·*kee*·no turkey
— alla gosutta *a*·la go·*zoo*·ta turkey casserole with fennel & broth
— con sugo di melagrana kon *soo*·go dee me·la·*gra*·na with pomegranate sauce
tagliatelle ⓕ ta·lya·*te*·le long, ribbon-shaped pasta
— alla salsa di noci *a*·la *sal*·sa dee *no*·chee with nuts, oil, butter, ricotta & parmesan
— con finocchio selvatico kon fee·*no*·kyo sel·*va*·tee·ko served with a fennel, bacon & parsley sauce
taglierini ⓜ pl ta·lye·*ree*·nee thin strips of pasta
— al ragù al ra·*goo* served with meat sauce
tagliolini (blò blò) ⓜ pl ta·lyo·*lee*·nee (blo blo) thin strips of pasta in broth, with grated cheese
tajarin ⓜ pl ta·ya·*reen* thin pasta usually served with meat sauce
taleggio ⓜ ta·le·jo sweet, soft & fatty cheese with a soft rind
taralli ⓜ pl ta·*ra*·lee boiled & baked pretzel-like biscuits

tartufo ⓜ tar·*too*·fo truffle (very expensive kind of fungus)
tè ⓜ te tea
tegamata ⓕ **di maiale** te·ga·*ma*·ta dee ma·*ya*·le casserole of pork & fennel seed
tegame, in te·*ga*·me, een fried • braised
tegole ⓕ pl **d'Aosta** *te*·go·le da·*os*·ta almond biscuits
testaió ⓜ tes·ta·*yo* squares of pasta served with pesto & parmesan
testaroli ⓜ pl tes·ta·*ro*·lee discs of pasta, like pancakes
tiramisù ⓜ tee·ra·mee·*soo* sponge cake or savoiardi soaked in coffee & arranged in layers with mascarpone, then sprinkled with cocoa
tòcco ⓜ **di carne** to·*ko* dee *kar*·ne veal sauce
toma ⓕ *to*·ma firm cow or sheep's cheese
— piemontese pye·mon·*te*·ze a softer variety of **toma**
tomaxelle ⓕ pl to·ma·*kse*·le veal roulade in wine & broth
tomino ⓜ to·*mee*·no small fresh cheese
tonno ⓜ *to*·no tuna
torciarelli ⓜ pl **al tartufo** tor·cha·*re*·lee al tar·*too*·fo pasta served with a sauce containing minced lean pork, spices, mushrooms, truffles & cheese
torcinelli ⓜ pl tor·chee·*ne*·lee stewed lamb or kid entrails
torcolo ⓜ **di San Costanzo** *tor*·ko·lo dee san kos·*tan*·dzo ring-shaped cake
torresani ⓜ pl to·re·*za*·nee pigeon kebabs
torrone ⓜ to·*ro*·ne nougat
— al cioccolato al cho·ko·*la*·to very soft chocolate nougat
torroni ⓜ pl **di semi di sesamo** to·*ro*·nee dee *se*·mee dee *se*·za·mo crunchy sweets with sesame seeds
torta ⓕ *tor*·ta cake • tart • pie
tortelli ⓜ tor·*te*·lee fat, stuffed pasta
— di San Leo dee san *le*·o with spinach & cheeses
— di zucca dee *tsoo*·ka with pumpkin
tortellini ⓜ pl tor·te·*lee*·nee pasta filled with meat, parmesan & egg
tortelloni ⓜ pl tor·te·*lo*·nee large **tortellini**
tosella ⓕ to·*ze*·la fresh fried cheese
totano ⓜ to·*ta*·no type of squid
tramezzino ⓜ tra·me·*dzee*·no sandwich
Trebbiano ⓜ tre·*bya*·no white grape found throughout Italy
trenette ⓕ pl **al pesto** tre·*ne*·te al *pes*·to long, flat pasta with **pesto**
trifola ⓕ *tree*·fo·la white truffle
triglia ⓕ *tree*·lya red mullet
trota ⓕ *tro*·ta trout
tubetti ⓜ pl too·*be*·tee short pasta tubes
turcinelli ⓜ pl **arrostiti** toor·chee·*ne*·lee a·ro·*stee*·tee lamb-offal stew

~ U ~

uardi ⓜ pl **e fasoi** ⓜ pl *war*·dee e fa·*zoy* soup with beans, barley, ham bone & spices
umbrici ⓜ pl oom·*bree*·chee hand-made, thick spaghetti
uova ⓜ pl *wo*·va eggs
uva ⓕ pl *oo*·va grapes
— bianca *byan*·ka green grapes
— nera *ne*·ra red grapes
— passa *pa*·sa raisins

~ V ~

vapore, cotto/a a ⓜ/ⓕ va·*po*·re, *ko*·to/a a steamed
vecchio/a ⓜ/ⓕ *ve*·kyo/a old • aged
ventresca ⓕ **di tonno** ven·*tres*·ka dee *to*·no tuna belly

verdura/verdure ⓕ ver·*doo*·ra/ ver·*doo*·re vegetable/vegetables
verza ⓕ *ver*·dza savoy cabbage
vialone nano ⓜ vya·*lo*·ne *na*·no short-grain rice used for risotto
vincisgrassi ⓜ pl veen·cheez·*gra*·see rich, baked dish made of offal, cheese & sometimes truffle
vino ⓜ *vee*·no wine
— bianco *byan*·ko white wine
— rosso *ro*·so red wine
— spumante spoo·*man*·te sparkling wine
viscidu ⓜ vee·*shee*·doo dry, salty & sour cheese, sliced & pickled
vitello ⓜ vee·*te*·lo veal
— tonnato to·*na*·to thin slices of veal covered with a tuna, capers & anchovy sauce
vongole ⓕ pl *von*·go·le clams

~ Z ~

zabaglione ⓜ dza·ba·*lyo*·ne mousse-like dessert made of beaten egg, marsala & sugar
zampetto ⓜ dzam·*pe*·to calf, lamb or pig trotter
zenzero ⓜ *dzen*·dze·ro ginger
zeppule ⓕ pl **'e cicenielli** ⓜ pl *dze*·poo·le e chee·che·*nye*·lee fritters with cheese & anchovies
zeppule ⓕ pl **'e San Giuseppe** *dze*·poo·le e san joo·*ze*·pe small, fried ring-shaped cakes
zimin ⓜ pl *dzee*·meen soup with beans, pork & chards • dish with calamari & chard
ziti ⓜ pl *dzee*·tee long fat hollow pasta
zucca ⓕ *tsoo*·ka pumpkin
— gialla in agrodolce *ja*·la een a·gro·*dol*·che fried & served with spices & capers
zucchero ⓜ *tsoo*·ke·ro sugar
zuccotto ⓜ **fiorentino** tsoo·*ko*·to fyo·ren·*tee*·no sponge cake with liqueur, custard, chocolate & whipped cream
zuppa ⓕ *tsoo*·pa soup, usually thick
— alla canavesana *a*·la ka·na·ve·*za*·na soup base of bread, cabbage, butter, lard, onions & garlic
— di ceci dee *che*·chee rich chickpea soup
— di pesce alla marinara dee *pe*·she a·la ma·ree·*na*·ra fish soup
— 'e zuffritto e tsoo·*free*·to sauce prepared with pig's offal, red wine & tomato sauce

Dictionary

ENGLISH *to* ITALIAN

Inglese–Italiano

Nouns in this dictionary, and adjectives affected by gender, have their gender indicated by ⓜ and/or ⓕ. If it's a plural noun, you'll also see pl. Where a word that could be either a noun or a verb has no gender indicated, it's a verb.

A

aboard a bordo a *bor*·do
abortion aborto ⓜ a·*bor*·to
above sopra *so*·pra
abroad all'estero a·*les*·te·ro
accident incidente ⓜ een·chee·*den*·te
accommodation alloggio ⓜ a·*lo*·jo
acupuncture agopuntura ⓕ a·go·poon·*too*·ra
adaptor spina ⓕ multipla *spee*·na *mool*·tee·pla
addicted dipendente ⓜ/ⓕ dee·pen·*den*·te
address indirizzo ⓜ een·dee·*ree*·tso
administration amministrazione ⓕ a·mee·nee·stra·*tsyo*·ne
admission price prezzo ⓜ d'ingresso *pre*·tso deen·*gre*·so
admit (let in) far entrare far en·*tra*·re
adult adulto/a ⓜ/ⓕ a·*dool*·to/a
adventure avventura ⓕ a·ven·*too*·ra
advertisement annuncio ⓜ a·*noon*·cho
aerobics aerobica ⓕ a·e·*ro*·bee·ka
after dopo *do*·po
afternoon pomeriggio ⓜ po·me·*ree*·jo
aftershave dopobarba ⓜ do·po·*bar*·ba
again di nuovo dee *nwo*·vo
age età ⓕ e·*ta*
aggressive aggressivo/a ⓜ/ⓕ a·gre·*see*·vo/a
agree essere d'accordo e·se·re da·*kor*·do
agriculture agricoltura ⓕ a·gree·kol·*too*·ra
AIDS AIDS ⓜ a·*eedz*
air aria ⓕ *a*·rya
airmail via ⓕ aerea *vee*·a a·e·re·a
air-conditioned ad aria condizionata ad *a*·rya kon·dee·*tsyo*·na·ta
airline linea ⓕ aerea *lee*·ne·a a·e·re·a
airport aeroporto ⓜ a·e·ro·*por*·to
airport tax tassa ⓕ aeroportuale *ta*·sa a·e·ro·por·*twa*·le
aisle (plane, train) corridoio ⓜ ko·ree·*do*·yo
alarm clock sveglia ⓕ *sve*·lya
alcohol alcol ⓜ *al*·kol
all (singular) tutto/a ⓜ/ⓕ *too*·to/a

all (plural) tutti/e ⓜ/ⓕ *too*·tee/ *too*·te
allergy allergia ⓕ a·ler·*jee*·a
almond mandorla ⓕ *man*·dor·la
alone da solo/a ⓜ/ⓕ da *so*·lo/a
already già ja
also anche *an*·ke
altar altare ⓜ al·*ta*·re
altitude quota ⓕ *kwo*·ta
always sempre *sem*·pre
ambassador ambasciatore/ ambasciatrice ⓜ/ⓕ am·ba·sha·*to*·re/ am·ba·sha·*tree*·che
ambulance ambulanza ⓕ am·boo·*lan*·tsa
amount quantità ⓕ kwan·tee·*ta*
ancient antico/a ⓜ/ⓕ an·*tee*·ko/a
and e e
angry arrabbiato/a ⓜ/ⓕ a·ra·*bya*·to/a
animal animale ⓜ a·nee·*ma*·le
ankle caviglia ⓕ ka·*vee*·lya
annual annuale a·noo·*a*·le
answer risposta ⓕ rees·*pos*·ta
ant formica ⓕ for·*mee*·ka
antibiotics antibiotici ⓜ pl an·tee·bee·*o*·tee·chee
antihistamines antistaminici ⓜ pl an·tee·sta·*mee*·nee·chee
antinuclear antinucleare an·tee·noo·kle·*a*·re
antique pezzo ⓜ di antiquariato *pe*·tso dee an·tee·kwa·*rya*·to
antiseptic antisettico ⓜ an·tee·*se*·tee·ko
appendix appendice ⓕ a·pen·*dee*·che
apple mela ⓕ *me*·la
appointment appuntamento ⓜ a·poon·ta·*men*·to
apricot albicocca ⓕ al·bee·*ko*·ka
archaeological archeologico/a ⓜ/ⓕ ar·ke·o·*lo*·jee·ko/a
architect architetto ⓜ ar·kee·*te*·to
architecture architettura ⓕ ar·kee·te·*too*·ra
argue litigare lee·tee·*ga*·re
arm braccio ⓜ *bra*·cho
aromatherapy aromaterapia ⓕ a·ro·ma·te·ra·*pee*·a
arrest arrestare a·res·*ta*·re
arrivals arrivi ⓜ pl a·*ree*·vee
arrive arrivare a·ree·*va*·re
art arte ⓕ *ar*·te
art gallery galleria ⓕ d'arte ga·le·*ree*·a *dar*·te
artist artista ⓜ&ⓕ ar·*tee*·sta
ashtray portacenere ⓜ por·ta·*che*·ne·re
ask (a question) domandare do·man·*da*·re
ask (for something) richiedere ree·*kye*·de·re
aspirin aspirina ⓕ as·pee·*ree*·na
asthma asma ⓕ *az*·ma
athletics atletica ⓕ at·*le*·tee·ka
aubergine melanzana ⓕ me·lan·*dza*·na
aunt zia ⓕ *tsee*·a
Australia Australia ⓕ ow·*stra*·lya
Austria Austria ⓕ *ow*·stree·a
automatic automatico/a ⓜ/ⓕ ow·to·*ma*·tee·ko/a
automatic teller machine (ATM) Bancomat ⓜ *ban*·ko·mat
autumn autunno ⓜ ow·*too*·no
avenue viale ⓜ vee·*a*·le
awful orrendo/a ⓜ/ⓕ o·*ren*·do/a

B

B&W (film) in bianco e nero een *byan*·ko e *ne*·ro
baby bimbo/a ⓜ/ⓕ *beem*·bo/a
baby food cibo ⓜ da bebè *chee*·bo da be·*be*
baby powder borotalco ⓜ bo·ro·*tal*·ko
back (body) schiena ⓕ *skye*·na
backpack zaino ⓜ *dzai*·no
bacon pancetta ⓕ pan·*che*·ta
bad cattivo/a ⓜ/ⓕ ka·*tee*·vo/a
bag (general) borsa ⓕ *bor*·sa
bag (shopping) sacchetto ⓜ sa·*ke*·to
baggage bagaglio ⓜ ba·*ga*·lyo

B

baggage allowance bagaglio ⓜ consentito ba·*ga*·lyo kon·sen·*tee*·to
baggage claim ritiro ⓜ bagagli ree·*tee*·ro ba·*ga*·lyee
bakery panetteria ⓕ pa·ne·te·*ree*·a
balance (account) saldo ⓜ *sal*·do
balcony balcone ⓜ bal·*ko*·ne
ball (dancing) ballo ⓜ *ba*·lo
ball (inflated) pallone ⓜ pa·*lo*·ne
ball (sports) palla ⓕ *pa*·la
ballet balletto ⓜ ba·*le*·to
band (music) gruppo ⓜ *groo*·po
bandage fascia ⓕ *fa*·sha
Band-Aids cerotti ⓜ pl che·*ro*·tee
bank (money) banca ⓕ *ban*·ka
bank account conto ⓜ in banca *kon*·to een *ban*·ka
banknote banconota ⓕ ban·ko·*no*·ta
baptism battesimo ⓜ ba·*te*·zee·mo
bar locale ⓜ lo·*ka*·le
bar fridge frigobar ⓜ *free*·go·bar
barber barbiere ⓜ bar·*bye*·re
basket cestino ⓜ ches·*tee*·no
basketball pallacanestro ⓕ pa·la·ka·*ne*·stro
bath bagno ⓜ *ba*·nyo
bathing suit costume ⓜ da bagno kos·*too*·me da *ba*·nyo
bathroom bagno ⓜ *ba*·nyo
battery (for car) batteria ⓕ ba·te·*ree*·a
battery (general) pila ⓕ *pee*·la
be essere *e*·se·re
beach spiaggia ⓕ *spya*·ja
beans fagioli ⓜ pl fa·*jo*·lee
beansprouts germogli ⓜ pl (di soia) jer·*mo*·lyee (dee *so*·ya)
beautician estetista ⓜ&ⓕ es·te·*tee*·sta
beautiful bello/a ⓜ/ⓕ *be*·lo/a
beauty salon parrucchiere ⓜ pa·roo·*kye*·re
because perché per·*ke*
bed letto ⓜ *le*·to
bedding coperte ⓕ pl e lenzuola ⓕ pl ko·*per*·te e len·*zwo*·la
bedroom camera ⓕ da letto *ka*·me·ra da *le*·to
bee ape ⓕ *a*·pe
beef manzo ⓜ *man*·dzo
beer birra ⓕ *bee*·ra
beetroot barbabietola ⓕ bar·ba·*bye*·to·la
before prima *pree*·ma
beggar mendicante ⓜ&ⓕ men·dee·*kan*·te
begin cominciare ko·meen·*cha*·re
behind dietro *dye*·tro
Belgium Belgio ⓜ *bel*·jo
below sotto *so*·to
best migliore mee·*lyo*·re
bet scommessa ⓕ sko·*me*·sa
better migliore mee·*lyo*·re
between fra fra
bible bibbia ⓕ *bee*·bya
bicycle bicicletta ⓕ bee·chee·*kle*·ta
big grande *gran*·de
bike chain catena ⓕ di bicicletta ka·*te*·na dee bee·chee·*kle*·ta
bike lock lucchetto ⓜ loo·*ke*·to
bike path ciclopista ⓕ chee·klo·*pee*·sta
bill (account) conto ⓜ *kon*·to
binoculars binocolo ⓜ bee·*no*·ko·lo
bird uccello ⓜ oo·*che*·lo
birthday compleanno ⓜ kom·ple·*a*·no
biscuit biscotto ⓜ bees·*ko*·to
bite (dog) morso ⓜ *mor*·so
bite (insect) puntura ⓕ poon·*too*·ra
black nero/a ⓜ/ⓕ *ne*·ro/a
blanket coperta ⓕ ko·*per*·ta
blind cieco/a ⓜ/ⓕ *chye*·ko/a
blister vescica ⓕ ve·*shee*·ka
blocked bloccato/a ⓜ/ⓕ blo·*ka*·to/a
blonde biondo/a ⓜ/ⓕ *byon*·do/a
blood sangue ⓜ *san*·gwe
blood group gruppo ⓜ sanguigno *groo*·po san·*gwee*·nyo
blood pressure pressione ⓕ del sangue pre·*syo*·ne del *san*·gwe
blood test analisi ⓕ del sangue a·*na*·lee·zee del *san*·gwe
blue (dark) blu bloo

DICTIONARY

blue (light) azzurro/a ⓜ/ⓕ a·*dzoo*·ro/a
board (plane/ship) salire su sa·*lee*·re soo
boarding house pensione ⓕ pen·*syo*·ne
boarding pass carta ⓕ d'imbarco *kar*·ta deem·*bar*·ko
boat barca ⓕ *bar*·ka
body corpo ⓜ *kor*·po
bone osso ⓜ *o*·so
book libro ⓜ *lee*·bro
book (make a booking) prenotare pre·no·*ta*·re
booked out completo/a ⓜ/ⓕ kom·*ple*·to/a
bookshop libreria ⓕ lee·bre·*ree*·a
boots stivali ⓜ pl stee·*va*·lee
boots (ski) scarponi ⓜ pl (da sci) skar·*po*·nee (da shee)
boots (soccer) scarpette ⓕ pl skar·*pe*·te
border confine ⓜ kon·*fee*·ne
bored annoiato/a ⓜ/ⓕ a·no·*ya*·to/a
boring noioso/a ⓜ/ⓕ no·*yo*·zo/a
borrow prendere in prestito *pren*·de·re een *pres*·tee·to
bottle bottiglia ⓕ bo·*tee*·lya
bottle opener apribottiglie ⓜ a·pree·bo·*tee*·lye
(at the) bottom (in) fondo ⓜ (een) *fon*·do
bowl piatto ⓜ fondo *pya*·to *fon*·do
box scatola ⓕ *ska*·to·la
boxing pugilato ⓜ poo·jee·*la*·to
boy bambino ⓜ bam·*bee*·no
boy(friend) ragazzo ⓜ ra·*ga*·tso
bra reggiseno ⓜ re·jee·*se*·no
brake freno ⓜ *fre*·no
brave coraggioso/a ⓜ/ⓕ ko·ra·*jo*·zo/a
bread pane ⓜ *pa*·ne
break rompere *rom*·pe·re
break down guastarsi gwas·*tar*·see
breakfast (prima) colazione ⓕ (*pree*·ma) ko·la·*tsyo*·ne
breast seno ⓜ *se*·no
breathe respirare res·pee·*ra*·re
brewery fabbrica di birra ⓕ *fa*·bree·ka dee *bee*·ra
bribe corrompere ko·*rom*·pe·re
bridge ponte ⓜ *pon*·te
briefcase valigetta ⓕ va·lee·*je*·ta
brilliant brillante ⓜ/ⓕ bree·*lan*·te
bring portare por·*ta*·re
broken rotto/a ⓜ/ⓕ *ro*·to/a
broken down guastato/a ⓜ/ⓕ gwas·*ta*·to/a
bronchitis bronchite ⓕ bron·*kee*·te
brother fratello ⓜ fra·*te*·lo
brown marrone ⓜ/ⓕ ma·*ro*·ne
bruise livido ⓜ *lee*·vee·do
bucket secchio ⓜ *se*·kyo
Buddhist buddista ⓜ&ⓕ boo·*dee*·sta
budget bilancio ⓜ bee·*lan*·cho
buffet (meal) pasto ⓜ freddo *pas*·to *fre*·do
bug insetto ⓜ een·*se*·to
build costruire kos·troo·*ee*·re
builder costruttore/costruttrice ⓜ/ⓕ kos·troo·*to*·re/ko·stroo·*tree*·che
building edificio ⓜ e·dee·*fee*·cho
burn bruciare broo·*cha*·re
bus (city) autobus ⓜ *ow*·to·boos
bus (coach) pullman ⓜ *pool*·man
bus station stazione ⓕ d'autobus sta·*tsyo*·ne *dow*·to·boos
bus stop fermata ⓕ d'autobus fer·*ma*·ta *dow*·to·boos
business affari ⓜ pl a·*fa*·ree
business class classe ⓕ business *kla*·se *beez*·nes
business person uomo/donna d'affari ⓜ/ⓕ *wo*·mo/*do*·na da·*fa*·ree
business studies commercio ⓜ ko·*mer*·cho
business trip viaggio ⓜ d'affari vee·*a*·jo da·*fa*·ree
busker musicista ⓜ&ⓕ di strada moo·zee·*chee*·sta dee *stra*·da
but ma ma
butcher's shop macelleria ⓕ ma·che·le·*ree*·a

butter burro ⓜ *boo*·ro
butterfly farfalla ⓕ far·*fa*·la
button bottone ⓜ bo·*to*·ne
buy comprare kom·*pra*·re

C

cabbage cavolo ⓜ *ka*·vo·lo
cable car funivia ⓕ foo·nee·*vee*·a
cafe bar ⓜ bar
cake torta ⓕ *tor*·ta
cake shop pasticceria ⓕ pa·stee·che·*ree*·a
calculator calcolatrice ⓕ kal·ko·la·*tree*·che
calendar calendario ⓜ ka·len·*da*·ryo
camera macchina ⓕ fotografica *ma*·kee·na fo·to·*gra*·fee·ka
camera shop fotografo ⓜ fo·*to*·gra·fo
camp campeggiare kam·pe·*ja*·re
camp site campeggio ⓜ kam·*pe*·jo
camping store negozio ⓜ da campeggio ne·*go*·tsyo da kam·*pe*·jo
can (tin) scatola ⓕ *ska*·to·la
can potere po·*te*·re
can opener apriscatole ⓜ a·pree·*ska*·to·le
cancel cancellare kan·che·*la*·re
cancer cancro ⓜ *kan*·kro
candle candela ⓕ kan·*de*·la
candy dolciumi ⓜ pl dol·*choo*·mee
cantaloupe melone ⓜ me·*lo*·ne
capsicum peperone ⓜ pe·pe·*ro*·ne
car macchina ⓕ *ma*·kee·na
car hire autonoleggio ⓜ ow·to·no·*le*·jo
car owner's title libretto ⓜ di circolazione lee·*bre*·to dee cheer·ko·la·*tsyo*·ne
car park parcheggio ⓜ par·*ke*·jo
car racing automobilismo ⓜ ow·to·mo·bee·*leez*·mo
car registration bollo ⓜ di circolazione *bo*·lo dee cheer·ko·la·*tsyo*·ne
caravan roulotte ⓕ roo·*lot*
cards carte ⓕ pl *kar*·te
carpenter carpentiere ⓜ kar·pen·*tye*·re
carrot carota ⓕ ka·*ro*·ta
carry portare por·*ta*·re
carry-on luggage bagaglio ⓜ a mano ba·*ga*·lyo a *ma*·no
carton scatola ⓕ *ska*·to·la
cash soldi ⓜ pl *sol*·dee
cash a cheque riscuotere un assegno ree·*skwo*·te·re oon a·*se*·nyo
cash register cassa ⓕ *ka*·sa
cashew noce ⓕ (di acagiù) *no*·che (dee a·ka·*joo*)
cashier cassiere/a ⓜ/ⓕ ka·*sye*·re/a
casino casinò ⓜ ka·zee·*no*
cassette cassetta ⓕ ka·*se*·ta
castle castello ⓜ kas·*te*·lo
cat gatto ⓜ *ga*·to
cathedral duomo ⓜ *dwo*·mo
Catholic cattolico/a ⓜ/ⓕ ka·*to*·lee·ko/a
cauliflower cavolfiore ⓜ ka·vol·*fyo*·re
cave grotta ⓕ *gro*·ta
caviar caviale ⓜ ka·*vya*·le
CD cidì ⓜ chee·*dee*
celebration celebrazione ⓕ che·le·bra·*tsyo*·ne
cell phone (telefono) cellulare ⓜ (te·*le*·fo·no) che·loo·*la*·re
cent centesimo ⓜ chen·*te*·zee·mo
centimetre centimetro ⓜ chen·*tee*·me·tro
central heating riscaldamento ⓜ centrale rees·kal·da·*men*·to chen·*tra*·le
centre centro ⓜ *chen*·tro
cereal cereali ⓜ pl che·re·*a*·lee
certificate certificato ⓜ cher·tee·fee·*ka*·to
chain catena ⓕ ka·*te*·na
chair sedia ⓕ *se*·dya
chairlift (skiing) seggiovia ⓕ se·jo·*vee*·a
championships campionato ⓜ kam·pyo·*na*·to
chance fortuna ⓕ for·*too*·na

change (coins) spiccioli ⓜ pl spee·cho·lee
change (money) resto ⓜ *res*·to
change cambiare kam·*bya*·re
change room (sport) spogliatoio ⓜ spo·lya·*to*·yo
:harming affascinante a·fa·shee·*nan*·te
chat up agganciare a·gan·*cha*·re
:heap economico/a ⓜ/ⓕ e·ko·*no*·mee·ko/a
cheat imbrogliare eem·bro·*lya*·re
:heck (bill) conto ⓜ *kon*·to
check controllare kon·tro·*la*·re
:heck-in (airport) accetazione ⓕ ı·che·ta·*tsyo*·ne
:heck-in (hotel) registrazione ⓕ 'e·jee·stra·*tsyo*·ne
:heese formaggio ⓜ for·*ma*·jo
:hef cuoco/a ⓜ/ⓕ *kwo*·ko/a
hemist farmacista ⓜ&ⓕ ar·ma·*chee*·sta
:heque assegno ⓜ a·*se*·nyo
hess scacchi ⓜ pl *ska*·kee
:hest petto ⓜ *pe*·to
:hicken pollo ⓜ *po*·lo
:hickpeas ceci ⓜ pl *che*·chee
:hild bambino/a ⓜ/ⓕ bam·*bee*·no/a
:hild seat seggiolino ⓜ se·jo·*lee*·no
:hild minding (group) asilo nido ⓜ ı·*zee*·lo *nee*·do
:hilli peperoncino ⓜ e·pe·ron·*chee*·no
:hilli sauce salsa ⓕ di peperoncino osso *sal*·sa dee pe·pe·ron·*chee*·no o·so
hiropractor chiropratico ⓜ ee·ro·*pra*·tee·ko
hocolate cioccolato ⓜ cho·ko·*la*·to
:hristian cristiano/a ⓜ/ⓕ rees·*tya*·no/a
:hristmas Natale ⓜ na·*ta*·le
hurch chiesa ⓕ *kye*·za
ider sidro ⓜ *see*·dro
igar sigaro ⓜ *see*·ga·ro
igarette sigaretta ⓕ see·ga·*re*·ta
cigarette lighter accendino ⓜ a·chen·*dee*·no
cinema cinema ⓜ *chee*·ne·ma
circus circo ⓜ *cheer*·ko
citizenship cittadinanza ⓕ chee·ta·dee·*nan*·tsa
city città ⓕ chee·*ta*
class classe ⓕ *kla*·se
classical classico/a ⓜ/ⓕ *kla*·see·ko/a
clean pulito/a ⓜ/ⓕ poo·*lee*·to/a
cleaning pulizia ⓕ poo·lee·*tsee*·a
client cliente ⓜ&ⓕ klee·*en*·te
cliff scogliera ⓕ sko·*lye*·ra
climb scalare ska·*la*·re
cloakroom guardaroba ⓜ gwar·da·*ro*·ba
clock orologio ⓜ o·ro·*lo*·jo
close (nearby) vicino/a ⓜ/ⓕ vee·*chee*·no/a
close (shut) chiudere *kyoo*·de·re
closed chiuso/a ⓜ/ⓕ *kyoo*·zo/a
clothes line corda ⓕ del bucato *kor*·da del boo·*ka*·to
clothing abbigliamento ⓜ a·*bee*·lya·men·to
clothing store negozio ⓜ di abbigliamento ne·*go*·tsyo dee a·*bee*·lya·men·to
cloud nuvola ⓕ *noo*·vo·la
cloudy nuvoloso/a ⓜ/ⓕ noo·vo·*lo*·zo/a
clutch frizione ⓕ free·*tsyo*·ne
coach (bus) pullman ⓜ *pool*·man
coast costa ⓕ *kos*·ta
coat cappotto ⓜ ka·*po*·to
cocaine cocaina ⓕ ko·ka·ee·na
cockroach scarafaggio ⓜ ska·ra·*fa*·jo
cocoa cacao ⓜ ka·*ka*·o
coffee caffè ⓜ ka·*fe*
coins monete ⓕ pl mo·*ne*·te
cold freddo/a ⓜ/ⓕ *fre*·do/a
(have a) cold essere raffreddato/a ⓜ/ⓕ e·se·re *ra*·fre·*da*·to/a
colleague collega ⓜ&ⓕ ko·*le*·ga

C

collect call chiamata ⓕ a carico del destinatario kya·*ma*·ta a *ka*·ree·ko del des·tee·na·*ta*·ryo
college collegio ⓜ universitario ko·*le*·jo oo·nee·ver·see·*ta*·ryo
colour colore ⓜ ko·*lo*·re
comb pettine ⓜ *pe*·tee·ne
come venire ve·*nee*·re
comedy commedia ⓕ comica ko·*me*·dya *ko*·mee·ka
comfortable comodo/a ⓜ/ⓕ *ko*·mo·do/a
commission commissione ⓕ ko·mee·*syo*·ne
communion comunione ⓕ ko·moo·*nyo*·ne
communist comunista ⓜ&ⓕ ko·moo·*nee*·sta
companion compagno/a ⓜ/ⓕ kom·*pa*·nyo/a
company (firm) ditta ⓕ *dee*·ta
compass bussola ⓕ *boo*·so·la
complain lamentarsi la·men·*tar*·see
complimentary (free) gratuito/a ⓜ/ⓕ gra·*too*·ee·to/a
computer game gioco ⓜ elettronico *jo*·ko e·le·*tro*·nee·ko
concert concerto ⓜ kon·*cher*·to
conditioner balsamo ⓜ per i capelli *bal*·sa·mo per ee ka·*pe*·lee
condom preservativo ⓜ pre·zer·va·*tee*·vo
confession (religious) confessione ⓕ kon·fe·*syo*·ne
confirm (a booking) confermare kon·fer·*ma*·re
connection (transport) coincidenza ⓕ ko·een·chee·*den*·tsa
conservative conservatore/conservatrice ⓜ/ⓕ kon·ser·va·*to*·re/kon·ser·va·*tree*·che
constipation stitichezza ⓕ stee·tee·*ke*·tsa
consulate consolato ⓜ kon·so·*la*·to
contact lenses lenti ⓕ pl a contatto *len*·tee a kon·*ta*·to
contraceptive contraccettivo ⓜ kon·tra·che·*tee*·vo
contract contratto ⓜ kon·*tra*·to
convenience store alimentari ⓜ a·lee·men·*ta*·ree
convent convento ⓜ kon·*ven*·to
cook cuoco/a ⓜ/ⓕ *kwo*·ko/a
cook cucinare koo·chee·*na*·re
cookie biscotto ⓜ bees·*ko*·to
corn flakes fiocchi ⓜ pl di mais *fyo*·kee dee *ma*·ees
corner angolo ⓜ *an*·go·lo
correct giusto/a ⓜ/ⓕ *joo*·sto/a
corrupt corrotto/a ⓜ/ⓕ ko·*ro*·to/a
cost costare kos·*ta*·re
cot culla ⓕ *koo*·la
cotton cotone ⓜ ko·*to*·ne
cotton balls batuffoli ⓜ pl di cotone ba·*too*·fo·lee dee ko·*to*·ne
cough tossire to·*see*·re
cough medicine sciroppo ⓜ per la tosse shee·*ro*·po per la *to*·se
count contare kon·*ta*·re
counter (at bar) bancone ⓜ ban·*ko*·ne
country (nation) paese ⓜ pa·*e*·ze
countryside campagna ⓕ kam·*pa*·nya
courgette zucchini ⓜ pl tsoo·*kee*·nee
court (legal) corte ⓕ *kor*·te
court (tennis) campo ⓜ da tennis *kam*·po da *te*·nees
cover charge (restaurant) coperto ⓜ ko·*per*·to
cover charge (venue) ingresso ⓜ een·*gre*·so
cow mucca ⓕ *moo*·ka
craft (product) pezzo ⓜ d'artigianato *pe*·tso dar·tee·ja·*na*·to
craft (trade) mestiere ⓜ mes·*tye*·re
crash (accident) incidente ⓜ een·chee·*den*·te
crazy pazzo/a ⓜ/ⓕ *pa*·tso/a
cream (food) panna ⓕ *pa*·na
cream cheese formaggio ⓜ fresco for·*ma*·jo *fres*·ko
creche asilo ⓜ nido a·*zee*·lo *nee*·do

:redit card carta ⓕ di credito *kar*·ta
!ee *kre*·dee·to
:rime (infringment) delitto ⓜ
!e·*lee*·to
:rime (issue) criminalità ⓕ
‹ree·mee·na·lee·*ta*
Croatia Croazia ⓜ kro·*a*·tsya
:ross (religious) croce ⓕ *kro*·che
:rowded affollato/a ⓜ/ⓕ
·fo·*la*·to/a
:ucumber cetriolo ⓜ che·tree·*o*·lo
:up tazza ⓕ *ta*·tsa
'urrency exchange cambio ⓜ valuta
'am·byo va·*loo*·ta
:urrent (electricity) corrente ⓕ
:o·*ren*·te
:urrent affairs attualità ⓕ
·too·a·lee·*ta*
:urry powder polvere ⓕ da curry
ol·ve·re da *koo*·ree
:ustoms dogana ⓕ do·*ga*·na
:ut tagliare ta·*lya*·re
:utlery posate ⓕ pl po·*za*·te
ycle andare in bicicletta an·*da*·re een
ee·chee·*kle*·ta
ycling ciclismo ⓜ chee·*kleez*·mo
yclist ciclista ⓜ&ⓕ chee·*klee*·sta
ystitis cistite ⓕ chees·*tee*·te

D

lad papà ⓜ pa·*pa*
'amage danno ⓜ *da*·no
ance ballare ba·*la*·re
lancing ballo ⓜ *ba*·lo
'angerous pericoloso/a ⓜ/ⓕ
e·ree·ko·*lo*·zo/a
lark scuro/a ⓜ/ⓕ *skoo*·ro/a
'ate (appointment) appuntamento
) a·poon·ta·*men*·to
ate (day) data ⓕ *da*·ta
ate (go out with) uscire con
o·*shee*·re kon
ate of birth data ⓕ di nascita *da*·ta
ee *na*·shee·ta
aughter figlia ⓕ *fee*·lya
ay giorno ⓜ *jor*·no
day after tomorrow dopodomani
do·po·do·*ma*·nee
day before yesterday altro ieri ⓜ
al·tro *ye*·ree
dead morto/a ⓜ/ⓕ *mor*·to/a
deaf sordo/a ⓜ/ⓕ *sor*·do/a
deep profondo/a ⓜ/ⓕ pro·*fon*·do/a
delay ritardo ⓜ ree·*tar*·do
delicatessen salumeria ⓕ
sa·loo·me·*ree*·a
democracy democrazia ⓕ
de·mo·kra·*tsee*·a
demonstration (protest)
manifestazione ⓕ ma·nee·fes·ta·*tsyo*·ne
Denmark Danimarca ⓕ
da·nee·*mar*·ka
dental floss filo ⓜ dentario *fee*·lo
den·*ta*·ree·o
dentist dentista ⓜ&ⓕ den·*tee*·sta
deodorant deodorante ⓜ
de·o·do·*ran*·te
depart partire par·*tee*·re
department store grande magazzino
ⓜ *gran*·de ma·ga·*dzee*·no
departure partenza ⓕ par·*ten*·tsa
deposit (bank) deposito ⓜ
de·*po*·zee·to
deposit (refundable) caparra ⓕ
ka·*pa*·ra
derailleur deragliatore ⓜ
de·ra·lya·*to*·re
dessert dolce ⓜ *dol*·che
destination destinazione ⓕ
des·tee·na·*tsyo*·ne
diabetes diabete ⓜ dee·a·*be*·te
dial tone segnale ⓜ (acustico)
se·*nya*·le (a·*koos*·tee·ko)
diaper pannolino ⓜ pa·no·*lee*·no
diaphragm diaframma ⓜ
dee·a·*fra*·ma
diarrhoea diarrea ⓕ dee·a·*re*·a
diary agenda ⓕ a·*jen*·da
dictionary vocabolario ⓜ
vo·ka·bo·*la*·ryo
die morire mo·*ree*·re
diet dieta ⓕ *dye*·ta

different diverso/a dee·*ver*·so/a
different (from) differente (da) dee·fe·*ren*·te (da)
difficult difficile dee·*fee*·chee·le
digital digitale dee·jee·*ta*·le
dining car carrozza ⓕ ristorante ka·*ro*·tsa rees·to·*ran*·te
dinner cena ⓕ *che*·na
direct diretto/a ⓜ/ⓕ dee·*re*·to/a
direct-dial telefono ⓜ diretto te·*le*·fo·no dee·*re*·to
direction direzione ⓕ dee·re·*tsyo*·ne
director (films) regista ⓜ&ⓕ re·*jee*·sta
dirty sporco/a ⓜ/ⓕ *spor*·ko/a
disabled disabile dee·*za*·bee·le
discount sconto ⓜ *skon*·to
discrimination discriminazione ⓕ dees·kree·mee·na·*tsyo*·ne
disease malattia ⓕ ma·la·*tee*·a
disinfectant disinfettante ⓜ deez·een·fe·*tan*·te
disk (computer) dischetto ⓜ dees·*ke*·to
disposable usa e getta *oo*·za e *je*·ta
dive tuffarsi ⓜ pl too·*far*·see
diving (sea) immersioni ⓕ pl ee·mer·*syo*·nee
divorced divorziato/a ⓜ/ⓕ dee·vor·*tsya*·to/a
dizzy stordito/a ⓜ/ⓕ stor·*dee*·to/a
do fare *fa*·re
doctor medico ⓜ *me*·dee·ko
dog cane ⓜ *ka*·ne
dole sussidio ⓜ di disoccupazione soo·*see*·dyo dee dee·zo·koo·pa·*tsyo*·ne
doll bambola ⓕ *bam*·bo·la
dollar dollaro ⓜ *do*·la·ro
door porta ⓕ *por*·ta
dope (drugs) roba ⓕ *ro*·ba
double doppio/a ⓜ/ⓕ *do*·pyo/a
double bed letto ⓜ matrimoniale *le*·to ma·tree·mo·*nya*·le
double room camera ⓕ doppia *ka*·mer·a *do*·pya
down giù joo
dozen dozzina ⓕ do·*dzee*·na
drag queen travestito ⓜ tra·ves·*tee*·to
drama dramma ⓜ *dra*·ma
dream sogno ⓜ *so*·nyo
dream sognare so·*nya*·re
dress abito ⓜ *a*·bee·to
drink bevanda ⓕ be·*van*·da
drink bere *be*·re
drinkable potabile po·*ta*·bee·le
drive guidare gwee·*da*·re
drivers licence patente ⓕ (di guida) pa·*ten*·te (dee *gwee*·da)
drug (medicinal) medicina ⓕ me·dee·*chee*·na
drug addiction tossicodipendenza ⓕ to·see·ko·dee·pen·*den*·tsa
drug dealer spacciatore/spacciatrice ⓜ/ⓕ spa·cha·*to*·re/spa·cha·*tree*·che
drugs (illegal) droga ⓕ sg *dro*·ga
drums batteria ⓕ ba·te·*ree*·a
drunk ubriaco/a ⓜ/ⓕ oo·bree·*a*·ko/a
dry secco/a ⓜ/ⓕ *se*·ko/a
dry asciugare a·*shoo*·ga·re
dry cleaning lavaggio ⓜ a secco la·*va*·jo a *se*·ko
duck anatra ⓕ *a*·na·tra
dummy (pacifier) ciucciotto ⓜ choo·*cho*·to
during durante doo·*ran*·te

E

each ciascuno/a ⓜ/ⓕ chas·*koo*·no/a
ear orecchio ⓜ o·*re*·kyo
early presto ⓜ/ⓕ *pres*·to
earplugs tappi ⓜ pl per le orecchie *ta*·pee per le o·*re*·kye
earrings orecchini ⓜ pl o·re·*kee*·nee
Earth Terra ⓕ *te*·ra
earthquake terremoto ⓜ te·re·*mo*·to
east est ⓜ est
Easter Pasqua ⓕ *pas*·kwa
easy facile *fa*·chee·le
eat mangiare man·*ja*·re
economy class classe ⓕ turistica *kla*·se too·*ree*·stee·ka

eczema eczema ⓜ ek·*dze*·ma
education istruzione ⓕ ees·troo·*tsyo*·ne
egg uovo ⓜ *wo*·vo
eggplant melanzana ⓕ me·lan·*dza*·na
elections elezioni ⓕ pl e·le·*tsyo*·nee
electrician elettricista ⓜ&ⓕ e·le·tree·*chee*·sta
electricity elettricità ⓕ e·le·tree·chee·*ta*
elevator ascensore ⓜ a·shen·*so*·re
email email ⓜ *e*·mayl
embarrassed imbarazzato/a ⓜ/ⓕ eem·ba·ra·*tsa*·to/a
embassy ambasciata ⓕ am·ba·*sha*·ta
emergency emergenza ⓕ e·mer·*jen*·tsa
emotional emotivo/a ⓜ/ⓕ e·mo·*tee*·vo/a
employee impiegato/a ⓜ/ⓕ eem·pye·*ga*·to/a
employer datore/datrice ⓜ/ⓕ di lavoro da·*to*·re/da·*tree*·ce dee la·*vo*·ro
empty vuoto/a ⓜ/ⓕ *vwo*·to/a
end fine ⓕ *fee*·ne
end finire fee·*nee*·re
endangered species specie ⓕ in via di estinzione *spe*·che een *vee*·a dee es·teen·*tsyo*·ne
engagement (couple) fidanzamento ⓜ fee·dan·tsa·*men*·to
engine motore ⓜ mo·*to*·re
engineer ingegnere ⓜ&ⓕ een·je·*nye*·re
England Inghilterra ⓕ een·geel·*te*·ra
English inglese een·*gle*·ze
enjoy (oneself) divertirsi dee·ver·*teer*·see
enough abbastanza a·bas·*tan*·tsa
enter entrare en·*tra*·re
entertainment guide guida ⓕ agli spettacoli *gwee*·da *a*·lyee spe·*ta*·ko·lee
entry entrata ⓕ en·*tra*·ta
(padded) envelope busta ⓕ (imbottita) *boo*·sta eem·bo·*tee*·ta
environment ambiente ⓜ am·*byen*·te
epilepsy epilessia ⓕ e·pee·le·*see*·a
equipment attrezzatura ⓕ a·tre·tsa·*too*·ra
escalator scala ⓕ mobile *ska*·la *mo*·bee·le
euro euro ⓜ e·*oo*·ro
Europe Europa ⓕ e·oo·*ro*·pa
European europeo/a ⓜ/ⓕ e·oo·ro·*pe*·o/a
euthanasia eutanasia ⓕ e·oo·ta·na·*zee*·a
evening sera ⓕ *se*·ra
everything tutto ⓜ *too*·to
example esempio ⓜ e·*zem*·pyo
excellent ottimo/a ⓜ/ⓕ o·tee·mo/a
excess bagage bagaglio ⓜ in eccedenza ba·*ga*·lyo een e·che·*den*·tsa
exchange cambio ⓜ *kam*·byo
exchange cambiare kam·*bya*·re
exchange rate tasso ⓜ di cambio *ta*·so dee *kam*·byo
excluded escluso/a ⓜ/ⓕ es·*kloo*·zo/a
exhaust (car) tubo ⓜ di scappamento *too*·bo dee ska·pa·*men*·to
exhibition esposizione ⓕ es·po·zee·*tsyo*·ne
exit uscita ⓕ oo·*shee*·ta
expensive caro/a ⓜ/ⓕ *ka*·ro/a
experience esperienza ⓕ es·pe·*ryen*·tsa
exploitation sfruttamento ⓜ sfroo·ta·*men*·to
express espresso/a ⓜ/ⓕ es·*pre*·so/a
express mail posta ⓕ prioritaria *pos*·ta pree·o·ree·*ta*·rya
extension (visa) proroga ⓕ *pro*·ro·ga
eye occhio ⓜ *o*·kyo
eye drops collirio ⓜ ko·*lee*·ryo

F

fabric stoffa ⓕ *sto*·fa
face faccia ⓕ *fa*·cha
factory fabbrica ⓕ *fa*·bree·ka
factory worker operaio/a ⓜ/ⓕ o·pe·*ra*·yo/a
fall (autumn) autunno ⓜ ow·*too*·no

F

family famiglia ⓕ fa·*mee*·lya
family name cognome ⓜ ko·*nyo*·me
famous famoso/a ⓜ/ⓕ fa·*mo*·zo/a
fan (person) tifoso/a ⓜ/ⓕ tee·*fo*·zo/a
fan (machine) ventilatore ⓜ ven·tee·la·*to*·re
fan belt cinghia ⓕ della ventola *cheen*·gya *de*·la *ven*·to·la
far lontano/a ⓜ/ⓕ lon·*ta*·no/a
farm fattoria ⓕ fa·to·*ree*·a
farmer agricoltore/agricoltrice ⓜ/ⓕ a·gree·kol·*to*·re/a·gree·kol·*tree*·che
fashion moda ⓕ *mo*·da
fast veloce ve·*lo*·che
fat grasso/a ⓜ/ⓕ *gra*·so/a
father padre ⓜ *pa*·dre
father-in-law suocero ⓜ *swo*·che·ro
faucet rubinetto ⓜ roo·bee·*ne*·to
fault (someone's) colpa ⓕ *kol*·pa
faulty difettoso/a ⓜ/ⓕ dee·fe·*to*·zo/a
favourite preferito/a ⓜ/ⓕ pre·fe·*ree*·to/a
fee compenso ⓜ kom·*pen*·so
feel sentire sen·*tee*·re
feelings sentimenti ⓜ pl sen·tee·*men*·tee
fence recinto ⓜ re·*cheen*·to
fencing (sport) scherma ⓕ *sker*·ma
ferry traghetto ⓜ tra·*ge*·to
festival festa ⓕ *fes*·ta
fever febbre ⓕ *fe*·bre
few pochi/e ⓜ/ⓕ *po*·kee/*po*·ke
fiance(e) fidanzato/a ⓜ/ⓕ fee·dan·*tsa*·to/a
fiction narrativa ⓕ na·ra·*tee*·va
fig fico ⓜ *fee*·ko
fight lite ⓕ *lee*·te
film (cinema) film ⓜ feelm
film (roll for camera) rullino ⓜ roo·*lee*·no
film speed ASA *a*·za
find trovare tro·*va*·re
fine (payment) multa ⓕ *mool*·ta
finger dito ⓜ *dee*·to
finish finire fee·*nee*·re
fire fuoco ⓜ *fwo*·ko
firewood legna ⓕ da ardere *le*·nya da *ar*·de·re
first primo/a ⓜ/ⓕ *pree*·mo/a
first class prima classe ⓕ *pree*·ma *kla*·se
first-aid kit valigetta ⓕ del pronto soccorso va·lee·*je*·ta del *pron*·to so·*kor*·so
fish pesce ⓜ *pe*·she
fish shop pescheria ⓕ pe·ske·*ree*·a
fishing pesca ⓕ *pe*·ska
flag bandiera ⓕ ban·*dye*·ra
flashlight (torch) torcia ⓕ elettrica *tor*·cha e·*le*·tree·ka
flat appartamento ⓜ a·par·ta·*men*·to
flat piatto/a ⓜ/ⓕ *pya*·to/a
flea pulce ⓕ *pool*·che
flight volo ⓜ *vo*·lo
flood inondazione ⓕ ee·non·da·*tzyo*·nee
floor (ground) pavimento ⓜ pa·vee·*men*·to
floor (storey) piano ⓜ *pya*·no
florist fioraio ⓜ&ⓕ fyo·*ra*·yo
flour farina ⓕ fa·*ree*·na
flower fiore ⓜ *fyo*·re
flu influenza ⓕ een·floo·*en*·tsa
fly mosca ⓕ *mos*·ka
fly volare vo·*la*·re
foggy nebbioso/a ⓜ/ⓕ ne·*byo*·zo/a
follow seguire se·*gwee*·re
food cibo ⓜ *chee*·bo
food poisoning intossicazione ⓕ alimentare een·to·see·ka·*tsyo*·ne a·lee·men·*ta*·re
food supplies provviste ⓜ pl alimentari pro·*vee*·ste a·lee·men·*ta*·re
foot piede ⓜ *pye*·de
football (soccer) calcio ⓜ *kal*·cho
footpath marciapiede ⓜ mar·cha·*pye*·de
foreign straniero/a ⓜ/ⓕ stra·*nye*·ro/a
forest foresta ⓕ fo·*res*·ta
forever per sempre per *sem*·pre

DICTIONARY

orget dimenticare dee·men·tee·*ka*·re
orgive perdonare per·do·*na*·re
ork forchetta ⓕ for·*ke*·ta
orm (paper) modulo ⓜ *mo*·doo·lo
ortnight quindici giorni ⓜ pl
:*ween*·dee·chee *jor*·nee
oyer atrio ⓜ *a*·tryo
ragile fragile *fra*·jee·le
rance Francia ⓕ *fran*·cha
ree (gratis) gratuito/a ⓜ/ⓕ
:ra·*too*·ee·to/a
ree (not bound) libero/a ⓜ/ⓕ
ee·be·ro/a
reeze congelare kon·je·*la*·re
resh fresco/a ⓜ/ⓕ *fres*·ko/a
ridge frigorifero ⓜ free·go·*ree*·fe·ro
riend amico/a ⓜ/ⓕ a·*mee*·ko/a
rozen congelato/a ⓜ/ⓕ
on·je·*la*·to/a
rozen foods surgelati ⓜ pl
oor·je·*la*·tee
ruit frutta ⓕ *froo*·ta
ruit juice (bottled) succo ⓜ di
rutta *soo*·ko dee *froo*·ta
ruit juice (fresh) spremuta ⓕ
ore·*moo*·ta
ry friggere *free*·je·re
rying pan padella ⓕ pa·*de*·la
ull pieno/a ⓜ/ⓕ *pye*·no/a
ull-time a tempo pieno a *tem*·po
ye·no
un divertimento ⓜ
ee·ver·tee·*men*·to
have) fun divertirsi dee·ver·*teer*·see
uneral funerale ⓜ foo·ne·*ra*·le
unny divertente dee·ver·*ten*·te
urniture mobili ⓜ pl *mo*·bee·lee
uture futuro ⓜ foo·*too*·ro

G

ame (play) gioco ⓜ *jo*·ko
ame (sport) partita ⓕ par·*tee*·ta
arage garage ⓜ ga·*raj*
arbage spazzatura ⓕ pl
a·tsa·*too*·ra
arden giardino ⓜ jar·*dee*·no
gardening giardinaggio ⓜ
jar·dee·*na*·jo
garlic aglio ⓜ *a*·lyo
gas (for cooking) gas ⓜ gaz
gas (petrol) benzina ⓕ ben·*dzee*·na
gas cartridge cartuccia ⓕ di
ricambio del gas kar·*too*·cha dee
ree·*kam*·byo del gaz
gastroenteritis gastroenterite ⓕ
gas·tro·en·te·*ree*·te
gate cancello ⓜ kan·*che*·lo
gay gay gei
gears (bicycle) cambio ⓜ *kam*·byo
general generale je·ne·*ra*·le
Germany Germania ⓕ jer·*ma*·nya
gift regalo ⓜ re·*ga*·lo
ginger zenzero ⓜ *dzen*·dze·ro
girl(friend) ragazza ⓕ ra·*ga*·tsa
give dare *da*·re
glandular fever mononucleosi ⓜ
mo·no·noo·kle·o·zee
glass (material) vetro ⓜ *ve*·tro
glass (drinking) bicchiere ⓜ
bee·*kye*·re
glasses (spectacles) occhiali ⓜ pl
o·*kya*·lee
gloves guanti ⓜ pl *gwan*·tee
go andare an·*da*·re
go out with uscire con oo·*shee*·re kon
goat capra ⓕ *ka*·pra
god (general) dio/dea ⓜ/ⓕ *dee*·o/
de·a
goggles (skiing) occhiali ⓜ pl (da
sci) o·*kya*·lee (da shee)
gold oro ⓜ *o*·ro
golf ball palla ⓕ da golf *pa*·la da golf
golf course campo ⓜ da golf *kam*·po
da golf
good buono/a ⓜ/ⓕ *bwo*·no/a
government governo ⓜ go·*ver*·no
grams grammi ⓜ pl *gra*·mee
grandchild nipote ⓜ&ⓕ nee·*po*·te
grandfather nonno ⓜ *no*·no
grandmother nonna ⓕ *no*·na
grapefruit pompelmo ⓜ pom·*pel*·mo
grapes uva ⓕ pl *oo*·va

grass erba ⓕ *er*·ba
grave (tomb) tomba ⓕ *tom*·ba
great ottimo/a ⓜ/ⓕ *o*·tee·mo/a
green verde *ver*·de
greengrocer fruttivendolo/a ⓜ/ⓕ froo·tee·*ven*·do·lo/a
grey grigio/a ⓜ/ⓕ *gree*·jo/a
grocery drogheria ⓕ dro·ge·*ree*·a
groundnut arachide ⓕ a·*ra*·kee·de
grow crescere *kre*·she·re
guesthouse pensione ⓕ pen·*syo*·ne
guide (audio) guida ⓕ audio *gwee*·da *ow*·dyo
guide (person) guida ⓕ *gwee*·da
guide dog cane ⓜ guida *ka*·ne *gwee*·da
guidebook guida ⓕ (turistica) *gwee*·da (too·*ree*·stee·ka)
guided tour visita ⓕ guidata vee·zee·ta gwee·*da*·ta
guilty colpevole kol·*pe*·vo·le
guitar chitarra ⓕ kee·*ta*·ra
gum (mouth) gengiva ⓕ jen·*jee*·va
gum (chewing) gomma ⓕ da masticare *go*·ma da ma·stee·*ka*·re
gym palestra ⓕ pa·*le*·stra
gymnastics ginnastica ⓕ jee·*nas*·tee·ka
gynaecologist ginecologo/a ⓜ/ⓕ jee·ne·*ko*·lo·go/a

H

hail grandine ⓕ *gran*·dee·ne
hailstorm grandinata ⓕ gran·dee·*na*·ta
haircut taglio ⓜ di capelli *ta*·lyo dee ka·*pe*·lee
hairdresser parrucchiere/a ⓜ/ⓕ pa·roo·*kye*·re/a
halal halal a·*lal*
half mezzo ⓜ *me*·dzo
hallucinate allucinare a·loo·chee·*na*·re
ham (boiled) prosciutto ⓜ (cotto) pro·*shoo*·to (*ko*·to)
hammer martello ⓜ mar·*te*·lo
hammock amaca ⓕ a·*ma*·ka
hand mano ⓕ *ma*·no
handbag borsetta ⓕ bor·*se*·ta
handball pallamuro ⓕ pa·la·*moo*·ro
handicrafts oggetti ⓜ pl d'artigianato o·*je*·tee dar·tee·ja·*na*·to
handkerchief fazzoletto ⓜ fa·tso·*le*·to
handlebars manubrio ⓜ ma·*noo*·bry
handmade fatto/a ⓜ/ⓕ a mano *fa*·to/a a *ma*·no
handsome bello/a ⓜ/ⓕ *be*·lo/a
happy felice ⓜ/ⓕ fe·*lee*·che
harassment molestia ⓕ mo·*les*·tya
harbour porto ⓜ *por*·to
hard (not easy) difficile dee·*fee*·chee·le
hard (not soft) duro/a ⓜ/ⓕ *doo*·ro/
hardware store ferramenta ⓕ fe·ra·*men*·ta
hash hashish ⓜ *a*·sheesh
hat cappello ⓜ ka·*pe*·lo
have avere a·*ve*·re
hay fever febbre ⓕ da fieno *fe*·bre da *fye*·no
he lui *loo*·ee
head testa ⓕ *tes*·ta
headache mal ⓜ di testa mal dee *tes*·ta
headlights fari ⓜ pl *fa*·ree
health salute ⓕ sa·*loo*·te
hear sentire sen·*tee*·re
hearing aid apparecchio ⓜ acustico a·pa·*re*·kyo a·*koos*·tee·ko
heart cuore ⓜ *kwo*·re
heart condition problema ⓜ cardiaco pro·*ble*·ma kar·*dee*·a·ko
heat caldo ⓜ *kal*·do
heater stufa ⓕ *stoo*·fa
heating riscaldamento ⓜ rees·kal·da·*men*·to
heavy pesante pe·*zan*·te
height altezza ⓕ al·*te*·tsa
helmet casco ⓜ *kas*·ko
help aiutare a·yoo·*ta*·re
hepatitis epatite ⓕ e·pa·*tee*·te

herbalist erborista ⓜ&ⓕ er·bo·*ree*·sta
herbs erbe ⓕ pl *er*·be
here qui kwee
heroin eroina ⓕ e·ro·*ee*·na
herring aringa ⓕ a·*reen*·ga
high alto/a ⓜ/ⓕ *al*·to/a
high school scuola ⓕ superiore *skwo*·la soo·pe·*ryo*·re
hike escursione ⓕ a piedi es·koor·*syo*·ne a *pye*·de
hiking escursionismo ⓜ a piedi es·koor·syo·*neez*·mo a *pye*·de
hiking boots scarponi ⓜ pl skar·*po*·nee
hiking route itinerario ⓜ escursionistico e·tee·ne·*ra*·ryo es·koor·syo·*nee*·stee·ko
hill collina ⓕ ko·*lee*·na
Hindu indù ⓜ&ⓕ een·*doo*
hire noleggiare no·le·*ja*·re
historical storico/a ⓜ/ⓕ *sto*·ree·ko/a
history storia ⓕ *sto*·rya
hitchhike fare l'autostop *fa*·re *low*·to·stop
HIV positive sieropositivo/a ⓜ/ⓕ sye·ro·po·zee·*tee*·vo/a
hobby passatempo ⓜ pa·sa·*tem*·po
hockey hockey ⓜ *o*·kee
holidays vacanze ⓕ pl va·*kan*·tse
Holy Week settimana ⓕ santa se·tee·*ma*·na *san*·ta
home casa ⓕ *ka*·za
homeless senzatetto ⓜ&ⓕ sen·tsa·*te*·to
homemaker casalingo/a ⓕ ka·za·*leen*·go/a
homeopathy omeopatia ⓕ o·me·o·pa·*tee*·a
homosexual omosessuale ⓜ&ⓕ o·mo·se·*swa*·le
honey miele ⓜ *mye*·le
honeymoon luna ⓕ di miele *loo*·na dee *mye*·le
horse cavallo ⓜ ka·*va*·lo
horse riding andare a cavallo an·*da*·re a ka·*va*·lo
horseradish rafano ⓜ *ra*·fa·no
hospital ospedale ⓜ os·pe·*da*·le
hospitality ospitalità ⓕ os·pee·ta·lee·*ta*
hot caldo/a ⓜ/ⓕ *kal*·do/a
hot water acqua ⓕ calda *a*·kwa *kal*·da
hotel albergo ⓜ al·*ber*·go
hour ora ⓕ *o*·ra
house casa ⓕ *ka*·za
how come *ko*·me
how much quanto/a ⓜ/ⓕ *kwan*·to/a
hug abbracciare a·bra·*cha*·re
huge enorme e·*nor*·me
human rights diritti ⓜ pl umani dee·*ree*·tee oo·*ma*·nee
(to be) hungry avere fame a·*ve*·re *fa*·me
hunting caccia ⓕ *ka*·cha
(to be in a) hurry avere fretta a·*ve*·re *fre*·ta
hurt fare male *fa*·re *ma*·le
husband marito ⓜ ma·*ree*·to
hydrating fluid fluido ⓜ idratante *floo*·ee·do ee·dra·*tan*·te

I

I io *ee*·o
ice ghiaccio ⓜ *gya*·cho
ice axe piccozza ⓕ pee·*ko*·tsa
ice cream gelato ⓜ je·*la*·to
ice-cream parlour gelateria ⓕ je·la·te·*ree*·a
ice hockey hockey ⓜ su ghiaccio *o*·kee soo *gya*·cho
identification documento ⓜ d'identità do·koo·*men*·to dee·den·tee·*ta*
identification card (ID) carta ⓕ d'identità *kar*·ta dee·den·tee·*ta*
idiot idiota ⓜ&ⓕ ee·*dyo*·ta
if se se
ill malato/a ⓜ/ⓕ ma·*la*·to/a
illegal illegale ee·le·*ga*·le
immigration immigrazione ⓕ ee·mee·gra·*tsyo*·ne

important importante *eem·por·tan·te*
impossible impossibile *eem·po·see·bee·le*
included compreso/a ⓜ/ⓕ *kom·pre·zo/a*
indicator (car) freccia ⓕ *fre·cha*
indigestion indigestione ⓕ *een·dee·je·styo·ne*
industry industria ⓕ *een·doos·trya*
infection infezione ⓕ *een·fe·tsyo·ne*
inflammation infiammazione ⓕ *een·fya·ma·tsyo·ne*
influenza influenza ⓕ *een·floo·en·tsa*
information informazioni ⓕ pl *een·for·ma·tsyo·nee*
ingredient ingrediente ⓜ *een·gre·dyen·te*
inhaler inalatore ⓜ *ee·na·la·to·re*
injection iniezione ⓕ *ee·nye·tsyo·ne*
injured ferito/a ⓜ/ⓕ *fe·ree·to/a*
injury ferita ⓕ *fe·ree·ta*
innocent innocente *ee·no·chen·te*
insect insetto ⓜ *een·se·to*
inside dentro *den·tro*
instructor (general) istruttore/istruttrice ⓜ/ⓕ *ee·stroo·to·re/ee·stroo·tree·che*
instructor (skiing) maestro/a ⓜ/ⓕ *ma·es·tro/a*
insurance assicurazione ⓕ *a·see·koo·ra·tsyo·ne*
interesting interessante *een·te·re·san·te*
intermission intervallo ⓜ *een·ter·va·lo*
international internazionale *een·ter·na·tsyo·na·le*
internet (cafe) Internet (point) ⓜ *een·ter·net (poynt)*
interpreter interprete ⓜ/ⓕ *een·ter·pre·te*
intersection incrocio ⓜ *een·kro·cho*
interview colloquio ⓜ (selettivo) *ko·lo·kwyo (se·le·tee·vo)*
invite invitare *een·vee·ta·re*
Ireland Irlanda ⓕ *eer·lan·da*
iron (for clothes) ferro ⓜ da stiro *fe·ro da stee·ro*
island isola ⓕ *ee·zo·la*
IT informatica ⓕ *een·for·ma·tee·ka*
Italian italiano/a ⓜ/ⓕ *ee·ta·lya·no/a*
Italy Italia ⓕ *ee·ta·lya*
itch prurito ⓜ *proo·ree·to*
itinerary itinerario ⓜ *ee·tee·ne·ra·ryo*
IUD spirale ⓕ *spee·ra·le*

J

jacket giacca ⓕ *ja·ka*
jail prigione ⓕ *pree·jo·ne*
jam marmellata ⓕ *mar·me·la·ta*
Japan Giappone ⓜ *ja·po·ne*
jar barattolo ⓜ *ba·ra·to·lo*
jealous geloso/a ⓜ/ⓕ *je·lo·zo/a*
jet lag disturbi ⓜ pl da fuso orario *dees·toor·bee da foo·zo o·ra·ryo*
jewellery gioielli ⓜ pl *jo·ye·lee*
Jewish ebreo/a ⓜ/ⓕ *e·bre·o/a*
job lavoro ⓜ *la·vo·ro*
jockey fantino ⓜ *fan·tee·no*
jogging footing ⓜ *foo·teeng*
joke scherzo ⓜ *sker·tso*
journalist giornalista ⓜ&ⓕ *jor·na·lee·sta*
judge giudice ⓜ *joo·dee·che*
judo giudò ⓜ *joo·do*
juice succo ⓜ *soo·ko*
jump saltare *sal·ta·re*
jumper maglione ⓜ *ma·lyo·ne*
jumper leads cavi ⓜ pl con morsetti *ka·vee kon mor·se·tee*

K

key chiave ⓕ *kya·ve*
keyboard tastiera ⓕ *tas·tye·ra*
kick dare un calcio *da·re oon kal·cho*
kill ammazzare *a·ma·tsa·re*
kilogram chilo ⓜ *kee·lo*
kilometre chilometro ⓜ *kee·lo·me·tro*
kind gentile *jen·tee·le*
kindergarten asilo ⓜ *a·zee·lo*
king re ⓜ *re*

kiss bacio ⓜ *ba*·cho
kiss baciare ba·*cha*·re
kitchen cucina ⓕ koo·*chee*·na
kitten gattino ⓜ ga·*tee*·no
knapsack zaino ⓜ *dzai*·no
knee ginocchio ⓜ jee·*no*·kyo
knife coltello ⓜ kol·*te*·lo
know (a person) conoscere ko·*no*·she·re
know (how to) sapere sa·*pe*·re
kosher kasher *ka*·sher

L

labourer lavoratore/lavoratrice ⓜ/ⓕ la·vo·ra·*to*·re/la·vo·ra·*tree*·che
lace merletto ⓜ mer·*le*·to
lager birra ⓕ chiara *bee*·ra *kya*·ra
lake lago ⓜ *la*·go
lamb agnello ⓜ a·*nye*·lo
land terra ⓕ *te*·ra
lane vicolo ⓜ *vee*·ko·lo
landlady padrona ⓕ di casa pa·*dro*·na dee *ka*·za
landlord padrone ⓜ di casa pa·*dro*·ne dee *ka*·za
language lingua ⓕ *leen*·gwa
laptop (computer) portatile ⓜ (kom·*pyoo*·ter) por·*ta*·tee·le
lard lardo ⓜ *lar*·do
large grande *gran*·de
last ultimo/a ⓜ/ⓕ *ool*·tee·mo/a
late in ritardo een ree·*tar*·do
laugh ridere *ree*·de·re
laundrette lavanderia ⓕ a gettone la·van·de·*ree*·a a je·*to*·ne
laundry lavanderia ⓕ la·van·de·*ree*·a
law legge ⓕ *le*·je
lawyer avvocato/a ⓜ/ⓕ a·vo·*ka*·to/a
laxatives lassativi ⓜ pl la·sa·*tee*·vee
lazy pigro/a ⓜ/ⓕ *pee*·gro/a
leader capo ⓜ *ka*·po
leaf foglia ⓕ *fo*·lya
learn imparare eem·pa·*ra*·re
leather cuoio ⓜ *kwo*·yo
leave partire par·*tee*·re
leek porro ⓜ *po*·ro
left (direction) sinistra ⓕ see·*nee*·stra
left luggage (office) deposito ⓜ bagagli de·*po*·zee·to ba·*ga*·lyee
left wing (di) sinistra (dee) see·*nee*·stra
leg (body part) gamba ⓕ *gam*·ba
leg (in race) tappa ⓕ *ta*·pa
legal legale le·*ga*·le
legume legume ⓜ le·*goo*·me
lemon limone ⓜ lee·*mo*·ne
lemonade limonata ⓕ lee·mo·*na*·ta
lens obiettivo ⓜ o·bye·*tee*·vo
Lent quaresima ⓕ kwa·*re*·zee·ma
lentil lenticchia ⓕ len·*tee*·kya
lesbian lesbica ⓕ *lez*·bee·ka
less (di) meno (dee) *me*·no
letter lettera ⓕ *le*·te·ra
lettuce lattuga ⓕ la·*too*·ga
level (tier) livello ⓜ lee·*ve*·lo
liar bugiardo/a ⓜ/ⓕ boo·*jar*·do/a
library biblioteca ⓕ bee·blyo·*te*·ka
lice pidocchi ⓜ pl pee·*do*·kee
licence plate number numero ⓜ di targa *noo*·me·ro dee *tar*·ga
lie (not stand) stendersi *sten*·der·see
life vita ⓕ *vee*·ta
life jacket giubbotto ⓜ di salvataggio joo·*bo*·to dee sal·va·*ta*·jo
lift (elevator) ascensore ⓜ a·shen·*so*·re
light luce ⓕ *loo*·che
light (colour) chiaro/a ⓜ/ⓕ *kya*·ro/a
light (not heavy) leggero/a ⓜ/ⓕ le·*je*·ro/a
light bulb lampadina ⓕ lam·pa·*dee*·na
light meter esposimetro ⓜ es·po·*zee*·me·tro
lighter accendino ⓜ a·chen·*dee*·no
lights (on car) fari ⓜ pl *fa*·ree
like piacere pya·*che*·re
lime limetta ⓕ lee·*me*·ta
line linea ⓕ *lee*·ne·a
lip balm burro ⓜ per le labbra *boo*·ro per le *la*·bra

lips labbra ⓕ pl *la*·bra
lipstick rossetto ⓜ ro·*se*·to
liquor store bottiglieria ⓕ bo·tee·lye·*ree*·a
list elenco ⓜ e·*len*·ko
listen ascoltare as·kol·*ta*·re
litre litro ⓜ *lee*·tro
(a) little un po' oon po
live vivere *vee*·ve·re
liver fegato ⓜ *fe*·ga·to
lizard lucertola ⓕ loo·*cher*·to·la
local locale lo·*ka*·le
lock (door) serratura ⓕ se·ra·*too*·ra
locked chiuso/a ⓜ/ⓕ (a chiave) *kyoo*·zo/a (a *kya*·ve)
locker armadietto ⓜ ar·ma·*dye*·to
lollies caramelle ⓕ pl ka·ra·*me*·le
long lungo/a ⓜ/ⓕ *loon*·go/a
long-distance (bus) interurbano/a ⓜ/ⓕ een·ter·oor·*ba*·no/a
look guardare gwar·*da*·re
look after curare koo·*ra*·re
look for cercare cher·*ka*·re
lookout veduta ⓕ ve·*doo*·ta
loose change spiccioli ⓜ pl *spee*·cho·lee
lose perdere *per*·de·re
lost perso/a ⓜ/ⓕ *per*·so/a
lost-property office ufficio ⓜ oggetti smarriti oo·*fee*·cho o·*je*·tee sma·*ree*·tee
(a) lot molto/a ⓜ/ⓕ *mol*·to/a
loud forte ⓜ/ⓕ *for*·te
love amare a·*ma*·re
lover amante ⓜ/ⓕ a·*man*·te
low basso/a ⓜ/ⓕ *ba*·so/a
lubricant lubrificante ⓜ loo·bree·fee·*kan*·te
luck fortuna ⓕ for·*too*·na
lucky fortunato/a ⓜ/ⓕ for·too·*na*·to/a
luggage bagaglio ⓜ ba·*ga*·lyo
luggage lockers armadietti ⓜ pl per i bagagli ar·ma·*dye*·tee per ee ba·*ga*·lyee
luggage tag etichetta ⓕ e·tee·*ke*·ta
lump nodulo ⓜ *no*·doo·lo
lunch pranzo ⓜ *pran*·dzo
lungs polmoni ⓜ pl pol·*mo*·nee
luxurious di lusso dee *loo*·so

M

machine macchina ⓕ *ma*·kee·na
made of (cotton) fatto/a ⓜ/ⓕ di (cotone) *fa*·to/a dee (ko·*to*·ne)
magazine rivista ⓕ ree·*vee*·sta
mail posta ⓕ *pos*·ta
mail box buca ⓕ delle lettere *boo*·ka de·le *le*·te·re
main principale preen·chee·*pa*·le
make fare *fa*·re
make-up trucco ⓜ *troo*·ko
mallet mazzuolo ⓜ ma·*tswo*·lo
mammogram mammografia ⓕ ma·mo·gra·*fee*·a
man uomo ⓜ *wo*·mo
manager manager ⓜ *me*·nee·je
mandarin mandarino ⓜ man·da·*ree*·no
manual manuale ma·noo·*a*·le
manual worker manovale ⓜ&ⓕ ma·no·*va*·le
many molti/e ⓜ/ⓕ pl *mol*·tee/*mol*·te
map pianta ⓕ *pyan*·ta
marble marmo ⓜ *mar*·mo
margarine margarina ⓕ mar·ga·*ree*·na
marijuana marijuana ⓕ ma·ree·*wa*·na
marital status stato ⓜ civile *sta*·to chee·*vee*·le
market mercato ⓜ mer·*ka*·to
marmalade marmellata ⓕ mar·me·*la*·ta
marriage matrimonio ⓜ ma·tree·*mo*·nyo
married sposato/a ⓜ/ⓕ spo·*za*·to/a
marry sposare spo·*za*·re
martial arts arti ⓕ pl marziali *ar*·tee mar·*tsya*·lee
mass (Catholic) messa ⓕ *me*·sa
massage massaggio ⓜ ma·*sa*·jo
mat tappeto ⓜ ta·*pe*·to
match (sport) partita ⓕ par·*tee*·ta

natches fiammiferi ⓜ pl
ya·mee·fe·ree
nattress materasso ⓜ ma·te·ra·so
naybe forse for·se
nayonnaise maionese ⓕ ma·yo·ne·ze
nayor sindaco ⓜ seen·da·ko
neasles morbillo ⓜ mor·bee·lo
neat carne ⓕ kar·ne
nechanic meccanico ⓜ&ⓕ
ne·ka·nee·ko
nedia mezzi ⓜ pl di comunicazione
ne·tsee dee ko·moo·nee·ka·tsyo·ne
nedicine medicina ⓕ
ne·dee·chee·na
neditation meditazione ⓕ
ne·dee·ta·tsyo·ne
neet incontrare een·kon·tra·re
nelon melone ⓜ me·lo·ne
nember socio/a ⓜ/ⓕ so·cho/a
nenstruation mestruazione ⓕ
ne·stroo·a·tsyo·ne
nenu menu ⓜ me·noo
message messaggio ⓜ me·sa·jo
metal metallo ⓜ me·ta·lo
netre (distance) metro ⓜ me·tro
netro station stazione ⓕ
lella metropolitana sta·tsyo·ne de·la
ne·tro·po·lee·ta·na
nicrowave oven forno ⓜ a
nicroonde for·no a mee·kro·on·de
midnight mezzanotte ⓕ me·dza·no·te
nigraine emicrania ⓕ e·mee·kra·nya
military le forze ⓕ pl armate le
or·tse ar·ma·te
nilitary service servizio ⓜ militare
ser·vee·tsyo mee·lee·ta·re
milk latte ⓜ la·te
nillimetre millimetro ⓜ
nee·lee·me·tro
mince carne ⓕ tritata kar·ne
ree·ta·ta
mineral water acqua ⓕ minerale
a·kwa mee·ne·ra·le
ninibar frigobar ⓜ free·go·bar
mints caramelle ⓕ pl alla menta
ka·ra·me·le a·la men·ta

minute minuto ⓜ mee·noo·to
mirror specchio ⓜ spe·kyo
miscarriage aborto ⓜ spontaneo
a·bor·to spon·ta·ne·o
miss (feel absence of) mancare
man·ka·re
mistake sbaglio ⓜ sba·lyo
mix mescolare mes·ko·la·re
mobile phone (telefono) cellulare ⓜ
(te·le·fo·no) che·loo·la·re
modern moderno/a ⓜ/ⓕ
mo·der·no/a
moisturiser idratante ⓜ ee·dra·tan·te
monastery monastero ⓜ
mo·nas·te·ro
money denaro ⓜ de·na·ro
month mese ⓜ me·ze
monument monumento ⓜ
mo·noo·men·to
(full) moon luna ⓕ (piena) loo·na
(pye·na)
more (di) più (dee) pyoo
morning mattina ⓕ ma·tee·na
morning after pill la pillola ⓕ
del mattino dopo la pee·lo·la del
ma·tee·no do·po
morning sickness nausea ⓕ
mattutina now·ze·a ma·too·tee·na
mosque moschea ⓕ mos·ke·a
mosquito zanzara ⓕ tsan·tsa·ra
mother madre ⓕ ma·dre
mother-in-law suocera ⓕ swo·che·ra
motorboat motoscafo ⓜ
mo·to·ska·fo
motorbike moto ⓕ mo·to
motorway (tollway) autostrada ⓕ
ow·to·stra·da
mountain montagna ⓕ mon·ta·nya
mountain path sentiero ⓜ di
montagna sen·tye·ro dee mon·ta·nya
mountain range catena ⓕ di
montagne ka·te·na dee mon·ta·nye
mountaineering alpinismo ⓜ
al·pee·neez·mo
mouse (rodent) topo ⓜ to·po
mouth bocca ⓕ bo·ka

movie film ⓜ feelm
mud fango ⓜ *fan*·go
mum mamma ⓕ *ma*·ma
muscle muscolo ⓜ *moo*·sko·lo
museum museo ⓜ moo·*ze*·o
mushroom fungo ⓜ *foon*·go
music musica ⓕ *moo*·zee·ka
musician musicista ⓜ&ⓕ moo·zee·*chee*·sta
Muslim musulmano/a ⓜ/ⓕ moo·sool·*ma*·no/a
mussels cozze ⓕ pl *ko*·tse
mustard senape ⓕ *se*·na·pe
mute muto/a ⓜ/ⓕ *moo*·to/a

N

nail clippers tagliaunghie ⓜ ta·lya·*oon*·gye
name nome ⓜ *no*·me
napkin tovagliolo ⓜ to·va·*lyo*·lo
nappy pannolino ⓜ pa·no·*lee*·no
nappy rash sfogo ⓜ da pannolino *sfo*·go da pa·no·*lee*·no
national nazionale na·tsyo·*na*·le
national park parco ⓜ nazionale *par*·ko na·tsyo·*na*·le
nationality nazionalità ⓕ na·tsyo·na·lee·*ta*
nature natura ⓕ na·*too*·ra
naturopathy naturopatia ⓕ na·too·ro·pa·*tee*·a
near (to) vicino (a) vee·*chee*·no (a)
nearby vicino/a ⓜ/ⓕ vee·*chee*·no/a
necessary necessario/a ⓜ/ⓕ ne·che·*sa*·ryo/a
neck collo ⓜ *ko*·lo
need avere bisogno di a·*ve*·re bee·*zo*·nyo dee
needle (sewing) ago ⓜ *a*·go
needle (syringe) ago ⓜ da siringa *a*·go da see·*reen*·ga
neither nessuno/a ⓜ/ⓕ ne·*soo*·no/a
net rete ⓕ *re*·te
Netherlands Paesi Bassi ⓜ pl pa·e·zee *ba*·see
never mai mai
new nuovo/a ⓜ/ⓕ *nwo*·vo/a
New Year's Day Capodanno ⓜ *ka*·po *da*·no
New Year's Eve San Silvestro ⓜ san seel·*ves*·tro
New Zealand Nuova Zelanda ⓕ *nwo*·va dze·*lan*·da
news notizie ⓕ pl no·*tee*·tsye
newsagency edicola ⓕ e·*dee*·ko·la
newspaper giornale ⓜ jor·*na*·le
next prossimo/a ⓜ/ⓕ *pro*·see·mo/a
next to accanto a a·*kan*·to a
nice (meal) buono/a ⓜ/ⓕ *bwo*·no/a
nice (person) gentile jen·*tee*·le
nice (weather) bello/a ⓜ/ⓕ *be*·lo/a
nickname soprannome ⓜ so·pra·*no*·me
night notte ⓕ *no*·te
no no no
noisy rumoroso/a ⓜ/ⓕ roo·mo·*ro*·zo/a
nondirect non-diretto/a ⓜ/ⓕ non·dee·*re*·to/a
none niente *nyen*·te
nonsmoking non fumatore non foo·ma·*to*·re
noodles pasta ⓕ *pas*·ta
noon mezzogiorno ⓜ *me*·dzo *jor*·no
north nord ⓜ nord
nose naso ⓜ *na*·zo
notebook quaderno ⓜ kwa·*der*·no
nothing niente *nyen*·te
novel romanzo ⓜ ro·*man*·dzo
now adesso a·*de*·so
nuclear energy energia ⓕ nucleare en·er·*jee*·a noo·kle·*a*·re
nuclear testing esperimenti ⓜ pl nucleari es·pe·ree·*men*·tee noo·kle·*a*·re
nuclear waste scorie ⓕ pl radioattiv *sko*·rye ra·dyo·a·*tee*·ve
number numero ⓜ *noo*·me·ro
number plate targa ⓕ *tar*·ga
nun suora ⓕ *swo*·ra
nurse infermiere/a ⓜ/ⓕ een·fer·*mye*·re/a
nut noce ⓕ *no*·che

O

ats avena ⓕ a·ve·na
ccupation (work) mestiere ⓜ
ıes·*tye*·re
cean oceano ⓜ o·*che*·a·no
ff (spoiled) guasto/a ⓜ/ⓕ
wa·sto/a
ffice ufficio ⓜ oo·*fee*·cho
ffice worker impiegato/a ⓜ/ⓕ
em·pye·*ga*·to/a
ften spesso *spe*·so
il olio ⓜ *o*·lyo
ld vecchio/a ⓜ/ⓕ *ve*·kyo/a
ld city centro ⓜ storico *chen*·tro
o·ree·ko
live oliva ⓕ o·*lee*·va
live oil olio ⓜ d'oliva o·lyo do·*lee*·va
n su soo
nce una volta ⓕ *oo*·na *vol*·ta
ne-way (ticket) (un biglietto di)
olo andata (oon bee·*lye*·to dee) so·lo
n·*da*·ta
nion cipolla ⓕ chee·*po*·la
nly solo *so*·lo
pen aperto/a ⓜ/ⓕ a·*per*·to/a
pen aprire a·*pree*·re
pening hours orario ⓜ di apertura
ra·ryo dee a·per·*too*·ra
pera opera ⓕ lirica *o*·pe·ra *lee*·ree·ka
pera house teatro ⓜ dell'opera
·a·tro del·o·per·a
peration (medical) intervento ⓜ
en·ter·*ven*·to
perator operatore/operatrice ⓜ/ⓕ
pe·ra·to·re/o·pe·ra·*tree*·che
pinion opinione ⓕ o·pee·*nyo*·ne
pposite di fronte a dee *fron*·te a
r o o
range (colour) arancione
ran·*cho*·ne
range (fruit) arancia ⓕ a·*ran*·cha
range juice (bottled) succo ⓜ
arancia *soo*·ko da·*ran*·cha
range juice (fresh) spremuta ⓜ
arancia spre·*moo*·ta da·*ran*·cha

orchestra orchestra ⓕ or·*kes*·tra
order ordine ⓜ *or*·dee·ne
order ordinare or·dee·*na*·re
ordinary ordinario/a ⓜ/ⓕ
or·dee·*na*·ryo/a
original originale ⓜ/ⓕ o·ree·jee·*na*·le
other altro/a ⓜ/ⓕ *al*·tro/a
outside fuori *fwo*·ree
ovarian cyst cisti ⓕ ovarica
chee·stee o·*va*·ree·ka
oven forno ⓜ *for*·no
over (above) sopra *so*·pra
overdose dose ⓕ eccessiva *do*·ze
e·che·*see*·va
owner proprietario/a ⓜ/ⓕ
pro·prye·*ta*·ryo/a
oxygen ossigeno ⓜ o·*see*·je·no
oyster ostrica ⓕ *o*·stree·ka
ozone layer strato ⓜ d'ozono *stra*·to
do·*dzo*·no

P

pacifier ciucciotto ⓜ choo·*cho*·to
package pacchetto ⓜ pa·*ke*·to
packet (general) pacchetto ⓜ
pa·*ke*·to
padded envelope busta ⓕ imbottita
boos·ta eem·bo·*tee*·ta
padlock lucchetto ⓜ loo·*ke*·to
page pagina ⓕ *pa*·jee·na
pain dolore ⓜ do·*lo*·re
painful doloroso/a ⓜ/ⓕ do·lo·*ro*·zo/a
painkillers analgesico ⓜ
an·al·*je*·zee·ko
paint dipingere dee·*peen*·je·re
painter pittore/pittrice ⓜ/ⓕ
pee·*to*·re/pee·*tree*·che
painting (the art) pittura ⓕ
pee·*too*·ra
painting (canvas) quadro ⓜ *kwa*·dro
pair paio ⓜ *pa*·yo
palace palazzo ⓜ pa·*la*·tso
pan pentola ⓕ *pen*·to·la
pants pantaloni ⓜ pl pan·ta·*lo*·nee
panty liners salva slip ⓜ pl *sal*·va
sleep

pantyhose collant ⓕ pl ko·*lant*
pap smear pap test ⓜ pap test
paper carta ⓕ *kar*·ta
papers documenti ⓜ pl do·koo·*men*·tee
paperwork moduli ⓜ pl *mo*·doo·lee
parcel pacchetto ⓜ pa·*ke*·to
parents genitori ⓜ pl je·nee·*to*·ree
park parco ⓜ *par*·ko
parliament parlamento ⓜ par·la·*men*·to
part parte ⓕ *par*·te
part-time ad orario ridotto ad o·*ra*·ryo ree·*do*·to
partner (intimate) compagno/a ⓜ/ⓕ kom·*pa*·nyo/a
party (celebration) festa ⓕ *fes*·ta
party (politics) partito ⓜ par·*tee*·to
pass (document) tessera ⓕ *te*·se·ra
pass (mountain) passo ⓜ *pa*·so
pass (sport) passaggio ⓜ pa·*sa*·jo
passenger passeggero/a ⓜ/ⓕ pa·se·*je*·ro/a
passport passaporto ⓜ pa·sa·*por*·to
past passato ⓜ pa·*sa*·to
pate (food) paté ⓜ pa·*te*
path sentiero ⓜ sen·*tye*·ro
pay pagare pa·*ga*·re
payment pagamento ⓜ pa·ga·*men*·to
pea pisello ⓜ pee·*ze*·lo
peace pace ⓕ *pa*·che
peach pesca ⓕ *pe*·ska
peak cima ⓕ *chee*·ma
peanuts arachidi ⓕ pl a·*ra*·kee·dee
pear pera ⓕ *pe*·ra
pedal pedale ⓜ pe·*da*·le
pedestrian pedone ⓜ/ⓕ pe·*do*·ne
pegs (tent) picchetti ⓜ pl pee·*ke*·tee
pen (ballpoint) penna ⓕ (a sfera) *pe*·na (a *sfe*·ra)
pencil matita ⓕ ma·*tee*·ta
penis pene ⓜ *pe*·ne
penicillin penicillina ⓕ pe·nee·chee·*lee*·na
penknife temperino ⓜ tem·pe·*ree*·no
pensioner pensionato/a ⓜ/ⓕ pen·syo·*na*·to/a
people gente ⓕ *jen*·te
pepper pepe ⓜ *pe*·pe
per (day) al (giorno) al (*jor*·no)
per cent per cento ⓕ per·*chen*·to
performance spettacolo ⓜ spe·*ta*·ko·lo
perfume profumo ⓜ pro·*foo*·mo
period pain dolori ⓜ pl mestruali do·*lo*·ree me·*stroo*·a·lee
permanent permanente ⓜ/ⓕ per·ma·*nen*·te
permission permesso ⓜ per·*me*·so
permit permesso ⓜ per·*me*·so
person persona ⓕ per·*so*·na
personal personale ⓜ/ⓕ per·so·*na*·l
petition petizione ⓕ pe·tee·*tsyo*·ne
petrol benzina ⓕ ben·*dzee*·na
petrol station distributore ⓜ dee·stree·boo·*to*·re
pharmacy farmacia ⓕ far·ma·*chee*·a
phone book elenco ⓜ telefonico e·*len*·ko te·le·*fo*·nee·ko
phone box cabina ⓕ telefonica ka·*bee*·na te·le·*fo*·nee·ka
phone call chiamata ⓕ kya·*ma*·ta
phonecard scheda ⓕ telefonica *ske*·da te·le·*fo*·nee·ka
photo foto ⓕ *fo*·to
photographer fotografo ⓜ fo·*to*·gra·fo
photography fotografia ⓕ fo·to·gra·*fee*·a
phrasebook vocabolarietto ⓜ vo·ka·bo·la·*rye*·to
pick (up) raccogliere ra·*ko*·lye·re
pickaxe piccone ⓜ pee·*ko*·ne
pickles sottoaceti ⓜ pl so·to·a·*che*·tee
pie torta ⓕ *tor*·ta
piece pezzo ⓜ *pe*·tso
pig maiale ⓜ ma·*ya*·le
pill pillola ⓕ *pee*·lo·la
(the) Pill la pillola ⓕ (anticoncezionale la *pee*·lo·la (an·tee·kon·che·tsyo·*na*·le

illow cuscino ⓜ koo·*shee*·no
illowcase federa ⓕ *fe*·de·ra
ineapple ananas ⓜ *a*·na·nas
ink rosa ⓜ&ⓕ *ro*·za
istachio pistacchio ⓜ pee·*sta*·kyo
lace (location) luogo ⓜ *lwo*·go
lace (seat) posto ⓜ *pos*·to
lace of birth luogo ⓜ di nascita
wo·go dee *na*·shee·ta
lane aereo ⓜ a·e·re·o
lanet pianeta ⓜ pya·*ne*·ta
lant pianta ⓕ *pyan*·ta
lastic plastica ⓕ *pla*·stee·ka
late piatto ⓜ *pya*·to
lateau altopiano ⓜ al·to·*pya*·no
latform binario ⓜ bee·*na*·ryo
lay (a game) giocare jo·*ka*·re
lay (guitar) suonare (la chitarra)
wo·*na*·re (la kee·*ta*·ra)
lay (soccer) giocare (a calcio)
o·*ka*·re (a *kal*·cho)
lay (sport) praticare pra·tee·*ka*·re
lay (theatre) commedia ⓕ
o·*me*·dya
layground parco ⓜ giochi *par*·ko
o·kee
lug (bath) tappo ⓜ *ta*·po
lug (electricity) spina ⓕ *spee*·na
lum prugna ⓕ *proo*·nya
ocket tasca ⓕ *tas*·ka
oetry poesia ⓕ po·e·*zee*·a
oint punto ⓜ *poon*·to
oint indicare een·dee·*ka*·re
oisonous velenoso/a ⓜ/ⓕ
e·le·*no*·zo/a
olice (civilian) polizia ⓕ po·lee·*tsee*·a
olice (military) carabinieri ⓜ pl
a·ra·bee·*nye*·ree
olice station posto ⓜ di polizia
os·to dee po·lee·*tsee*·a
olitician politico ⓜ po·*lee*·tee·ko
olitics politica ⓕ po·*lee*·tee·ka
ollen polline ⓜ *po*·lee·ne
olls elezioni ⓕ pl e·le·*tsyo*·nee
ollution inquinamento ⓜ
en·kwee·na·*men*·to

pony cavallino ⓜ ka·va·*lee*·no
pool (game) biliardo ⓜ beel·*yar*·do
pool (swimming) piscina ⓕ
pee·*shee*·na
poor povero/a ⓜ/ⓕ *po*·ve·ro/a
popular popolare po·po·*la*·re
pork maiale ⓜ ma·*ya*·le
port porto ⓜ *por*·to
possible possibile po·*see*·bee·le
post code codice ⓜ postale
ko·dee·che pos·*ta*·le
poste restante fermo ⓜ posta *fer*·mo
pos·ta
post office ufficio ⓜ postale
oo·*fee*·cho pos·*ta*·le
postage tariffa ⓕ postale ta·*ree*·fa
pos·*ta*·le
postcard cartolina ⓕ kar·to·*lee*·na
pot (ceramics) pignatta ⓕ pee·*nya*·ta
pot (dope) erba ⓕ *er*·ba
pot (cooking) pentola ⓕ *pen*·to·la
potato patata ⓕ pa·*ta*·ta
pottery oggetti ⓜ pl in ceramica
o·*je*·tee een che·*ra*·mee·ka
pound (money) sterlina ⓕ ster·*lee*·na
poverty povertà ⓕ po·ver·*ta*
power potere ⓜ po·*te*·re
prawn gambero ⓜ *gam*·be·ro
prayer preghiera ⓕ pre·*gye*·ra
prefer preferire pre·fe·*ree*·re
pregnancy test kit test ⓜ di
gravidanza test dee gra·vee·*dan*·tsa
pregnant incinta een·*cheen*·ta
premenstrual tension tensione ⓕ
premestruale ten·*syo*·ne
pre·me·*stroo*·a·le
prepare preparare pre·pa·*ra*·re
prescription ricetta ⓕ ree·*che*·ta
present (gift) regalo ⓜ re·*ga*·lo
president presidente ⓜ/ⓕ
pre·zee·*den*·te
pressure pressione ⓕ pre·*syo*·ne
pretty carino/a ⓜ/ⓕ ka·*ree*·no/a
previous precedente pre·che·*den*·te
price prezzo ⓜ *pre*·tso
priest prete ⓜ *pre*·te

prime minister primo ministro ⓜ/ⓕ *pree*·mo mee·*nee*·stro
printer (computer) stampante ⓕ stam·*pan*·te
prison prigione ⓕ pree·*jo*·ne
prisoner prigioniero/a ⓜ/ⓕ pree·jo·*nye*·ro/a
private privato/a ⓜ/ⓕ pree·*va*·to/a
produce produrre pro·*doo*·re
profit profitto ⓜ pro·*fee*·to
program programma ⓜ pro·*gra*·ma
projector proiettore ⓜ pro·ye·*to*·re
promise promessa ⓕ pro·*me*·sa
protect proteggere pro·*te*·je·re
protected (species) (specie) ⓕ protetta (*spe*·che) pro·*te*·ta
protest manifestazione ⓕ ma·nee·fes·ta·*tsyo*·ne
protest protestare pro·tes·*ta*·re
provisions provviste ⓕ pl pro·*vee*·ste
prune prugna ⓕ *proo*·nya
pub pub ⓜ poob
public holiday festa ⓕ *fes*·ta
public telephone telefono ⓜ pubblico te·*le*·fo·no *poo*·blee·ko
public toilet gabinetto ⓜ pubblico ga·bee·*ne*·to *poo*·blee·ko
pull tirare tee·*ra*·re
pump pompa ⓕ pom·*pa*
pumpkin zucca ⓕ *tsoo*·ka
puncture bucatura ⓕ boo·ka·*too*·ra
puppy cucciolo ⓜ *koo*·cho·lo
pure puro/a ⓜ/ⓕ *poo*·ro/a
purple viola vee·*o*·la
push spingere *speen*·je·re
put mettere *me*·te·re

Q

qualifications titoli ⓜ pl di studio *tee*·to·lee dee *stoo*·dee·o
quality qualità ⓕ kwa·lee·*ta*
quantity quantità ⓕ kwan·tee·*ta*
quarantine quarantena ⓕ kwa·ran·*te*·na
quarrel bisticcio ⓜ bees·*tee*·cho
quarter quarto ⓜ *kwar*·to
queen regina ⓕ re·*jee*·na
question domanda ⓕ do·*man*·da
queue coda ⓕ *ko*·da
quick rapido/a ⓜ/ⓕ *ra*·pee·do/a
quiet tranquillo/a ⓜ/ⓕ tran·*kwee*·lo/a

R

rabbit coniglio ⓜ ko·*nee*·lyo
race (sport) gara ⓜ *ga*·ra
racetrack pista ⓕ *pee*·sta
racing bike bici ⓕ da corsa *bee*·chee da *kor*·sa
racism razzismo ⓜ ra·*tseez*·mo
racquet racchetta ⓕ ra·*ke*·ta
radiator radiatore ⓜ ra·dya·*to*·re
railway station stazione ⓕ ferroviaria sta·*tsyo*·ne fe·ro·vee·*a*·ree·a
rain pioggia ⓜ *pyo*·ja
raincoat impermeabile ⓜ eem·per·me·*a*·bee·le
raisin uva ⓕ passa *oo*·va *pa*·sa
rape stupro ⓜ *stoo*·pro
rare raro/a ⓜ/ⓕ *ra*·ro/a
rash sfogo ⓜ *sfo*·go
raspberry lampone ⓜ lam·*po*·ne
rat topo ⓜ *to*·po
raw crudo/a ⓜ/ⓕ *kroo*·do/a
razor rasoio ⓜ ra·*zo*·yo
razor blades lamette ⓕ pl (da barba) la·*me*·te (da *bar*·ba)
read leggere *le*·je·re
ready pronto/a ⓜ/ⓕ *pron*·to/a
realistic realistico/a ⓜ/ⓕ re·a·*lee*·stee·ko/a
reason ragione ⓕ ra·*jo*·ne
receipt ricevuta ⓕ ree·che·*voo*·ta
receive ricevere ree·*che*·ve·re
recently di recente dee re·*chen*·te
recommend raccomandare ra·ko·man·*da*·re
recyclable riciclabile ree·chee·*kla*·bee·le
recycle riciclare ree·chee·*kla*·re
red rosso/a ⓜ/ⓕ *ro*·so/a
referee arbitro ⓜ *ar*·bee·tro

reflexology riflessologia ⓕ ree·fle·so·lo·*jee*·a
refrigerator frigo ⓜ *free*·go
refugee rifugiato/a ⓜ/ⓕ ree·foo·*gya*·to/a
refund rimborso ⓜ reem·*bor*·so
refuse rifiutare ree·fyoo·*ta*·re
region regione ⓕ re·*jo*·ne
registered mail posta raccomandata ⓕ *pos*·ta ra·ko·man·*da*·ta
regular normale nor·*ma*·le
relationship rapporto ⓜ ra·*por*·to
relax rilassarsi ree·la·*sar*·see
relic reliquia ⓕ re·*lee*·kwee·a
religion religione ⓕ re·lee·*jo*·ne
religious religioso/a ⓜ/ⓕ re·lee·*jo*·zo/a
remote remoto/a ⓜ/ⓕ re·*mo*·to/a
remote control telecomando ⓜ te·le·ko·*man*·do
rent affitto ⓜ a·*fee*·to
rent prendere in affitto *pren*·de·re een a·*fee*·to
repair riparare ree·pa·*ra*·re
reservation prenotazione ⓕ pre·no·ta·*tsyo*·ne
rest riposare ree·po·*za*·re
restaurant ristorante ⓜ rees·to·*ran*·te
retired pensionato/a ⓜ/ⓕ pen·syo·*na*·to/a
return ritornare ree·tor·*na*·re
return (ticket) (biglietto) di andata e ritorno (bee·*lye*·to) dee an·*da*·ta e ree·*tor*·no
reverse-charges call chiamata ⓕ a carico del destinatario kya·*ma*·ta a *ka*·ree·ko del des·tee·na·*ta*·ryo
rhythm ritmo ⓜ *reet*·mo
rice riso ⓜ *ree*·zo
rich (wealthy) ricco/a ⓜ/ⓕ *ree*·ko/a
ride corsa ⓕ *kor*·sa
ride (a bike) andare in bicicletta an·*da*·re een bee·chee·*kle*·ta
ride (a horse) cavalcare ka·val·*ka*·re
right (correct) giusto/a ⓜ/ⓕ *joo*·sto/a
right (direction) a destra *a de*·stra
right-wing (di) destra (dee) *de*·stra
ring (on finger) anello ⓜ a·*ne*·lo
ring (by phone) telefonare te·le·fo·*na*·re
rip-off bidone ⓜ bee·*do*·ne
risk rischio ⓜ *rees*·kyo
river fiume ⓜ *fyoo*·me
road strada ⓕ *stra*·da
rob derubare de·roo·*ba*·re
rock roccia ⓕ *ro*·cha
rock (music) (musica) ⓕ rock (*moo*·zee·ka) rok
rock climbing (andare su) roccia ⓜ (an·*da*·re soo) *ro*·cha
rock group gruppo ⓜ rock *groo*·po rok
roll (bread) panino ⓜ pa·*nee*·no
romantic romantico/a ⓜ/ⓕ ro·*man*·tee·ko/a
room camera ⓕ *ka*·me·ra
rope corda ⓕ *kor*·da
round rotondo/a ⓜ/ⓕ ro·*ton*·do/a
roundabout rotonda ⓜ ro·*ton*·da
route itinerario ⓜ ee·tee·ne·*ra*·ryo
rowing canottaggio ⓜ ka·no·*ta*·jo
rubbish spazzatura ⓕ spa·tsa·*too*·ra
rug tappeto ⓜ ta·*pe*·to
rugby rugby ⓜ *roog*·bee
ruins rovine ⓕ pl ro·*vee*·ne
rules regole ⓕ pl *re*·go·le
run correre *ko*·re·re
running (sport) footing ⓜ *foo*·teeng

S

sad triste *tree*·ste
saddle sella ⓕ *se*·la
safe cassaforte ⓕ ka·sa·*for*·te
safe sicuro/a ⓜ/ⓕ see·*koo*·ro/a
safe sex rapporti ⓜ pl protetti ra·*por*·tee pro·*te*·tee
safety gear corredo ⓜ antinfortunistico ko·*re*·do an·teen·for·too·*nee*·stee·ko
saint santo/a ⓜ/ⓕ *san*·to/a
salad insalata ⓕ een·sa·*la*·ta
salami salame ⓜ sa·*la*·me

S

salary stipendio ⓜ stee·*pen*·dyo
(on) sale in vendita een *ven*·dee·ta
sales tax IVA ⓕ *ee*·va
salmon salmone ⓜ sal·*mo*·ne
salt sale ⓜ *sa*·le
same stesso/a ⓜ/ⓕ *ste*·so/a
sand sabbia ⓕ *sa*·bya
sandals sandali ⓜ pl *san*·da·lee
sandwich tramezzino ⓜ tra·me·*dzee*·no
sanitary napkins assorbenti ⓜ pl igienici as·or·*ben*·tee ee·*je*·nee·chee
sardines sardine ⓕ pl sar·*dee*·ne
sauce sugo ⓜ *soo*·go
sauna sauna ⓕ *sow*·na
sausage salsiccia ⓕ sal·*see*·cha
say dire *dee*·re
scanner scanner ⓜ *ska*·ner
scarf sciarpa ⓕ *shar*·pa
school scuola ⓕ *skwo*·la
science scienza ⓕ *shen*·tsa
scissors forbici ⓕ pl *for*·bee·chee
score punteggio ⓜ poon·*te*·jo
score segnare se·*nya*·re
scoreboard tabellone ⓜ segnapunti ta·be·*lo*·ne se·nya·*poon*·tee
Scotland Scozia ⓕ *sko*·tsya
sculpture scultura ⓕ skool·*too*·ra
sea mare ⓜ *ma*·re
seasickness mal ⓜ di mare mal dee *ma*·re
seaside al mare al *ma*·re
season stagione ⓕ sta·*jo*·ne
seat (chair) sedile ⓜ se·*dee*·le
seat (place) posto ⓜ *pos*·to
seatbelt cintura ⓕ di sicurezza cheen·*too*·ra dee see·koo·*re*·tsa
second secondo ⓜ se·*kon*·do
second secondo/a ⓜ/ⓕ se·*kon*·do/a
second class seconda classe ⓕ se·*kon*·da *kla*·se
secondhand di seconda mano ⓜ/ⓕ dee se·*kon*·da *ma*·no
secretary segretario/a ⓜ/ⓕ se·gre·*ta*·ryo/a
see vedere ve·*de*·re
(to be) self-employed lavorare in proprio la·vo·*ra*·re een *pro*·pryo
selfish egoista ⓜ/ⓕ e·go·*ee*·sta
sell vendere *ven*·de·re
send mandare man·*da*·re
sensual sensuale ⓜ/ⓕ sen·soo·*a*·le
separate separato/a ⓜ/ⓕ se·pa·*ra*·to/a
(TV) series serie ⓕ (televisiva) *se*·ree·e (te·le·vee·*see*·va)
serious serio/a ⓜ/ⓕ *se*·ryo/a
service servizio ⓜ ser·*vee*·tsyo
service charge servizio ⓜ ser·*vee*·tsyo
service station stazione ⓕ di servizio sta·*tsyo*·ne dee ser·*vee*·tsyo
several diversi/e ⓜ/ⓕ pl dee·*ver*·see/ dee·*ver*·se
sew cucire koo·*chee*·re
sex sesso ⓜ *se*·so
sexism sessismo ⓜ se·*seez*·mo
sexy erotico/a ⓜ/ⓕ e·*ro*·tee·ko/a
shade ombra ⓕ *om*·bra
shadow ombra ⓕ *om*·bra
shape forma ⓕ *for*·ma
share (with) condividere kon·dee·*vee*·de·re
sharp affilato/a ⓜ/ⓕ a·fee·*la*·to/a
shave rasatura ⓕ ra·za·*too*·ra
shave fare la barba *fa*·re la *bar*·ba
shaving cream crema ⓕ da barba *kre*·ma da *bar*·ba
she lei lay
sheep pecora ⓕ *pe*·ko·ra
sheet (bed) lenzuolo ⓜ len·*tswo*·lo
ship nave ⓕ *na*·ve
shirt camicia ⓕ ka·*mee*·cha
shoe shop negozio ⓜ di scarpe ne·*go*·tsyo dee *skar*·pe
shoes scarpe ⓕ pl *skar*·pe
shop negozio ⓜ ne·*go*·tsyo
shopping centre centro ⓜ commerciale *chen*·tro ko·mer·*cha*·le
short (height) basso/a ⓜ/ⓕ *ba*·so/a
short (length) corto/a ⓜ/ⓕ *kor*·to/a

shorts pantaloncini ⓜ pl pan·ta·lon·*chee*·nee
shoulder spalla ⓕ *spa*·la
shout urlare oor·*la*·re
show spettacolo ⓜ spe·*ta*·ko·lo
show mostrare mos·*tra*·re
shower doccia ⓕ *do*·cha
shrine santuario ⓜ san·too·*a*·ryo
shut chiuso/a ⓜ/ⓕ *kyoo*·zo/a
shy timido/a ⓜ/ⓕ *tee*·mee·do/a
sick malato/a ⓜ/ⓕ ma·*la*·to/a
side lato ⓜ *la*·to
sign segno ⓜ *se*·nyo
signature firma ⓕ *feer*·ma
silk seta ⓕ *se*·ta
silver argento ⓜ ar·*jen*·to
similar simile ⓜ/ⓕ *see*·mee·le
simple semplice ⓜ/ⓕ *sem*·plee·che
since (time) da da
sing cantare kan·*ta*·re
singer cantante ⓜ/ⓕ kan·*tan*·te
single (man) celibe ⓜ *che*·lee·be
single (woman) nubile ⓕ *noo*·bee·le
single room camera ⓕ singola *ka*·me·ra *seen*·go·la
singlet canottiera ⓕ ka·no·*tye*·ra
sister sorella ⓕ so·*re*·la
sit sedere se·*de*·re
size (clothes) taglia ⓕ *ta*·lya
size (general) dimensioni ⓕ pl dee·men·*syo*·nee
ski sciare shee·*a*·re
ski lift sciovia ⓕ shee·o·*vee*·a
skiing sci ⓜ shee
ski(s) sci ⓜ sg&pl shee
skimmed milk latte ⓜ scremato *la*·te skre·*ma*·to
skin pelle ⓕ *pe*·le
skirt gonna ⓕ *go*·na
sky cielo ⓜ *che*·lo
sleep dormire dor·*mee*·re
sleeping bag sacco ⓜ a pelo *sa*·ko a *pe*·lo
sleeping car vagone ⓜ letto va·*go*·ne *le*·to

sleeping pills sonniferi ⓜ pl so·*nee*·fe·ree
(to be) sleepy avere sonno ⓜ a·*ve*·re *so*·no
slice fetta ⓕ *fe*·ta
slide (film) diapositiva ⓜ dee·a·po·zee·*tee*·va
slope pista ⓕ *pee*·sta
Slovenia Slovenia ⓕ slo·*ve*·nya
slow lento/a ⓜ/ⓕ *len*·to/a
slowly lentamente len·ta·*men*·te
small piccolo/a ⓜ/ⓕ *pee*·ko·lo/a
smell odore ⓜ o·*do*·re
smile sorridere so·*ree*·de·re
smoke fumare foo·*ma*·re
snack spuntino ⓜ spoon·*tee*·no
snail lumaca ⓕ loo·*ma*·ka
snake serpente ⓜ ser·*pen*·te
snorkel boccaglio ⓜ bo·*ka*·lyo
snow neve ⓕ *ne*·ve
snowboarding surf ⓜ da neve soorf da *ne*·ve
snow chains catene ⓕ pl da neve ka·*te*·ne da *ne*·ve
soap sapone ⓜ sa·*po*·ne
soap opera telenovela ⓕ te·le·no·*ve*·la
soccer calcio ⓜ *kal*·cho
social welfare assistenza ⓕ sociale a·sees·*ten*·tsa so·*cha*·le
socialist socialista ⓜ&ⓕ so·cha·*lee*·sta
socks calzini ⓜ pl cal·*tsee*·nee
soft morbido/a ⓜ/ⓕ *mor*·bee·do/a
soft drink bibita ⓕ *bee*·bee·ta
soldier soldato ⓜ sol·*da*·to
some alcuni/e ⓜ/ⓕ pl al·*koo*·nee/al·*koo*·ne
someone qualcuno/a ⓜ/ⓕ kwal·*koo*·no/a
something qualcosa kwal·*ko*·za
sometimes a volte a *vol*·te
son figlio ⓜ *fee*·lyo
song canzone ⓕ kan·*tso*·ne
soon fra poco fra *po*·ko
sore doloroso/a ⓜ/ⓕ do·lo·*ro*·zo/a
soup minestra ⓕ mee·*nes*·tra

S

sour cream panna ⓕ acida *pa*·na a·*chee*·da
south sud ⓜ sood
souvenir ricordino ⓜ ree·kor·*dee*·no
souvenir shop negozio ⓜ di souvenir ne·*go*·tsyo dee *soo*·ve·neer
soy milk latte ⓜ di soia *la*·te dee *so*·ya
soy sauce salsa ⓕ di soia *sal*·sa dee *so*·ya
space spazio ⓜ *spa*·tsyo
spade vanga ⓕ *van*·ga
Spain Spagna ⓕ *spa*·nya
speak parlare par·*la*·re
special speciale spe·*cha*·le
specialist specialista ⓜ&ⓕ spe·cha·*lee*·sta
speed velocità ⓕ ve·lo·chee·*ta*
speed limit limite ⓜ di velocità *lee*·mee·te dee ve·lo·chee·*ta*
speedometer tachimetro ⓜ ta·*kee*·me·tro
spermicide spermicida ⓕ sper·mee·*chee*·da
spider ragno ⓜ *ra*·nyo
spinach spinaci ⓜ pl spee·*na*·chee
spoke(s) raggio/raggi ⓜ *ra*·jo/*ra*·jee
spoon cucchiaio ⓜ koo·*kya*·yo
sports store negozio ⓜ di articoli sportivi ne·*go*·tsyo dee ar·*tee*·ko·lee spor·*tee*·vee
sportsperson sportivo/a ⓜ/ⓕ spor·*tee*·vo/a
sprain storta ⓕ *stor*·ta
spring (season) primavera ⓕ pree·ma·*ve*·ra
square (town) piazza ⓕ *pya*·tsa
stadium stadio ⓜ *sta*·dyo
stage (theatre) palcoscenico ⓜ pal·ko·*she*·nee·ko
stage (in race) tappa ⓕ *ta*·pa
stairway scale ⓕ pl *ska*·le
stamp francobollo ⓜ fran·ko·*bo*·lo
standby (ticket) (in lista) d'attesa (een *lee*·sta) da·*te*·za
(four-)star (a quattro) stelle (a *kwa*·tro) *ste*·le
stars stelle ⓕ pl *ste*·le
start inizio ⓜ ee·*nee*·tsyo
start cominciare ko·meen·*cha*·re
station stazione ⓕ sta·*tsyo*·ne
stationer cartolaio ⓜ kar·to·*la*·yo
statue statua ⓕ *sta*·too·a
stay (at a hotel) fermarsi fer·*mar*·see
steak (beef) bistecca ⓕ bees·*te*·ka
steal rubare roo·*ba*·re
steep ripido/a ⓜ/ⓕ *ree*·pee·do/a
stingy avaro/a ⓜ/ⓕ a·*va*·ro/a
stockings calze ⓕ pl *kal*·tse
stolen rubato/a ⓜ/ⓕ roo·*ba*·to/a
stomach stomaco ⓜ *sto*·ma·ko
stomachache mal ⓜ di pancia mal dee *pan*·cha
stone pietra ⓕ *pye*·tra
stoned (drugged) fumato/a ⓜ/ⓕ foo·*ma*·to/a
stop fermata ⓕ fer·*ma*·ta
stop fermare fer·*ma*·re
storm temporale ⓜ tem·po·*ra*·le
story racconto ⓜ ra·*kon*·to
stove stufa ⓕ (a gas) *stoo*·fa a gaz
straight diritto/a ⓜ/ⓕ dee·*ree*·to/a
strange strano/a ⓜ/ⓕ *stra*·no/a
stranger sconosciuto/a ⓜ/ⓕ sko·no·*shoo*·to/a
strawberry fragola ⓕ *fra*·go·la
stream ruscello ⓜ roo·*she*·lo
street strada ⓕ *stra*·da
(on) strike (in) sciopero ⓜ een *sho*·pe·ro
string spago ⓜ *spa*·go
strong forte ⓜ/ⓕ *for*·te
student studente/studentessa ⓜ/ⓕ stoo·*den*·te/stoo·den·*te*·sa
stupid stupido/a ⓜ/ⓕ *stoo*·pee·do/a
style stile ⓜ *stee*·le
subtitles sottotitoli ⓜ pl so·to·*tee*·to·lee
suburb quartiere ⓜ kwar·*tye*·re
subway metropolitana ⓕ me·tro·po·lee·*ta*·na

DICTIONARY

sugar zucchero ⓜ *tsoo*·ke·ro
suitcase valigia ⓕ va·*lee*·ja
summer estate ⓕ es·*ta*·te
sun sole ⓜ *so*·le
sunblock crema ⓕ solare *kre*·ma so·*la*·re
sunburn scottatura ⓕ sko·ta·*too*·ra
sunglasses occhiali ⓜ pl da sole o·*kya*·lee da *so*·le
sunny soleggiato/a ⓜ/ⓕ so·le·*ja*·to/a
sunrise alba ⓕ *al*·ba
sunscreen crema ⓕ solare *kre*·ma so·*la*·re
sunset tramonto ⓜ tra·*mon*·to
supermarket supermercato ⓜ soo·per·mer·*ka*·to
superstition superstizione ⓕ soo·per·stee·*tsyo*·ne
supplies provviste ⓜ pl pro·*vee*·ste
support (cheer on) fare il tifo *fa*·re eel *tee*·fo
supporters tifosi ⓜ pl tee·*fo*·zee
surf praticare il surf pra·tee·*ka*·re eel soorf
surface mail posta ⓕ ordinaria pos·ta or·dee·*na*·rya
surfboard tavola da surf *ta*·vo·la da soorf
surname cognome ⓜ ko·*nyo*·me
surprise sorpresa ⓕ sor·*pre*·sa
sweater maglione ⓜ ma·*lyo*·ne
Sweden Svezia ⓕ *sve*·tsee·a
sweet dolce *dol*·che
swelling gonfiore ⓜ gon·*fyo*·re
swim nuotare nwo·*ta*·re
swimming nuoto ⓜ *nwo*·to
swimming pool piscina ⓕ pee·*shee*·na
swimsuit costume ⓜ da bagno ko·*stoo*·me da *ba*·nyo
Switzerland Svizzera ⓕ svee·*tse*·ra
synagogue sinagoga ⓕ see·na·*go*·ga
synthetic sintetico/a ⓜ/ⓕ seen·*te*·tee·ko/a
syringe siringa ⓕ see·*reen*·ga

T

table tavola ⓕ *ta*·vo·la
table tennis ping-pong ⓜ peeng·*pong*
tablecloth tovaglia ⓕ to·*va*·lya
tailor sarto ⓜ *sar*·to
take prendere *pren*·de·re
take (photo) fare *fa*·re
talk parlare par·*la*·re
tall alto/a ⓜ/ⓕ *al*·to/a
tampons tamponi ⓜ pl tam·*po*·nee
tanning lotion lozione ⓕ abbronzante lo·*tsyo*·ne a·bron·*dzan*·te
tap (faucet) rubinetto ⓜ roo·bee·*ne*·to
tasty gustoso/a ⓜ/ⓕ goo·*sto*·zo/a
tax tassa ⓕ *ta*·sa
taxi tassì ⓜ ta·*see*
taxi stand posteggio ⓜ di tassì po·*ste*·jo dee ta·*see*
tea tè ⓜ te
teacher (general) insegnante ⓜ&ⓕ een·sen·*yan*·te
teacher (primary) maestro/a ⓜ/ⓕ ma·*es*·tro/a
teacher (secondary) professore/professoressa ⓜ/ⓕ pro·fe·*so*·re/pro·fe·so·*re*·sa
team squadra ⓕ *skwa*·dra
teaspoon cucchiaino ⓜ koo·kya·*ee*·no
teeth denti ⓜ pl *den*·tee
telegram telegramma ⓜ te·le·*gra*·ma
telephone telefono ⓜ te·*le*·fo·no
telephone telefonare te·le·fo·*na*·re
telephone centre centro ⓜ telefonico *chen*·tro te·le·*fo*·nee·ko
telephoto lens teleobiettivo ⓜ te·le·o·bye·*tee*·vo
television televisione ⓕ te·le·vee·*zyo*·ne
tell raccontare ra·kon·*ta*·re
temperature (fever) febbre ⓕ *fe*·bre
temperature (weather) temperatura ⓕ tem·pe·ra·*too*·ra

temple tempio ⓜ *tem*·pyo
tennis court campo ⓜ da tennis *kam*·po da *te*·nees
tent tenda ⓕ *ten*·da
tent pegs picchetti ⓜ pl (per la tenda) pee·*ke*·tee (per la *ten*·da)
terrible terribile ⓜ/ⓕ te·*ree*·bee·le
test esame ⓜ e·*za*·me
thank ringraziare reen·gra·*tsya*·re
theatre teatro ⓜ te·*a*·tro
there là la
they loro *lo*·ro
thick spesso/a ⓜ/ⓕ *spe*·so/a
thief ladro/a ⓜ/ⓕ *la*·dro/a
thin magro/a ⓜ/ⓕ *ma*·gro/a
think pensare pen·*sa*·re
third terzo/a ⓜ/ⓕ *ter*·tso/a
(to be) thirsty avere sete ⓕ a·*ve*·re *se*·te
this (one) questo/a ⓜ/ⓕ *kwe*·sto/a
thread (sewing) filo ⓜ *fee*·lo
throat gola ⓕ *go*·la
thrush (medical) mughetto ⓜ moo·*ge*·to
ticket biglietto ⓜ bee·*lye*·to
ticket collector controllore ⓜ kon·tro·*lo*·re
ticket machine distributore ⓜ automatico di biglietti dee·stree·boo·*to*·re ow·to·*ma*·tee·ko dee bee·*lye*·tee
ticket office biglietteria ⓕ bee·lye·te·*ree*·a
tide marea ⓕ ma·*re*·a
tight stretto/a ⓜ/ⓕ *stre*·to/a
time tempo ⓜ *tem*·po
time difference differenza ⓕ di fuso orario dee·fe·*ren*·tsa dee *foo*·zo o·*ra*·ryo
timetable orario ⓜ o·*ra*·ryo
tin (can) scatoletta ⓕ ska·to·*le*·ta
tin opener apriscatole ⓜ a·pree·*ska*·to·le
tiny minuscolo/a ⓜ/ⓕ mee·*noos*·ko·lo/a
tip (gratuity) mancia ⓕ *man*·cha
tired stanco/a ⓜ/ⓕ *stan*·ko/a
tissues fazzolettini ⓜ pl di carta fa·tso·le·*tee*·nee dee *kar*·ta
toast pane ⓜ tostato *pa*·ne tos·*ta*·to
toaster tostapane ⓜ tos·ta·*pa*·ne
tobacco tabacco ⓜ ta·*ba*·ko
tobacconist tabaccheria ⓕ ta·ba·ke·*ree*·a
tobogganing andare in slitta an·*da*·re een *slee*·ta
today oggi *o*·jee
toe dito ⓜ del piede *dee*·to del *pye*·de
together insieme een·*sye*·me
toilet gabinetto ⓜ ga·bee·*ne*·to
toilet paper carta ⓕ igienica *kar*·ta ee·*je*·nee·ka
toilets servizi ⓜ pl igienici ser·*vee*·tse ee·*je*·nee·chee
token gettone ⓜ je·*to*·ne
tomato pomodoro ⓜ po·mo·*do*·ro
tomato sauce salsa ⓕ di pomodoro *sal*·sa dee po·mo·*do*·ro
tomorrow domani do·*ma*·nee
tonight stasera sta·*se*·ra
too (expensive) troppo (caro/a) *tro*·po (*ka*·ro/a)
too many troppi/e ⓜ/ⓕ pl *tro*·pee/*tro*·pe
too much troppo/a ⓜ/ⓕ sg *tro*·po/a
tooth (front) dente ⓜ *den*·te
toothache mal ⓜ di denti mal dee *den*·tee
toothbrush spazzolino ⓜ da denti spa·tso·*lee*·no da *den*·tee
toothpaste dentifricio ⓜ den·tee·*free*·cho
toothpick stuzzicadenti ⓜ stoo·tsee·ka·*den*·tee
torch (flashlight) torcia ⓕ elettrica *tor*·cha e·*le*·tree·ka
touch toccare to·*ka*·re
tour gita ⓕ *jee*·ta
tourist turista ⓜ&ⓕ too·*ree*·sta
tourist office ufficio ⓜ del turismo oo·*fee*·cho del too·*reez*·mo

towel asciugamano ⓜ a·shoo·ga·*ma*·no
tower torre ⓕ *to*·re
toxic waste rifiuti ⓜ pl tossici ree·*fyoo*·tee *to*·see·chee
toyshop negozio ⓜ di giocattoli ne·*go*·tsyo dee jo·*ka*·to·lee
track (path) sentiero ⓜ sen·*tye*·ro
track (sports) pista ⓕ *pee*·sta
trade commercio ⓜ ko·*mer*·cho
traffic traffico ⓜ *tra*·fee·ko
traffic jam ingorgo ⓜ een·*gor*·go
traffic lights semaforo ⓜ se·*ma*·fo·ro
trail pista ⓜ *pee*·sta
train treno ⓜ *tre*·no
train station stazione ⓕ (ferroviaria) sta·*tsyo*·ne (fe·ro·*vyar*·ya)
tram tram ⓜ tram
transit lounge sala ⓕ di transito *sa*·la dee *tran*·zee·to
translate tradurre tra·*doo*·re
transport trasporto ⓜ tras·*por*·to
travel viaggiare vee·a·*ja*·re
travel agency agenzia ⓕ di viaggio a·jen·*tsee*·a dee vee·*a*·jo
travel sickness (air) mal ⓜ di aereo mal dee a·*e*·re·o
travel sickness (car) mal ⓜ di macchina mal dee *ma*·kee·na
travel sickness (sea) mal ⓜ di mare mal dee *ma*·re
travellers cheque assegno ⓜ di viaggio a·*se*·nyo dee vee·*a*·jo
tree albero ⓜ *al*·be·ro
trip gita ⓕ *jee*·ta
trolley (luggage) carrello ⓜ ka·*re*·lo
trousers pantaloni ⓜ pl pan·ta·*lo*·nee
truck camion ⓜ *ka*·myon
true vero/a ⓜ/ⓕ *ve*·ro/a
try (attempt) provare pro·*va*·re
T-shirt maglietta ⓕ ma·*lye*·ta
tube (tyre) camera ⓕ d'aria *ka*·me·ra *da*·rya
tuna tonno ⓜ *to*·no
tune melodia ⓕ me·lo·*dee*·a
turkey tacchino ⓜ ta·*kee*·no
turn girare jee·*ra*·re
TV TV ⓕ tee·*voo*
tweezers pinzette ⓕ pl peen·*tse*·te
twice due volte *doo*·e *vol*·te
twin beds due letti *doo*·e *le*·tee
twins gemelli/e ⓜ/ⓕ pl je·*me*·lee/ je·*me*·le
type tipo ⓜ *tee*·po
typical tipico/a ⓜ/ⓕ *tee*·pee·ko/a
tyre gomma ⓕ *go*·ma

U

ugly brutto/a ⓜ/ⓕ *broo*·to/a
ultrasound ecografia ⓕ e·ko·gra·*fee*·a
umbrella ombrello ⓜ om·*bre*·lo
uncomfortable scomodo/a ⓜ/ⓕ *sko*·mo·do/a
understand capire ka·*pee*·re
underwear biancheria ⓕ intima byan·ke·*ree*·a *een*·tee·ma
unemployed disoccupato/a ⓜ/ⓕ dee·zo·koo·*pa*·to/a
uniform divisa ⓕ dee·*vee*·za
universe universo ⓜ oo·nee·*ver*·so
university università ⓕ oo·nee·ver·see·*ta*
unleaded senza piombo *sen*·tsa *pyom*·bo
unsafe pericoloso/a ⓜ/ⓕ pe·ree·ko·*lo*·zo/a
until fino a *fee*·no a
unusual insolito/a ⓜ/ⓕ een·*so*·lee·to/a
up su soo
uphill in salita een sa·*lee*·ta
urgent urgente ⓜ/ⓕ oor·*jen*·te
USA Stati ⓜ pl Uniti d'America *sta*·tee oo·*nee*·tee da·*me*·ree·ka
useful utile *oo*·tee·le

V

vacant libero/a ⓜ/ⓕ *lee*·be·ro/a
vacation vacanza ⓕ va·*kan*·tsa
vaccination vaccinazione ⓕ va·chee·na·*tsyo*·ne

vagina vagina ⓕ va·*jee*·na
validate convalidare kon·va·lee·*da*·re
valley valle ⓕ *va*·le
valuable prezioso/a ⓜ/ⓕ pre·*tsyo*·zo/a
valuables oggetti ⓜ pl di valore o·*je*·tee dee va·*lo*·re
value (price) valore ⓜ va·*lo*·re
van furgone ⓜ foor·*go*·ne
veal vitello ⓜ vee·*te*·lo
vegetable verdura ⓕ ver·*doo*·ra
vegetarian vegetariano/a ⓜ/ⓕ ve·je·ta·*rya*·no/a
venereal disease malattia ⓕ venerea ma·la·*tee*·a ve·*ne*·re·a
venue locale ⓜ lo·*ka*·le
very molto *mol*·to
video videoregistratore ⓜ vee·de·o·re·jee·stra·*to*·re
video camera videocamera ⓕ vee·de·o·*ka*·me·ra
video tape videonastro ⓜ vee·de·o·*nas*·tro
view vista ⓕ *vee*·sta
village villaggio ⓜ vee·*la*·jo
vinegar aceto ⓜ a·*che*·to
vineyard vigneto ⓜ vee·*nye*·to
virus virus ⓜ *vee*·roos
visa visto ⓜ *vee*·sto
visit (person) andare a trovare an·*da*·re a tro·*va*·re
visit (place) fare una visita *fa*·re *oo*·na *vee*·see·ta
vitamins vitamine ⓕ pl vee·ta·*mee*·ne
voice voce ⓕ *vo*·che
volleyball pallavolo ⓕ pa·la·*vo*·lo
vomit vomitare vo·mee·*ta*·re
vote votare vo·*ta*·re

W

wage salario ⓜ sa·*la*·ryo
wait aspettare as·pe·*ta*·re
waiter cameriere/a ⓜ/ⓕ ka·mer·*ye*·re/a
waiting room sala ⓕ d'attesa *sa*·la da·*te*·sa
wake up svegliarsi sve·*lyar*·see
Wales Galles ⓜ *ga*·les
walk passeggiata ⓕ pa·se·*ja*·ta
walk camminare ka·mee·*na*·re
wall (external) muro ⓜ *moo*·ro
wall (internal) parete ⓕ pa·*re*·te
wallet portafoglio ⓜ por·ta·*fo*·lyo
want volere vo·*le*·re
war guerra ⓕ *gwe*·ra
wardrobe armadio ⓜ ar·*ma*·dyo
warm tiepido/a ⓜ/ⓕ *tye*·pee·do/a
warn avvertire a·ver·*tee*·re
wash (oneself) lavarsi la·*var*·see
wash (something) lavare la·*va*·re
washing machine lavatrice ⓕ la·va·*tree*·che
washing powder detersivo ⓜ de·ter·*see*·vo
watch orologio ⓜ o·ro·*lo*·jo
watch guardare gwar·*da*·re
water acqua ⓕ *a*·kwa
water bottle borraccia ⓕ bo·*ra*·cha
waterfall cascata ⓕ kas·*ka*·ta
watermelon anguria ⓕ an·*goo*·rya
waterproof impermeabile eem·per·me·*a*·bee·le
water skiing sci ⓜ acquatico shee a·*kwa*·tee·ko
watersports sport ⓜ acquatici sport a·*kwa*·tee·chee
wave onda ⓕ *on*·da
way via ⓕ *vee*·a
we noi noy
weak debole *de*·bo·le
wealthy ricco/a ⓜ/ⓕ *ree*·ko/a
wear indossare een·do·*sa*·re
weather tempo ⓜ *tem*·po
wedding matrimonio ⓜ ma·tree·*mo*·nyo
wedding present regalo ⓜ di nozze re·*ga*·lo dee *no*·tse
week settimana ⓕ se·tee·*ma*·na
weekend fine settimana ⓜ *fee*·ne se·tee·*ma*·na
weight peso ⓜ *pe*·zo

welcome dare il benvenuto a *da*·re eel ben·ve·*noo*·to a
well in buona salute een *bwo*·na sa·*loo*·te
west ovest ⓜ *o*·vest
wet bagnato/a ⓜ/ⓕ ba·*nya*·to/a
wetsuit muta ⓕ *moo*·ta
what che (cosa) ke (*ko*·za)
wheel ruota ⓕ *rwo*·ta
wheelchair sedia ⓕ a rotelle *se*·dya a ro·*te*·le
when quando *kwan*·do
where dove *do*·ve
white bianco/a ⓜ/ⓕ *byan*·ko/a
who chi kee
why perché per·*ke*
wide largo/a ⓜ/ⓕ *lar*·go/a
widow vedova ⓕ ve·*do*·va
widower vedovo ⓜ ve·*do*·vo
wife moglie ⓕ *mo*·lye
win vincere *veen*·che·re
wind vento ⓜ *ven*·to
window (car, plane) finestrino ⓜ fee·nes·*tree*·no
window (general) finestra ⓕ fee·*nes*·tra
windscreen parabrezza ⓜ pa·ra·*bre*·dza
wine vino ⓜ *vee*·no
wine cellar cantina ⓕ kan·*tee*·na
wine tasting degustazione ⓕ dei vini de·goos·ta·*tsyo*·ne day *vee*·nee
winery cantina ⓕ kan·*tee*·na
wings ali ⓕ pl *a*·lee
winner vincitore/vincitrice ⓜ/ⓕ veen·chee·*to*·re/veen·chee·*tree*·che
winter inverno ⓜ een·*ver*·no
wish desiderare de·see·de·*ra*·re
with con kon
within (an hour) entro (un'ora) *en*·tro (oon·*o*·ra)
without senza *sen*·tsa
woman donna ⓕ *do*·na
wonderful meraviglioso/a ⓜ/ⓕ me·ra·vee·*lyo*·zo/a
wood legno ⓜ *le*·nyo
wool lana ⓕ *la*·na
word parola ⓕ pa·*ro*·la
work (occupation) lavoro ⓜ la·*vo*·ro
work (of art) opera ⓕ (d'arte) *o*·pe·ra (*dar*·te)
work lavorare la·vo·*ra*·re
workout allenamento ⓜ a·le·na·*men*·to
workshop laboratorio ⓜ la·bo·ra·*to*·ryo
world mondo ⓜ *mon*·do
World Cup Coppa ⓕ del Mondo *ko*·pa del *mon*·do
worried preoccupato/a ⓜ/ⓕ pre·o·koo·*pa*·to/a
worship (pray) pregare pre·*ga*·re
wrist polso ⓜ *pol*·so
write scrivere *skree*·ve·re
writer scrittore/scrittrice ⓜ/ⓕ skree·*to*·re/skree·*tree*·che
wrong sbagliato/a ⓜ/ⓕ sba·*lya*·to/a

Y

year anno ⓜ *a*·no
yellow giallo/a ⓜ/ⓕ *ja*·lo/a
yes sì see
yesterday ieri *ye*·ree
(not) yet (non) ancora (non) an·*ko*·ra
you sg inf tu too
you sg pol Lei lay
you pl inf voi voy
you pl pol Loro *lo*·ro
young giovane *jo*·va·ne
youth hostel ostello ⓜ della gioventù os·*te*·lo *de*·la jo·ven·*too*

Z

zoo giardino ⓜ zoologico jar·*dee*·no dzo·o·*lo*·jee·ko

A

Dictionary

ITALIAN to ENGLISH

Italiano–Inglese

Nouns in this dictionary, and adjectives affected by gender, have their gender indicated by ⓜ and/or ⓕ. If it's a plural noun, you'll also see pl. Where a word that could be either a noun or a verb has no gender indicated, it's a verb.

A

a a in • at • to • until • per
a bordo a *bor*·do aboard
abbastanza a·bas·*tan*·tsa enough
abbigliamento ⓜ a·bee·lya·*men*·to clothing
abbracciare a·bra·*cha*·re hug
abitare a·bee·*ta*·re live (somewhere)
abito ⓜ *a*·bee·to dress
aborto ⓜ a·*bor*·to abortion
— spontaneo spon·*ta*·ne·o miscarriage
accanto a·*kan*·to nearby
accanto a a·*kan*·to a next to
accendino ⓜ a·chen·*dee*·no (cigarette) lighter
accetazione ⓕ a·che·ta·*tsyo*·ne check-in (airport)
aceto ⓜ a·*che*·to vinegar
acqua ⓕ *a*·kwa water
— bollita bo·*lee*·ta boiled water
— calda *kal*·da hot water
— del rubinetto del roo·bee·*ne*·to tap water
— minerale mee·ne·*ra*·le mineral water
— non gassata non ga·*sa*·ta still water
adesso a·*de*·so now
adulto/a ⓜ/ⓕ a·*dool*·to/a adult
aereo ⓜ a·e·re·o plane
aerobica ⓕ a·e·*ro*·bee·ka aerobics
aeroporto ⓜ a·e·ro·*por*·to airport
affari ⓜ pl a·*fa*·ree business
affascinante a·fa·shee·*nan*·te charming • attractive
affilato/a ⓜ/ⓕ a·fee·*la*·to/a sharp
affitto ⓜ a·*fee*·to rent
affollato/a ⓜ/ⓕ a·fo·*la*·to/a crowded
agenda ⓕ a·*jen*·da diary
agenzia ⓕ **di viaggio** a·jen·*tsee*·a dee vee·*a*·jo travel agency
agganciare a·gan·*cha*·re chat up
aggiustare a·joo·*sta*·re repair
aggressivo/a ⓜ/ⓕ a·gre·*see*·vo/a aggressive
aglio ⓜ *a*·lyo garlic
agnello ⓜ a·*nye*·lo lamb
ago ⓜ *a*·go needle (sewing)
agopuntura ⓕ a·go·poon·*too*·ra acupuncture
agricoltore/agricoltrice ⓜ/ⓕ a·gree·kol·*to*·re/a·gree·kol·*tree*·che farmer

agricoltura ⓕ a·gree·kol·*too*·ra agriculture
aiutare a·yoo·*ta*·re help
alba ⓕ *al*·ba sunrise
albergo ⓜ al·*ber*·go hotel
albero ⓜ *al*·be·ro tree
albicocca ⓕ al·bee·*ko*·ka apricot
alcuni/e ⓜ/ⓕ pl al·*koo*·nee/al·*koo*·ne some
ali ⓕ pl *a*·lee wings
alimentari ⓜ a·lee·men·*ta*·ree grocery store • convenience store
alimento ⓜ a·lee·*men*·to food
al giorno al *jor*·no per day
al mare al *ma*·re seaside
all'estero a·*les*·te·ro abroad
allenamento ⓜ a·le·na·*men*·to workout
allergia ⓕ a·ler·*jee*·a allergy
alloggio ⓜ a·*lo*·jo accommodation
allucinare a·loo·chee·*na*·re hallucinate
alpinismo ⓜ al·pee·*neez*·mo mountaineering
altare ⓜ al·*ta*·re altar
altezza ⓕ al·*te*·tsa height
alto/a ⓜ/ⓕ *al*·to/a high • tall
altopiano ⓜ al·to·*pya*·no plateau
altro/a ⓜ/ⓕ *al*·tro/a other
— ieri ⓜ *ye*·ree day before yesterday
amaca ⓕ a·ma·ka hammock
amante ⓜ/ⓕ a·*man*·te lover
amare a·*ma*·re love
ambasciata ⓕ am·ba·*sha*·ta embassy
ambasciatore/ambasciatrice ⓜ/ⓕ am·ba·sha·*to*·re/am·ba·sha·*tree*·che ambassador
ambiente ⓜ am·*byen*·te environment
ambulanza ⓕ am·boo·*lan*·tsa ambulance
amico/a ⓜ/ⓕ a·*mee*·ko/a friend
ammazzare a·ma·*tsa*·re kill
amministrazione ⓕ a·mee·nee·stra·*tsyo*·ne administration
analgesico ⓜ an·al·*je*·zee·ko painkillers
analisi ⓕ **del sangue** a·*na*·lee·zee del *san*·gwe blood test
ananas ⓜ *a*·na·nas pineapple
anatra ⓕ *a*·na·tra duck
anche *an*·ke also
ancora an·*ko*·ra still • yet
andare an·*da*·re go
— a cavallo a ka·*va*·lo horse riding
— a vedere a ve·*de*·re visit
— in bicicletta een bee·chee·*kle*·ta cycle • ride (a bike)
— in slitta een *slee*·ta tobogganing
— su roccia soo *ro*·cha rock climbing
andata ⓕ an·*da*·ta outward journey
anello ⓜ a·*ne*·lo ring (on finger)
angolo ⓜ *an*·go·lo corner
anguria ⓕ an·*goo*·rya watermelon
animale ⓜ a·nee·*ma*·le animal
anno ⓜ *a*·no year
annoiato/a ⓜ/ⓕ a·no·*ya*·to/a bored
annuale a·noo·*a*·le annual
annuncio ⓜ a·*noon*·cho advertisement
antibiotici ⓜ pl an·tee·bee·*o*·tee·chee antibiotics
antico/a ⓜ/ⓕ an·*tee*·ko/a ancient
antinucleare an·tee·noo·kle·*a*·re antinuclear
antisettico ⓜ an·tee·*se*·tee·ko antiseptic
antistaminici ⓜ pl an·tee·sta·*mee*·nee·chee antihistamines
ape ⓕ *a*·pe bee
aperto/a ⓜ/ⓕ a·*per*·to/a open
apparecchio ⓜ **acustico** a·pa·*re*·kyo a·*koos*·tee·ko hearing aid
appartamento ⓜ a·par·ta·*men*·to flat
appendice ⓕ a·pen·*dee*·che appendix
appuntamento ⓜ a·poon·ta·*men*·to appointment • date
apribottiglie ⓜ a·pree·bo·*tee*·lye bottle opener
aprire a·*pree*·re open
apriscatole ⓜ a·pree·*ska*·to·le can opener

arachidi ⓕ pl a·*ra*·kee·dee peanuts • groundnuts
arancia ⓕ a·*ran*·cha orange (fruit)
arancione a·ran·*cho*·ne orange (colour)
arbitro ⓜ *ar*·bee·tro referee
archeologico/a ⓜ/ⓕ ar·ke·o·*lo*·jee·ko/a archaeological
architetto ⓜ ar·kee·*te*·to architect
architettura ⓕ ar·kee·te·*too*·ra architecture
argento ⓜ ar·*jen*·to silver
aria ⓕ *a*·rya air
— condizionata kon·dee·*tsyo*·na·ta air-conditioning
aringa ⓕ a·*reen*·ga herring
armadietti ⓜ pl ar·ma·*dye*·tee lockers
— per i bagagli per ee ba·*ga*·lyee luggage lockers
armadio ⓜ ar·*ma*·dyo wardrobe
arrabbiato/a ⓜ/ⓕ a·ra·*bya*·to/a angry
arrestare a·res·*ta*·re arrest
arrivare a·ree·*va*·re arrive
arrivi ⓜ pl a·*ree*·vee arrivals
arte ⓕ *ar*·te art
arti ⓕ pl **marziali** *ar*·tee mar·*tsya*·lee martial arts
artista ⓜ&ⓕ ar·*tee*·sta artist
ASA *a*·za film speed
ascensore ⓜ a·shen·*so*·re elevator
asciugamano ⓜ a·shoo·ga·*ma*·no towel
asciugare a·*shoo*·ga·re dry
ascoltare as·kol·*ta*·re listen
asilo ⓜ a·*zee*·lo kindergarten
— nido *nee*·do creche
asma ⓕ *az*·ma asthma
asparagi ⓜ pl as·*pa*·ra·jee asparagus
aspettare as·pe·*ta*·re wait
aspirina ⓕ as·pee·*ree*·na aspirin
assegno ⓜ a·*se*·nyo cheque
— di viaggio dee vee·*a*·jo travellers cheque
assicurazione ⓕ a·see·koo·ra·*tsyo*·ne insurance
assistenza ⓕ **sociale** a·sees·*ten*·tsa so·*cha*·le (social) welfare
assorbenti ⓜ pl **igienici** a·sor·*ben*·tee ee·*je*·nee·chee sanitary napkins
atletica ⓕ at·*le*·tee·ka athletics
atrio ⓜ *a*·tryo foyer
attesa ⓕ a·*te*·sa wait
attrezzatura ⓕ a·tre·tsa·*too*·ra equipment
attualità ⓕ a·too·a·lee·*ta* current affairs
autobus ⓜ *ow*·to·boos bus (city)
autostop ⓜ *ow*·to·stop hitchhiking
automatico/a ⓜ/ⓕ ow·to·*ma*·tee·ko/a automatic
automobilismo ⓜ ow·to·mo·bee·*leez*·mo car racing
autonoleggio ⓜ ow·to·no·*le*·jo car hire
autostrada ⓕ *ow*·to·stra·da motorway • tollway
autunno ⓜ ow·*too*·no autumn
a volte a *vol*·te sometimes
avaro/a ⓜ/ⓕ a·*va*·ro/a stingy
avena ⓕ a·*ve*·na oats
avere a·*ve*·re have
— bisogno di bee·*zo*·nyo dee need
— fame ⓕ *fa*·me (to be) hungry
— fretta ⓕ *fre*·ta (to be) in a hurry
— mal ⓜ **di mare** mal dee *ma*·re (to be) seasick
— sete ⓕ *se*·te (to be) thirsty
— sonno ⓜ *so*·no (to be) sleepy
avventura ⓕ a·ven·*too*·ra adventure
avvertire a·ver·*tee*·re warn
avvocato/a ⓜ/ⓕ a·vo·*ka*·to/a lawyer
azzurro/a ⓜ/ⓕ a·*dzoo*·ro/a blue (light)

B

baciare ba·*cha*·re kiss
bacio ⓜ *ba*·cho kiss
bagaglio ⓜ ba·*ga*·lyo luggage
— a mano a *ma*·no carry-on luggage

— consentito kon·sen·*tee*·to baggage allowance
— in eccedenza een e·che·*den*·tsa excess bagage
bagnato/a ⓜ/ⓕ ba·*nya*·to/a wet
bagno ⓜ *ba*·nyo bath • bathroom
balcone ⓜ bal·*ko*·ne balcony
ballare ba·*la*·re dance
balletto ⓜ ba·*le*·to ballet
ballo ⓜ *ba*·lo ball (dancing) • dancing
balsamo ⓜ **per i capelli** *bal*·sa·mo per ee ka·*pe*·lee conditioner
bambino/a ⓜ/ⓕ bam·*bee*·no/a child
bambola ⓕ *bam*·bo·la doll
banca ⓕ *ban*·ka bank (money)
Bancomat ⓜ *ban*·ko·mat automatic teller machine (ATM)
bancone ⓜ ban·*ko*·ne counter (at bar)
banconota ⓕ ban·ko·*no*·ta banknote
bandiera ⓕ ban·*dye*·ra flag
bar ⓜ bar cafe
barattolo ⓜ ba·*ra*·to·lo jar
barbabietola ⓕ bar·ba·*bye*·to·la beetroot
barbiere ⓜ bar·*bye*·re barber
barca ⓕ *bar*·ka boat
basso/a ⓜ/ⓕ *ba*·so/a low • short (height)
batteria ⓕ ba·te·*ree*·a battery (for car) • drums
battesimo ⓜ ba·*te*·zee·mo baptism
batuffoli ⓜ pl **di cotone** ba·*too*·fo·lee dee ko·*to*·ne cotton balls
bebé ⓜ&ⓕ be·*be* baby
bello/a ⓜ/ⓕ *be*·lo/a beautiful • handsome • good (weather)
benessere ⓜ be·*ne*·se·re welfare (well-being)
benzina ⓕ ben·*dzee*·na gas (petrol)
bere *be*·re drink
bevanda ⓕ be·*van*·da drink
biancheria ⓕ **intima** byan·ke·*ree*·a *een*·tee·ma underwear
bianco/a ⓜ/ⓕ *byan*·ko/a white
bibbia ⓕ *bee*·bya bible
bibita ⓕ *bee*·bee·ta soft drink
biblioteca ⓕ beeb·lyo·*te*·ka library
bicchiere ⓜ bee·*kye*·re glass (drinking)
bici ⓕ **(da corsa)** *bee*·chee (da *kor*·sa) (racing) bike
bicicletta ⓕ bee·chee·*kle*·ta bicycle
bidone ⓜ bee·*do*·ne rip-off • bin
biglietteria ⓕ bee·lye·te·*ree*·a ticket office
biglietto ⓜ bee·*lye*·to ticket
— di andata e ritorno dee an·*da*·ta e ree·*tor*·no return ticket
— di solo andata dee *so*·lo an·*da*·ta one-way ticket
bilancio ⓜ bee·*lan*·cho budget
biliardo ⓜ beel·*yar*·do pool (game)
bimbo/a ⓜ/ⓕ *beem*·bo/a baby
binario ⓜ bee·*na*·ryo platform
binocolo ⓜ bee·*no*·ko·lo binoculars
biondo/a ⓜ/ⓕ *byon*·do/a blonde
birra ⓕ *bee*·ra beer
— chiara *kya*·ra lager
biscotto ⓜ bees·*ko*·to biscuit • cookie
bisogno ⓜ bee·*zo*·nyo need • necessity
bistecca ⓕ bees·*te*·ka steak (beef)
bisticcio ⓜ bees·*tee*·cho quarrel
bloccato/a ⓜ/ⓕ blo·*ka*·to/a blocked
blu bloo blue (dark)
bocca ⓕ *bo*·ka mouth
boccaglio ⓜ bo·*ka*·lyo snorkel
bollo ⓜ *bo*·lo stamp • seal
— di circolazione dee cheer·ko·la·*tsyo*·ne car registration
bordo ⓜ *bor*·do edge • border
borotalco ⓜ bo·ro·*tal*·ko baby powder
borraccia ⓕ bo·*ra*·cha water bottle
borsa ⓕ *bor*·sa bag (general)
borsetta ⓕ bor·*se*·ta handbag
bottiglia ⓕ bo·*tee*·lya bottle
bottiglieria ⓕ bo·tee·lye·*ree*·a liquor store
bottone ⓜ bo·*to*·ne button
braccio ⓜ *bra*·cho arm

brillante ⓜ/ⓕ bree·*lan*·te brilliant
bronchite ⓕ bron·*kee*·te bronchitis
bruciare broo·*cha*·re burn
brutto/a ⓜ/ⓕ *broo*·to/a ugly
buca ⓕ *boo*·ka hole • pit
— delle lettere *de*·le *le*·te·re mail box
bucatura ⓕ boo·ka·*too*·ra puncture
buddista ⓜ&ⓕ boo·*dee*·sta Buddhist
bugiardo/a ⓜ/ⓕ boo·*jar*·do/a liar
buono/a ⓜ/ⓕ *bwo*·no/a good • nice (meal)
burro ⓜ *boo*·ro butter
— per le labbra per le *la*·bra lip balm
bussola ⓕ *boo*·so·la compass
busta ⓕ **(imbottita)** *boo*·sta (eem·bo·*tee*·ta) (padded) envelope

C

cabina ⓕ ka·*bee*·na cabin • cubicle
— telefonica te·le·*fo*·nee·ka phone box
cacao ⓜ ka·*ka*·o cocoa
caccia ⓕ *ka*·cha hunting
caffè ⓜ ka·*fe* coffee
calcio ⓜ *kal*·cho soccer
calcolatrice ⓕ kal·ko·la·*tree*·che calculator
caldo ⓜ *kal*·do heat
caldo/a ⓜ/ⓕ *kal*·do/a hot
calendario ⓜ ka·len·*da*·ryo calendar
calze ⓕ pl *kal*·tse stockings
calzini ⓜ pl kal·*tsee*·nee socks
cambiare kam·*bya*·re change
cambio ⓜ *kam*·byo exchange
— valuta ⓕ va·*loo*·ta currency exchange
camera ⓕ *ka*·me·ra room
— d'aria *da*·rya tube (tyre)
— da letto da *le*·to bedroom
— doppia *do*·pya double room
— singola *seen*·go·la single room
cameriere/a ⓜ/ⓕ ka·mer·*ye*·re/a waiter
camicia ⓕ ka·*mee*·cha shirt
camion ⓜ *ka*·myon truck
camminare ka·mee·*na*·re walk
camminata ⓕ ka·mee·*na*·ta (long) walk
campagna ⓕ kam·*pa*·nya countryside
campeggiare kam·pe·*ja*·re camp
campeggio ⓜ kam·*pe*·jo campsite
campionato ⓜ kam·pyo·*na*·to championships
campo ⓜ *kam*·po field • pitch • court
— da golf da golf golf course
— da tennis da *te*·nees tennis court
cancellare kan·che·*la*·re cancel
cancello ⓜ kan·*che*·lo gate
cancro ⓜ *kan*·kro cancer
candela ⓕ kan·*de*·la candle • spark plug
cane ⓜ *ka*·ne dog
— guida *gwee*·da guide dog
canottaggio ⓜ ka·no·*ta*·jo rowing • canoeing
canottiera ⓕ ka·no·*tye*·ra singlet
cantante ⓜ/ⓕ kan·*tan*·te singer
cantare kan·*ta*·re sing
cantina ⓕ kan·*tee*·na wine cellar • winery
canzone ⓕ kan·*tso*·ne song
caparra ⓕ ka·*pa*·ra deposit (refundable)
capire ka·*pee*·re understand
capo ⓜ *ka*·po leader
Capodanno ⓜ *ka*·po·*da*·no New Year's Day
cappello ⓜ ka·*pe*·lo hat
cappotto ⓜ ka·*po*·to coat
capra ⓕ *ka*·pra goat
carabinieri ⓜ pl ka·ra·bee·*nye*·ree police (military)
caramelle ⓕ pl ka·ra·*me*·le lollies
— alla menta *a*·la *men*·ta mints
carcere ⓜ *kar*·che·re jail
carino/a ⓜ/ⓕ ka·*ree*·no/a pretty • cute
carne ⓕ *kar*·ne meat
— tritata tree·*ta*·ta mince meat
caro/a ⓜ/ⓕ *ka*·ro/a expensive
carota ⓕ ka·*ro*·ta carrot

carpentiere (m) kar·pen·*tye*·re carpenter
carrello (m) ka·*re*·lo trolley
carrozza (f) ka·*ro*·tsa carriage
— ristorante rees·to·*ran*·te dining car
carta (f) *kar*·ta paper
— d'identità dee·den·tee·*ta* identification card (ID)
— d'imbarco deem·*bar*·ko boarding pass
— di credito dee *kre*·dee·to credit card
— igienica ee·*je*·nee·ka toilet paper
— telefonica te·le·*fo*·nee·ka phone card
carte (f) pl *kar*·te cards
cartolaio (m) kar·to·*la*·yo stationer
cartolina (f) kar·to·*lee*·na postcard
cartuccia (f) kar·*too*·cha cartridge
— di ricambio del gas dee ree·*kam*·byo del gaz gas cartridge
casa (f) *ka*·za house • home
casalingo/a (m)/(f) ka·za·*leen*·go/a homemaker
cascata (f) kas·*ka*·ta waterfall
casco (m) *kas*·ko helmet
casinò (m) ka·zee·*no* casino
cassa (f) *ka*·sa cash register
cassaforte (f) ka·sa·*for*·te safe
cassetta (f) ka·*se*·ta cassette
cassiere/a (m)/(f) ka·*sye*·re/a cashier
castello (m) kas·*te*·lo castle
catena (f) ka·*te*·na chain
— di montagne dee mon·*ta*·nye mountain range
catene (f) pl **da neve** ka·*te*·ne da *ne*·ve snow chains
cattivo/a (m)/(f) ka·*tee*·vo/a bad
cattolico/a (m)/(f) ka·*to*·lee·ko/a Catholic
cavalcare ka·val·*ka*·re ride (horse)
cavallino (m) ka·va·*lee*·no pony
cavallo (m) ka·*va*·lo horse
cavi (m) pl **con morsetti** *ka*·vee kon mor·*se*·tee jumper leads
caviale (m) ka·*vya*·le caviar
caviglia (f) ka·*vee*·lya ankle
cavo (m) *ka*·vo cable
cavoletti (m) pl **di Bruxelles** ka·vo·*le*·tee dee brook·*sel* Brussels sprouts
cavolfiore (m) ka·vol·*fyo*·re cauliflower
cavolo (m) *ka*·vo·lo cabbage
ceci (m) pl *che*·chee chickpeas
celebrazione (f) che·le·bra·*tsyo*·ne celebration
celibe (m) *che*·lee·be single (man)
cellulare (m) che·loo·*la*·re mobile phone
cena (f) *che*·na dinner
centesimo (m) chen·*te*·zee·mo cent
centimetro (m) chen·*tee*·me·tro centimetre
centro (m) *chen*·tro centre
— commerciale ko·mer·*cha*·le shopping centre
— storico *sto*·ree·ko old city
— telefonico te·le·*fo*·nee·ko telephone centre
cercare cher·*ka*·re look for
cereali (m) pl che·re·*a*·lee cereal
cerotti (m) pl che·*ro*·tee Band-aids
certificato (m) cher·tee·fee·*ka*·to certificate
cestino (m) ches·*tee*·no basket
cetriolo (m) che·tree·*o*·lo cucumber
che (cosa) ke (*ko*·za) what
chi kee who
chiamata (f) kya·*ma*·ta phone call
— a carico del destinatario a *ka*·ree·ko del des·tee·na·*ta*·ryo reverse-charges call • collect call
chiaro/a (m)/(f) *kya*·ro/a light (colour)
chiave (f) *kya*·ve key
chiesa (f) *kye*·za church
chilo (m) *kee*·lo kilogram
chilometro (m) kee·*lo*·me·tro kilometre
chitarra (f) kee·*ta*·ra guitar
chiudere *kyoo*·de·re close
chiuso/a (m)/(f) *kyoo*·zo/a closed • shut • locked
ciascuno/a (m)/(f) chas·*koo*·no/a each

C

cibo ⓜ *chee*·bo food
— da bebè da be·*be* baby food
ciclismo ⓜ chee·*kleez*·mo cycling
ciclista ⓜ&ⓕ chee·*klee*·sta cyclist
ciclopista ⓕ chee·klo·*pee*·sta bike path
cidì ⓜ chee·*dee* CD
cieco/a ⓜ/ⓕ *chye*·ko/a blind
cielo ⓜ *che*·lo sky
cima ⓕ *chee*·ma peak
cinema ⓜ *chee*·ne·ma cinema
cinghia ⓕ **della ventola** *cheen*·gya *de*·la *ven*·to·la fanbelt
cintura ⓕ **di sicurezza** cheen·*too*·ra dee see·koo·*re*·tsa seatbelt
cioccolato ⓜ cho·ko·*la*·to chocolate
cipolla ⓕ chee·*po*·la onion
circo ⓜ *cheer*·ko circus
cisti ⓕ **ovarica** *chee*·stee o·*va*·ree·ka ovarian cyst
cistite ⓕ chees·*tee*·te cystitis
città ⓕ chee·*ta* city
cittadinanza ⓕ chee·ta·dee·*nan*·tsa citizenship
ciucciotto ⓜ choo·*cho*·to dummy (pacifier)
classe ⓕ *kla*·se class
— business *beez*·nes business class
— turistica too·*ree*·stee·ka economy class
classico/a ⓜ/ⓕ *kla*·see·ko/a classical
cliente ⓜ&ⓕ klee·*en*·te client
cocaina ⓕ ko·ka·*ee*·na cocaine
coda ⓕ *ko*·da queue
codice ⓜ **postale** *ko*·dee·che pos·*ta*·le postcode
cognome ⓜ ko·*nyo*·me surname
coincidenza ⓕ ko·een·chee·*den*·tsa coinicidence • connection (transport)
collant ⓕ pl ko·*lant* pantyhose
colazione ⓕ ko·la·*tsyo*·ne breakfast
collega ⓜ&ⓕ ko·*le*·ga colleague
collegio ⓜ **universitario** ko·*le*·jo oo·nee·ver·see·*ta*·ryo college
collina ⓕ ko·*lee*·na hill
collirio ⓜ ko·*lee*·ryo eye drops
collo ⓜ *ko*·lo neck
colloquio ⓜ **(selettivo)** ko·*lok*·wyo (se·le·*tee*·vo) interview
colore ⓜ ko·*lo*·re colour
colpa ⓕ *kol*·pa fault (someone's)
colpevole kol·*pe*·vo·le guilty
coltello ⓜ kol·*te*·lo knife
come *ko*·me how
cominciare ko·meen·*cha*·re begin • start
commedia ⓕ ko·*me*·dya play (theatre)
— comica *ko*·mee·ka comedy
commercio ⓜ ko·*mer*·cho trade • business studies
commissione ⓕ ko·mee·*syo*·ne commission
comodo/a ⓜ/ⓕ *ko*·mo·do/a comfortable
compagno/a ⓜ/ⓕ kom·*pa*·nyo/a companion • partner (intimate)
compenso ⓜ kom·*pen*·so fee
compleanno ⓜ kom·ple·*a*·no birthday
complesso ⓜ **rock** kom·*ple*·so rok rock group
completo/a ⓜ/ⓕ kom·*ple*·to/a booked out
comprare kom·*pra*·re buy
compreso/a ⓜ/ⓕ kom·*pre*·zo/a included
computer ⓜ **portatile** kom·*pyoo*·ter por·*ta*·tee·le laptop
comunione ⓕ ko·moo·*nyo*·ne communion
comunista ⓜ&ⓕ ko·moo·*nee*·sta communist
con kon with
— filtro ⓜ *feel*·tro filtered
concerto ⓜ kon·*cher*·to concert
condividere kon·dee·*vee*·de·re share (with)
confermare kon·fer·*ma*·re confirm (a booking)

DICTIONARY

confessione ⓕ kon·fe·*syo*·ne confession (religious)
confine ⓜ kon·*fee*·ne border
congelare kon·je·*la*·re freeze
congelato/a ⓜ/ⓕ kon·je·*la*·to/a frozen
coniglio ⓜ ko·*nee*·lyo rabbit
conoscere ko·*no*·she·re know (a person)
conservatore/conservatrice ⓜ/ⓕ kon·ser·va·*to*·re/kon·ser·va·*tree*·che conservative
consigliare kon·see·*lya*·re recommend
consolato ⓜ kon·so·*la*·to consulate
contanti ⓜ pl kon·*tan*·tee count
contare kon·*ta*·re count
conto ⓜ *kon*·to bill (account)
— in banca een *ban*·ka bank account
contraccettivi ⓜ pl kon·tra·che·*tee*·vee contraceptives
contratto ⓜ kon·*tra*·to contract
controllare kon·tro·*la*·re check
controllare kon·tro·*la*·re check
controllore ⓜ kon·tro·*lo*·re ticket collector
convalidare kon·va·lee·*da*·re validate
convento ⓜ kon·*ven*·to convent
coperta ⓕ ko·*per*·ta blanket
coperte ⓕ pl **e lenzuola** ⓕ pl ko·*per*·te e len·*zwo*·la bedding
coperto ⓜ ko·*per*·to cover charge (restaurant)
Coppa ⓕ **del Mondo** *ko*·pa del *mon*·do World Cup
coraggioso/a ⓜ/ⓕ ko·ra·*jo*·zo/a brave
corda ⓕ *kor*·da rope
— del bucato del boo·*ka*·to clothesline
corpo ⓜ *kor*·po body
corrente ⓕ ko·*ren*·te current (electricity)
correre *ko*·re·re run
corridoio ⓜ ko·ree·*do*·yo aisle (in plane, train)
corrompere ko·*rom*·pe·re bribe
corrotto/a ⓜ/ⓕ ko·*ro*·to/a corrupt
corsa ⓕ *kor*·sa ride • race
corte ⓕ *kor*·te court (legal)
corto/a ⓜ/ⓕ *kor*·to/a short (length)
cosa ⓕ *ko*·za thing • object • matter
costa ⓕ *kos*·ta coast
costare kos·*ta*·re cost
costruire kos·troo·*ee*·re build
costruttore/costruttrice ⓜ/ⓕ kos·troo·*to*·re/ko·stroo·*tree*·che builder
costume ⓜ **da bagno** kos·*too*·me da *ba*·nyo bathing suit
cotone ⓜ ko·*to*·ne cotton
cozza ⓕ *ko*·tsa mussel
crema ⓕ *kre*·ma cream
— da barba da *bar*·ba shaving cream
— solare so·*la*·re sunscreen
crescere *kre*·she·re grow
criminalità ⓕ kree·mee·na·lee·*ta* crime (issue)
cristiano/a ⓜ/ⓕ krees·*tya*·no/a Christian
croce ⓕ *kro*·che cross (religious)
crudo/a ⓜ/ⓕ *kroo*·do/a raw
cucchiaino ⓜ koo·kya·*ee*·no teaspoon
cucchiaio ⓜ koo·*kya*·yo spoon
cucciolo ⓜ *koo*·cho·lo puppy
cucina ⓕ koo·*chee*·na kitchen
cucinare koo·chee·*na*·re cook
cucire koo·*chee*·re sew
culla ⓕ *koo*·la cot
cuoco/a ⓜ/ⓕ *kwo*·ko/a cook • chef (restaurant)
cuoio ⓜ *kwo*·yo leather
cuore ⓜ *kwo*·re heart
curare koo·*ra*·re look after
cuscino ⓜ koo·*shee*·no pillow

D

da da from • at • to • since
da solo/a ⓜ/ⓕ da *so*·lo/a alone
danno ⓜ *da*·no damage

D

dare *da*·re give
— **il benvenuto a** eel ben·ve·*noo*·to a welcome
— **un calcio** oon *kal*·cho kick
data ⓕ *da*·ta date (day)
— **di arrivo** dee a·*ree*·vo date of arrival
— **di nascita** dee *na*·shee·ta date of birth
— **di partenza** dee par·*ten*·tsa date of departure
datore/datrice ⓜ/ⓕ **di lavoro** da·*to*·re/da·*tree*·che dee la·*vo*·ro employer
dea ⓕ *de*·a goddess
debole *de*·bo·le weak
degustazione ⓕ **(dei vini)** de·goos·ta·*tsyo*·ne day *vee*·nee (wine) tasting
delitto ⓜ de·*lee*·to crime (infringement)
democrazia ⓕ de·mo·kra·*tsee*·a democracy
denaro ⓜ de·*na*·ro money
dente ⓜ *den*·te tooth (front)
denti ⓜ pl *den*·tee teeth
dentifricio ⓜ den·tee·*free*·cho toothpaste
dentista ⓜ&ⓕ den·*tee*·sta dentist
dentro *den*·tro inside
deodorante ⓜ de·o·do·*ran*·te deodorant
deposito ⓜ de·*po*·zee·to deposit (bank)
— **bagagli** ba·*ga*·lyee left luggage (office)
derubare de·roo·*ba*·re rob
desiderare de·see·de·*ra*·re wish • desire
destinazione ⓕ des·tee·na·*tsyo*·ne destination
destra *de*·stra right (direction) • right-wing
detersivo ⓜ de·ter·*see*·vo washing powder
di dee from • by • of
— **andata e ritorno** an·*da*·ta e ree·*tor*·no return (ticket)
— **destra** *de*·stra right-wing
— **fronte a** *fron*·te a opposite
— **lusso** *loo*·so luxurious
— **meno** *me*·no less
— **nuovo** *nwo*·vo again
— **più** pyoo more
— **recente** re·*chen*·te recently
— **seconda mano** se·*kon*·da *ma*·no second-hand
— **sinistra** see·*nee*·stra left-wing
— **solo andata** *so*·lo an·*da*·ta one-way ticket
diabete ⓜ dee·a·*be*·te diabetes
diaframma ⓜ dee·a·*fra*·ma diaphragm
diapositiva ⓜ dee·a·po·zee·*tee*·va slide (film)
diarrea ⓕ dee·a·*re*·a diarrhoea
diesel ⓜ *dee*·zel diesel
dieta ⓕ *dye*·ta diet
dietro *dye*·tro behind
difettoso/a ⓜ/ⓕ dee·fe·*to*·zo/a faulty
differente (da) dee·fe·*ren*·te (da) different
differenza ⓕ dee·fe·*ren*·tsa difference
— **di fuso orario** dee *foo*·zo o·*ra*·ryo time difference
difficile dee·*fee*·chee·le difficult
digitale dee·jee·*ta*·le digital
dimensioni ⓕ pl dee·men·*syo*·nee size (general)
dimenticare dee·men·tee·*ka*·re forget
dio/dea ⓜ/ⓕ *dee*·o/*de*·a god (general)
dipendente ⓜ/ⓕ dee·pen·*den*·te addicted • dependant
dipingere dee·*peen*·je·re paint
dire *dee*·re say
diretto/a ⓜ/ⓕ dee·*re*·to/a direct
direzione ⓕ dee·re·*tsyo*·ne direction
diritti ⓜ pl **umani** dee·*ree*·tee oo·*ma*·nee human rights
diritto ⓜ dee·*ree*·to/a straight • right (prerogative)
disabile dee·*za*·bee·le disabled

DICTIONARY

ischetto ⓜ dees·*ke*·to disk
computer)
iscriminazione ⓕ
ees·kree·mee·na·*tsyo*·ne
iscrimination
isinfettante ⓜ deez·een·fe·*tan*·te
isinfectant
isoccupato/a ⓜ/ⓕ
ee·zo·koo·*pa*·to/a unemployed
istributore ⓜ dee·stree·boo·*to*·re
etrol/service station
– automatico di biglietti
w·to·*ma*·tee·ko dee bee·*lye*·tee ticket
nachine
isturbo ⓜ dees·*toor*·bo trouble
isturbi ⓜ pl **da fuso orario**
ees·*toor*·bee da *foo*·zo o·*ra*·ryo
et lag
ito ⓜ *dee*·to finger
– del piede del *pye*·de toe
itta ⓕ *dee*·ta company (firm)
iversi/e ⓜ/ⓕ pl dee·*ver*·see/
ee·*ver*·se several
iverso/a dee·*ver*·so/a different •
arious
ivertente dee·ver·*ten*·te funny •
ntertaining
ivertimento ⓜ dee·ver·tee·*men*·to
un
ivertirsi dee·ver·*teer*·see enjoy
oneself)
ivorziato/a ⓜ/ⓕ dee·vor·*tsya*·to/a
ivorced
ivisa ⓕ dee·*vee*·za uniform
occia ⓕ *do*·cha shower
ocumenti ⓜ pl do·koo·*men*·tee
apers
ocumento ⓜ **d'identità**
o·koo·*men*·to dee·den·tee·*ta*
dentification
ogana ⓕ do·*ga*·na customs
olce ⓜ *dol*·che sweet • dessert
olce *dol*·che sweet • soft
olciumi ⓜ pl dol·*choo*·mee candy
ollaro ⓜ *do*·la·ro dollar
olore ⓜ do·*lo*·re pain

dolori ⓜ pl **mestruali** do·*lo*·ree
me·*stroo*·a·lee period pain
doloroso/a ⓜ/ⓕ do·lo·*ro*·zo/a
painful • sore
domanda ⓕ do·*man*·da question
domandare do·man·*da*·re ask (a
question)
domani do·*ma*·nee tomorrow
— mattina ma·*tee*·na tomorrow
morning
— pomeriggio po·me·*ree*·jo tomorrow
afternoon
— sera *se*·ra tomorrow evening
donna ⓕ *do*·na woman
— d'affari da·*fa*·ree businesswoman
dopo *do*·po after
dopobarba ⓜ do·po·*bar*·ba
aftershave
dopodomani do·po·do·*ma*·nee day
after tomorrow
doppio/a ⓜ/ⓕ *do*·pyo/a double
dormire dor·*mee*·re sleep
dose ⓕ *do*·ze dose
— eccessiva e·che·*see*·va overdose
dove *do*·ve where
dozzina ⓕ do·*dzee*·na dozen
dramma ⓜ *dra*·ma drama
droga ⓕ *dro*·ga drug/drugs
drogheria ⓕ dro·ge·*ree*·a grocery
due *doo*·e two
— letti *le*·tee twin/two beds
— volte *vol*·te twice
duomo ⓜ *dwo*·mo cathedral
durante doo·*ran*·te during
duro/a ⓜ/ⓕ *doo*·ro/a hard (not soft)

E

e e and
ebreo/a ⓜ/ⓕ e·*bre*·o/a Jewish
ecografia ⓕ e·ko·gra·*fee*·a
ultrasound
economico/a ⓜ/ⓕ e·ko·*no*·mee·ko/a
cheap
edicola ⓕ e·*dee*·ko·la newsagency
edificio ⓜ e·dee·*fee*·cho building
egoista ⓜ/ⓕ e·go·*ee*·sta selfish

F

elenco ⓜ **telefonico** e·*len*·ko te·le·*fo*·nee·ko phone book
elettricista ⓜ&ⓕ e·le·tree·*chee*·sta electrician
elettricità ⓕ e·le·tree·chee·*ta* electricity
elezioni ⓕ pl e·le·*tsyo*·nee elections • polls
emergenza ⓕ e·mer·*jen*·tsa emergency
emicrania ⓕ e·mee·*kra*·nya migraine
emotivo/a ⓜ/ⓕ e·mo·*tee*·vo/a emotional
energia ⓕ **(nucleare)** en·er·*jee*·a (noo·kle·*a*·re) (nuclear) energy
enorme e·*nor*·me huge
entrare en·*tra*·re enter
entrata ⓕ en·*tra*·ta entry
entro (un'ora) *en*·tro (oon·*o*·ra) within (an hour)
epatite ⓕ e·pa·*tee*·te hepatitis
epilessia ⓕ e·pee·le·*see*·a epilepsy
erba ⓕ *er*·ba grass • pot (dope)
erbe ⓕ pl *er*·be herbs
erborista ⓜ&ⓕ er·bo·*ree*·sta herbalist
eroina ⓕ e·ro·*ee*·na heroin
erotico/a ⓜ/ⓕ e·*ro*·tee·ko/a sexy
errore ⓜ e·*ro*·re mistake
esame ⓜ e·*za*·me test
escluso/a ⓜ/ⓕ es·*kloo*·zo/a excluded
escursione ⓕ es·koor·*syo*·ne excursion • trip
— a piedi a *pye*·dee hike
escursionismo ⓜ es·koor·syo·*neez*·mo touring
— a piedi a *pye*·dee hiking
esecuzione ⓕ e·se·koo·*tsyo*·ne performance
esempio ⓜ e·*zem*·pyo example
esperienza ⓕ es·pe·*ryen*·tsa experience
esperimenti ⓜ pl **nucleari** es·pe·ree·*men*·tee noo·kle·*a*·ree nuclear testing
esposimetro ⓜ es·po·*zee*·me·tro light meter
esposizione ⓕ es·po·zee·*tsyo*·ne exhibition
espresso/a ⓜ/ⓕ es·*pre*·so/a express
essere *e*·se·re be
— d'accordo da·*kor*·do agree
— raffreddato/a ⓜ/ⓕ ra·fre·*da*·to/a have a cold
est ⓜ est east
estate ⓕ es·*ta*·te summer
estetista ⓜ&ⓕ es·te·*tee*·sta beautician
estero/a ⓜ/ⓕ *es*·te·ro/a foreign
età ⓕ e·*ta* age
etichetta ⓕ e·tee·*ke*·ta luggage tag
etto ⓜ *e*·to 100 grams
europeo/a ⓜ/ⓕ e·oo·ro·*pe*·o/a European
eutanasia ⓕ e·oo·ta·na·*zee*·a euthanasia

F

fabbrica ⓕ *fa*·bree·ka factory
faccia ⓕ *fa*·cha face
facile *fa*·chee·le easy
fagioli ⓜ pl fa·*jo*·lee beans
fame ⓕ *fa*·me hunger
famiglia ⓕ fa·*mee*·lya family
famoso/a ⓜ/ⓕ fa·*mo*·zo/a famous
fango ⓜ *fan*·go mud
fantastico/a ⓜ/ⓕ fan·*tas*·tee·ko/a great
fantino ⓜ fan·*tee*·no jockey
fare *fa*·re do • make
— il tifo eel *tee*·fo support (cheer on)
— l'autostop *low*·to·stop hitchhike
— la barba la *bar*·ba shave
— male *ma*·le hurt
— una camminata *oo*·na ka·mee·*na*·ta hike
— una foto *oo*·na *fo*·to take a photo
farfalla ⓕ far·*fa*·la butterfly
fari ⓜ pl *fa*·ree headlights
farina ⓕ fa·*ree*·na flour
farmacia ⓕ far·ma·*chee*·a pharmacy

farmacista ⓜ&ⓕ far·ma·*chee*·sta chemist
fascia ⓕ *fa*·sha bandage
fatto/a ⓜ/ⓕ *fa*·to/a made
— a mano a *ma*·no handmade
— di (cotone) dee (ko·*to*·ne) made of (cotton)
fattoria ⓕ fa·to·*ree*·a farm
fazzolettini ⓜ pl **di carta** fa·tso·le·*tee*·nee dee *kar*·ta tissues
fazzoletto ⓜ fa·tso·*le*·to handkerchief
febbre ⓕ *fe*·bre temperature (fever)
— da fieno da *fye*·no hay fever
federa ⓕ *fe*·de·ra pillowcase
fegato ⓜ *fe*·ga·to liver
felice ⓜ&ⓕ fe·*lee*·che happy
ferita ⓕ fe·*ree*·ta injury
ferito/a ⓜ/ⓕ fe·*ree*·to/a injured
fermare fer·*ma*·re stop
fermarsi fer·*mar*·see stay (at a hotel)
fermata ⓕ fer·*ma*·ta stop
fermo ⓜ **posta** *fer*·mo *pos*·ta poste restante
ferramenta ⓕ fe·ra·*men*·ta hardware store
ferro ⓜ *fe*·ro iron
— da stiro da *stee*·ro iron (clothes)
festa ⓕ *fes*·ta festival • public holiday • party (celebration)
fetta ⓕ *fe*·ta slice
fiammiferi ⓜ pl fya·*mee*·fe·ree matches
fico ⓜ *fee*·ko fig
fidanzamento ⓜ fee·dan·tsa·*men*·to engagement (couple)
fidanzato/a ⓜ/ⓕ fee·dan·*tsa*·to/a fiance(e)
figlia ⓕ *fee*·lya daughter
figlio ⓜ *fee*·lyo son
film ⓜ feelm movie
filo ⓜ *fee*·lo thread (sewing)
— dentario den·*ta*·ree·o dental floss
fine ⓕ *fee*·ne end
fine settimana ⓜ *fee*·ne se·tee·*ma*·na weekend
finestra ⓕ fee·*nes*·tra window (general)
finestrino ⓜ fee·nes·*tree*·no window (car, plane)
finire fee·*nee*·re end • finish • run out of
finito/a ⓜ/ⓕ fee·*nee*·to finished
fino a (giugno) *fee*·no a (*joo*·nyo) until (June)
fiocchi ⓜ pl **di mais** *fyo*·kee dee *ma*·ees cornflakes
fioraio ⓜ&ⓕ fyo·*ra*·yo florist
fiore ⓜ *fyo*·re flower
firma ⓕ *feer*·ma signature
fiume ⓜ *fyoo*·me river
fluido ⓜ **idratante** *floo*·ee·do ee·dra·*tan*·te hydrating fluid
foglia ⓕ *fo*·lya leaf
fondo ⓜ *fon*·do bottom
fondo/a ⓜ/ⓕ *fon*·do/a deep
footing ⓜ *foo*·teeng jogging • running (sport)
forbici ⓕ pl *for*·bee·chee scissors
forchetta ⓕ for·*ke*·ta fork
foresta ⓕ fo·*res*·ta forest
forma ⓕ *for*·ma shape
formaggio ⓜ for·*ma*·jo cheese
— fresco *fres*·ko cream cheese
formica ⓕ for·*mee*·ka ant
forno ⓜ *for*·no oven
— a microonde a mee·kro·*on*·de microwave (oven)
forse *for*·se maybe
forte ⓜ/ⓕ *for*·te strong • loud
fortuna ⓕ for·*too*·na chance • luck
fortunato/a ⓜ/ⓕ for·too·*na*·to/a lucky
forza ⓕ *for*·tsa strength • force
forze ⓕ pl **armate** *for*·tse ar·*ma*·te military
foto ⓕ *fo*·to photo
fotografia ⓕ fo·to·gra·*fee*·a photography
fotografo ⓜ fo·*to*·gra·fo photographer • camera shop

G

fra fra between
— poco *po*·ko soon
fragile *fra*·jee·le fragile
fragola ⓕ *fra*·go·la strawberry
francobollo ⓜ fran·ko·*bo*·lo stamp
fratello ⓜ fra·*te*·lo brother
freccia ⓕ *fre*·cha indicator (car)
freddo/a ⓜ/ⓕ *fre*·do/a cold
freno ⓜ *fre*·no brake
fresco/a ⓜ/ⓕ *fres*·ko/a fresh
fretta ⓕ *fre*·ta hurry
friggere *free*·je·re fry
frigo ⓜ *free*·go fridge
frigobar ⓜ *free*·go·bar bar fridge • minibar
frigorifero ⓜ free·go·*ree*·fe·ro refrigerator
frizione ⓕ free·*tsyo*·ne clutch
frutta ⓕ *froo*·ta fruit
— secca *se*·ka dried fruit
fruttivendolo/a ⓜ/ⓕ froo·tee·*ven*·do·lo/a greengrocer
fumare foo·*ma*·re smoke
fumato/a ⓜ/ⓕ foo·*ma*·to/a smoked • stoned (drugged)
funerale ⓜ foo·ne·*ra*·le funeral
fungo ⓜ *foon*·go mushroom
funivia ⓕ foo·nee·*vee*·a cable car
fuoco ⓜ *fwo*·ko fire
fuori *fwo*·ree outside
furgone ⓜ foor·*go*·ne van
futuro ⓜ foo·*too*·ro future

G

gabinetto ⓜ **(pubblico)** ga·bee·*ne*·to (*poo*·blee·ko) (public) toilet
galleria ⓕ **d'arte** ga·le·*ree*·a *dar*·te art gallery
Galles ⓜ *ga*·les Wales
gamba ⓕ *gam*·ba leg (body part)
gambero ⓜ *gam*·be·ro prawn
gara ⓜ *ga*·ra race (sport) • competition
garage ⓜ ga·*raj* garage
gas ⓜ gaz gas (for cooking)
gasolio ⓜ ga·*zo*·lyo diesel
gastroenterite ⓕ gas·tro·en·te·*ree*·te gastroenteritis
gattino ⓜ ga·*tee*·no kitten
gatto ⓜ *ga*·to cat
gelateria ⓕ je·la·te·*ree*·a ice-cream parlour
gelato ⓜ je·*la*·to ice cream
geloso/a ⓜ/ⓕ je·*lo*·zo/a jealous
gemelli/e ⓜ/ⓕ pl je·*me*·lee/je·*me*·le twins
generale je·ne·*ra*·le general
gengiva ⓕ jen·*jee*·va gum (mouth)
genitori ⓜ pl je·nee·*to*·ree parents
gente ⓕ *jen*·te people
gentile jen·*tee*·le kind • nice (person)
germogli ⓜ pl **(di soia)** jer·*mo*·lyee (dee *so*·ya) beansprouts
gettone ⓜ je·*to*·ne token
ghiaccio ⓜ *gya*·cho ice
già ja already
giacca ⓕ *ja*·ka jacket
giallo/a ⓜ/ⓕ *ja*·lo/a yellow
Giappone ⓜ ja·*po*·ne Japan
giardinaggio ⓜ jar·dee·*na*·jo gardening
giardino ⓜ jar·*dee*·no garden
— zoologico dzo·o·*lo*·jee·ko zoo
ginecologo/a ⓜ/ⓕ jee·ne·*ko*·lo·go/a gynaecologist
ginnastica ⓕ jee·*nas*·tee·ka gymnastics
ginocchio ⓜ jee·*no*·kyo knee
giocare jo·*ka*·re play
— a calcio a *kal*·cho play soccer
gioco ⓜ *jo*·ko game (play)
— elettronico e·le·*tro*·nee·ko computer game
gioielli ⓜ pl jo·*ye*·lee jewellery
giornale ⓜ jor·*na*·le newspaper
giornalista ⓜ&ⓕ jor·na·*lee*·sta journalist
giorno ⓜ *jor*·no day
giovane *jo*·va·ne young
girare jee·*ra*·re turn
gita ⓕ *jee*·ta tour • trip
giù joo down

giubbotto ⓜ **di salvataggio** joo·*bo*·to dee sal·va·*ta*·jo life jacket
giudice ⓜ *joo*·dee·che judge
giudò ⓜ joo·*do* judo
giusto/a ⓜ/ⓕ *joo*·sto/a right (correct)
gola ⓕ *go*·la throat
gomma ⓕ *go*·ma tyre
— da masticare da ma·stee·*ka*·re (chewing) gum
gonfiore ⓜ gon·*fyo*·re swelling
gonna ⓕ *go*·na skirt
governo ⓜ go·*ver*·no government
grammi ⓜ pl *gra*·mee grams
grande *gran*·de big • large
grande magazzino ⓜ *gran*·de ma·ga·*dzee*·no department store
grandinata ⓕ gran·dee·*na*·ta hailstorm
grandine ⓕ *gran*·dee·ne hail
grasso/a ⓜ/ⓕ *gra*·so/a fat
gratuito/a ⓜ/ⓕ gra·*too*·ee·to/a free (gratis) • complimentary
grigio/a ⓜ/ⓕ *gree*·jo/a grey
grotta ⓕ *gro*·ta cave
gruppo ⓜ *groo*·po band (music)
— sanguigno san·*gwee*·nyo blood group
guanti ⓜ *gwan*·tee gloves
guardare gwar·*da*·re look • watch
— le vetrine le ve·*tree*·ne go window-shopping
guardaroba ⓜ gwar·da·*ro*·ba cloakroom
guastarsi gwas·*tar*·see break down
guastato/a ⓜ/ⓕ gwas·*ta*·to/a broken down
guasto/a ⓜ/ⓕ *gwa*·sto/a off (food)
guerra ⓕ *gwe*·ra war
guida ⓕ *gwee*·da guide (person) • guidebook
— agli spettacoli *a*·lyee spe·*ta*·ko·lee entertainment guide
— audio *ow*·dyo guide (audio)
— turistica too·*ree*·stee·ka guidebook
guidare gwee·*da*·re drive
gustoso/a ⓜ/ⓕ goo·*sto*·zo/a tasty

H

halal a·*lal* halal
hashish ⓜ *a*·sheesh hash
hockey ⓜ *o*·kee hockey
— su ghiaccio soo *gya*·cho ice hockey

I

idiota ⓜ&ⓕ ee·*dyo*·ta idiot
idratante ⓜ ee·dra·*tan*·te moisturiser
ieri *ye*·ree yesterday
illegale ee·le·*ga*·le illegal
imbarazzato/a ⓜ/ⓕ eem·ba·ra·*tsa*·to/a embarrassed
imbrogliare eem·bro·*lya*·re cheat
immersione ⓕ ee·mer·*syo*·ne submersion • dive
— in apnea een ap·*ne*·a snorkelling
— subacquea soo·*ba*·kwe·a scuba diving
immigrazione ⓕ ee·mee·gra·*tsyo*·ne immigration
imparare eem·pa·*ra*·re learn
impermeabile eem·per·me·*a*·bee·le waterproof
impiegato/a ⓜ/ⓕ eem·pye·*ga*·to/a employee • office worker
importante eem·por·*tan*·te important
impossibile eem·po·*see*·bee·le impossible
in een in • to
— bianco e nero *byan*·ko e *ne*·ro B&W
— buona salute *bwo*·na sa·*loo*·te in good health
— fondo *fon*·do at the bottom • after all
— fretta *fre*·ta in a hurry
— lista d'attesa *lee*·sta da·*te*·za standby (ticket)
— omaggio o·*ma*·jo complimentary (free gift)
— ritardo ree·*tar*·do late
— salita sa·*lee*·ta uphill

— **sciopero** ⓜ *sho*·pe·ro on strike
— **vendita** *ven*·dee·ta on sale
inalatore ⓜ ee·na·la·*to*·re inhaler
incidente ⓜ een·chee·*den*·te accident • crash
incinta een·*cheen*·ta pregnant
incontrare een·kon·*tra*·re meet
incrocio ⓜ een·*kro*·cho intersection
indicare een·dee·*ka*·re point
indigestione ⓕ een·dee·je·*styo*·ne indigestion
indirizzo ⓜ een·dee·*ree*·tso address
indossare een·do·*sa*·re wear
indù ⓜ&ⓕ een·*doo* Hindu
industria ⓕ een·*doos*·trya industry
infermiere/a ⓜ/ⓕ een·fer·*mye*·re/a nurse
infezione ⓕ een·fe·*tsyo*·ne infection
infiammazione ⓕ een·fya·ma·*tsyo*·ne inflammation
influenza ⓕ een·floo·*en*·tsa flu • influenza
informatica ⓕ een·for·*ma*·tee·ka IT
informazioni ⓕ pl een·for·ma·*tsyo*·nee information
infortunato/a ⓜ/ⓕ een·for·too·*na*·to/a injured
ingegnere ⓜ&ⓕ een·je·*nye*·re engineer
Inghilterra ⓕ een·geel·*te*·ra England
inglese een·*gle*·ze English
ingorgo ⓜ een·*gor*·go traffic jam
ingrediente ⓜ een·gre·*dyen*·te ingredient
ingresso ⓜ een·*gre*·so cover charge (venue) • entrance
iniezione ⓕ ee·nye·*tsyo*·ne injection
inizio ⓜ ee·*nee*·tsyo start (beginning)
innocente ee·no·*chen*·te innocent
inquinamento ⓜ een·kwee·na·*men*·to pollution
insalata ⓕ een·sa·*la*·ta salad
insegnante ⓜ&ⓕ een·sen·*yan*·te teacher (general)
insetto ⓜ een·*se*·to insect
insieme een·*sye*·me together
insolito/a ⓜ/ⓕ een·*so*·lee·to/a unusual
interessante een·te·re·*san*·te interesting
internazionale een·ter·na·tsyo·*na*·le international
Internet (point) ⓜ *een*·ter·net (poynt) internet (cafe)
interprete ⓜ/ⓕ een·*ter*·pre·te interpreter
interurbano/a ⓜ/ⓕ een·ter·oor·*ba*·no/a long-distance (bus)
intervallo ⓜ een·ter·*va*·lo intermission
intervento ⓜ een·ter·*ven*·to operation (medical) • intervention (police) • speech
intossicazione ⓕ **alimentare** een·to·see·ka·*tsyo*·ne a·lee·men·*ta*·re food poisoning
inverno ⓜ een·*ver*·no winter
invitare een·vee·*ta*·re invite
io *ee*·o I
isola ⓕ *ee*·zo·la island
istruttore/istrutrice ⓜ/ⓕ ee·stroo·*to*·re/ee·stroo·*tree*·che instructor (general)
istruzione ⓕ ees·troo·*tsyo*·ne education
itinerario ⓜ ee·tee·ne·*ra*·ryo itinerary • route
— **escursionistico** es·koor·syo·*nee*·stee·ko hiking route
IVA ⓕ *ee*·va sales tax

K

kiwi ⓜ *kee*·wee kiwifruit
kosher *ka*·sher kasher

L

là la there
labbra ⓕ pl *la*·bra lips
laboratorio ⓜ la·bo·ra·*to*·ryo workshop

ladro/a ⓜ/ⓕ *la*·dro/a thief
lago ⓜ *la*·go lake
lamentarsi la·men·*tar*·see complain
lamette ⓕ pl **(da barba)** la·*me*·te (da *bar*·ba) razor blades
lampadina ⓕ lam·pa·*dee*·na light bulb
lampone ⓜ lam·*po*·ne raspberry
lana ⓕ *la*·na wool
lardo ⓜ *lar*·do lard
largo/a ⓜ/ⓕ *lar*·go/a wide
lassativi ⓜ pl la·sa·*tee*·vee laxatives
lato ⓜ *la*·to side
latte ⓜ *la*·te milk
— di soia dee *so*·ya soy milk
— scremato skre·*ma*·to skimmed milk
lattuga ⓕ la·*too*·ga lettuce
lavaggio ⓜ **a secco** la·*va*·jo a *se*·ko dry cleaning
lavanderia la·van·de·*ree*·a laundry (room)
— a gettone je·*to*·ne laundrette
lavare la·*va*·re wash (something)
lavarsi la·*var*·see wash (oneself)
lavatrice ⓕ la·va·*tree*·che washing machine
lavorare la·vo·*ra*·re work
— in proprio een *pro*·pryo (to be) self-employed
lavoratore/lavoratrice ⓜ/ⓕ la·vo·ra·*to*·re/la·vo·ra·*tree*·che worker
lavoro ⓜ la·*vo*·ro job • occupation • work
legale le·*ga*·le legal
legge ⓕ *le*·je law
leggere *le*·je·re read
leggero/a ⓜ/ⓕ le·*je*·ro/a light (not heavy)
legna ⓕ **(da ardere)** *le*·nya (da *ar*·de·re) (fire)wood
legno ⓜ *le*·nyo wood
legume ⓜ le·*goo*·me legume
lei lay she
Lei sg pol lay you
lentamente len·ta·*men*·te slowly
lenti ⓕ pl **a contatto** *len*·tee a kon·*ta*·to contact lenses
lenticchia ⓕ len·*tee*·kya lentil
lento/a ⓜ/ⓕ *len*·to/a slow
lenzuolo ⓜ len·*tswo*·lo sheet (bed)
lesbica ⓕ *lez*·bee·ka lesbian
lettera ⓕ *le*·te·ra letter
letto ⓜ *le*·to bed
— matrimoniale ma·tree·mo·*nya*·le double bed
libero/a ⓜ/ⓕ *lee*·be·ro/a free (not bound) • vacant
libreria ⓕ lee·bre·*ree*·a bookshop
libretto ⓜ lee·*bre*·to booklet
— di circolazione dee cheer·ko·la·*tsyo*·ne car owner's title
libro ⓜ *lee*·bro book
licenza ⓕ lee·*chen*·tsa permit
limetta ⓕ lee·*me*·ta lime (fruit) • nail file
limite ⓜ **di velocità** *lee*·mee·te dee ve·lo·chee·*ta* speed limit
limonata ⓕ lee·mo·*na*·ta lemonade
limone ⓜ lee·*mo*·ne lemon
linea ⓕ *lee*·ne·a line
— aerea a·e·re·a airline
lingua ⓕ *leen*·gwa tongue • language
lista ⓕ *lee*·sta list
— d'atteza da·*te*·za waiting list
lite ⓕ *lee*·te fight
litigare lee·tee·*ga*·re argue
litro ⓜ *lee*·tro litre
livello ⓜ lee·*ve*·lo level (tier)
livido ⓜ *lee*·vee·do bruise
locale ⓜ lo·*ka*·le bar • venue
locale lo·*ka*·le local
lontano/a ⓜ/ⓕ lon·*ta*·no/a far
loro *lo*·ro they
Loro pl pol *lo*·ro you
lozione ⓕ lo·*tsyo*·ne lotion
— abbronzante a·bron·*dzan*·te tanning lotion
lubrificante ⓜ loo·bree·fee·*kan*·te lubricant
lucchetto ⓜ loo·*ke*·to bike lock • padlock

luce ⓕ *loo*·che light
lucertola ⓕ loo·*cher*·to·la lizard
lui *loo*·ee he
lumaca ⓕ loo·*ma*·ka snail
luminoso/a ⓜ/ⓕ loo·meen·*o*·zo/a light (not dark)
luna ⓕ *loo*·na moon
— di miele dee *mye*·le honeymoon
— piena *pye*·na full moon
lungo/a ⓜ/ⓕ *loon*·go/a long
luogo ⓜ *lwo*·go place (location)
— di nascita dee *na*·shee·ta place of birth
lusso ⓜ *loo*·so luxury

M

ma ma but
macchina ⓕ *ma*·kee·na car • machine
— fotografica fo·to·*gra*·fee·ka camera
macelleria ⓕ ma·che·le·*ree*·a butcher's shop
madre ⓕ *ma*·dre mother
maestro/a ⓜ/ⓕ ma·*es*·tro/a teacher (primary school or music) • instructor (skiing)
maglietta ⓕ ma·*lye*·ta T-shirt
maglione ⓜ ma·*lyo*·ne jumper • sweater
magro/a ⓜ/ⓕ *ma*·gro/a thin • lean
mai mai never
maiale ⓜ ma·*ya*·le pig • pork
maionese ⓕ ma·yo·*ne*·ze mayonnaise
male ⓜ *ma*·le pain • harm • evil
mal ⓜ mal
— di aereo dee a·e·re·o travel sickness (air)
— di denti dee *den*·tee toothache
— di macchina dee *ma*·kee·na travel sickness (car)
— di mare dee *ma*·re travel sickness (sea)
— di pancia dee *pan*·cha stomach ache
— di testa dee *tes*·ta headache
malato/a ⓜ/ⓕ ma·*la*·to/a ill • sick
malattia ⓕ ma·la·*tee*·a disease
— venerea ve·*ne*·re·a venereal disease
mamma ⓕ *ma*·ma mum
mammografia ⓕ ma·mo·gra·*fee*·a mammogram
mancare man·*ka*·re miss • be lacking
mancia ⓕ *man*·cha tip (gratuity)
mandare man·*da*·re send
mandarino ⓜ man·da·*ree*·no mandarin
mandorla ⓕ *man*·dor·la almond
mangiare man·*ja*·re eat
manifestazione ⓕ ma·nee·fes·ta·*tsyo*·ne demonstration (protest)
mano ⓕ *ma*·no hand
manovale ⓜ&ⓕ ma·no·*va*·le manual worker
manuale ma·noo·*a*·le manual
manubrio ⓜ ma·*noo*·bryo handlebars
manzo ⓜ *man*·dzo beef
marciapiede ⓜ mar·cha·*pye*·de footpath
mare ⓜ *ma*·re sea
marea ⓕ ma·*re*·a tide
margarina ⓕ mar·ga·*ree*·na margarine
marito ⓜ ma·*ree*·to husband
marmellata ⓕ mar·me·*la*·ta jam
— d'arance da·*ran*·che marmalade
marmo ⓜ *mar*·mo marble
marrone ⓜ/ⓕ ma·*ro*·ne brown
martello ⓜ mar·*te*·lo hammer
massaggio ⓜ ma·*sa*·jo massage
materasso ⓜ ma·te·*ra*·so mattress
matita ⓕ ma·*tee*·ta pencil
matrimonio ⓜ ma·tree·*mo*·nyo marriage
mattina ⓕ ma·*tee*·na morning
mazzuolo ⓜ ma·*tswo*·lo mallet
meccanico ⓜ&ⓕ me·*ka*·nee·ko mechanic
medicina ⓕ me·dee·*chee*·na medicine
medicinale ⓜ me·dee·chee·*na*·le drug (medicinal)

medico ⓜ *me*·dee·ko doctor
meditazione ⓕ me·dee·ta·*tsyo*·ne meditation
mela ⓕ *me*·la apple
melanzana ⓕ me·lan·*dza*·na aubergine • eggplant
melodia ⓕ me·lo·*dee*·a tune
melone ⓜ me·*lo*·ne melon
membro ⓜ *mem*·bro member
mendicante ⓜ&ⓕ men·dee·*kan*·te beggar
meno *me*·no less
menù ⓜ me·*noo* menu
meraviglioso/a ⓜ/ⓕ me·ra·vee·*lyo*·zo/a wonderful
mercato ⓜ mer·*ka*·to market
merletto ⓜ mer·*le*·to lace
mescolare mes·ko·*la*·re mix
mese ⓜ *me*·ze month
messa ⓕ *me*·sa Mass
messaggio ⓜ me·*sa*·jo message
mestiere ⓜ mes·*tye*·re craft (trade) • occupation (work)
mestruazione ⓕ me·stroo·a·*tsyo*·ne menstruation
metallo ⓜ me·*ta*·lo metal
metro ⓜ *me*·tro metre (distance)
metropolitana ⓕ me·tro·po·lee·*ta*·na subway
mettere *me*·te·re put
mezzanotte ⓕ *me*·dza·*no*·te midnight
mezzi ⓜ pl **di comunicazione** *me*·tsee dee ko·moo·nee·ka·*tsyo*·ne media
mezzo ⓜ *me*·dzo half
mezzogiorno ⓜ *me*·dzo·*jor*·no noon
microonda ⓕ *mee*·kro·*on*·da microwave
miele ⓜ *mye*·le honey
migliore mee·*lyo*·re better • best
millimetro ⓜ mee·*lee*·me·tro millimetre
minestra ⓕ mee·*nes*·tra soup
minibar ⓜ *mee*·nee·bar minibar • bar fridge
minuto ⓜ mee·*noo*·to minute
minuto/a ⓜ/ⓕ mee·*noo*·to/a tiny
mobili ⓜ pl *mo*·bee·lee furniture
moda ⓕ *mo*·da fashion
moderno/a ⓜ/ⓕ mo·*der*·no/a modern
moduli ⓜ pl *mo*·doo·lee paperwork
modulo ⓜ *mo*·doo·lo form (paper)
moglie ⓕ *mo*·lye wife
molestia ⓕ mo·*les*·tya harassment
molto *mol*·to very
molto/a ⓜ/ⓕ *mol*·to/a a lot (of) • many
monastero ⓜ mo·nas·*te*·ro monastery
mondo ⓜ *mon*·do world
monete ⓕ pl mo·*ne*·te coins
mononucleosi ⓜ mo·no·noo·kle·*o*·zee glandular fever
montagna ⓕ mon·*ta*·nya mountain
monumento ⓜ mo·noo·*men*·to monument
morbillo ⓜ mor·*bee*·lo measles
morire mo·*ree*·re die
morso ⓜ *mor*·so bite (dog)
morto/a ⓜ/ⓕ *mor*·to/a dead
mosca ⓕ *mos*·ka fly
moschea ⓕ mos·*ke*·a mosque
mostrare mos·*tra*·re show
moto ⓕ *mo*·to motorbike
motore ⓜ mo·*to*·re engine
motoscafo ⓜ mo·to·*ska*·fo motorboat
mucca ⓕ *moo*·ka cow
mughetto ⓜ moo·*ge*·to thrush (medical)
multa ⓕ *mool*·ta fine (payment)
muro ⓜ *moo*·ro wall (outer)
muscolo ⓜ *moo*·sko·lo muscle
museo ⓜ moo·*ze*·o museum
musica ⓕ *moo*·zee·ka music
musicista ⓜ&ⓕ moo·zee·*chee*·sta musician
— di strada dee *stra*·da busker
musulmano/a ⓜ/ⓕ moo·sool·*ma*·no/a Muslim

muta ⓕ di subacqueo *moo*·ta dee soo·*ba*·kwe·o wetsuit
muto/a ⓜ/ⓕ *moo*·to/a mute

N

narrativa ⓕ na·ra·*tee*·va fiction
naso ⓜ *na*·zo nose
Natale ⓜ na·*ta*·le Christmas
natura ⓕ na·*too*·ra nature
nausea ⓕ *now*·ze·a nausea
— mattutina ma·too·*tee*·na morning sickness
nave ⓕ *na*·ve ship • boat
nazionale na·tsyo·*na*·le national
nazionalità ⓕ na·tsyo·na·lee·*ta* nationality
nebbioso/a ⓜ/ⓕ ne·*byo*·zo/a foggy
necessario/a ⓜ/ⓕ ne·che·*sa*·ryo/a necessary
negozio ⓜ ne·*go*·tsyo shop
— da campeggio da kam·*pe*·jo camping store
— di abbigliamento dee a·*bee*·lya·men·to clothing store
— di articoli sportivi dee ar·*tee*·ko·lee spor·*tee*·vee sports store
— di giocattoli dee jo·*ka*·to·lee toyshop
— di scarpe dee *skar*·pe shoe shop
— di souvenir dee *soo*·ve·neer souvenir shop
nero/a ⓜ/ⓕ *ne*·ro/a black
nessuno/a dei due ⓜ/ⓕ ne·*soo*·no/a day *doo*·e neither
neve ⓕ *ne*·ve snow
nido ⓜ *nee*·do nest • childminding (group)
niente *nyen*·te nothing • none
nipote ⓜ&ⓕ nee·*po*·te grandchild
no no no
noce ⓕ *no*·che nut • walnut
— di acagiù dee a·ka·*joo* cashew
nodulo ⓜ *no*·doo·lo lump
noi noy we
noioso/a ⓜ/ⓕ no·*yo*·zo/a boring
noleggiare no·le·*ja*·re hire
nome ⓜ *no*·me name
non non no • not
— ancora an·*ko*·ra not yet
— fumatore foo·ma·*to*·re nonsmoking
— diretto/a ⓜ/ⓕ dee·*re*·to/a nondirect
nonna ⓕ *no*·na grandmother
nonno ⓜ *no*·no grandfather
nord ⓜ nord north
normale nor·*ma*·le regular
notizie ⓕ pl no·*tee*·tsye news
notte ⓕ *no*·te night
nubile ⓕ *noo*·bee·le single (woman)
numero ⓜ *noo*·me·ro number
— di camera dee *ka*·me·ra room number
— di targa dee *tar*·ga licence plate number
— di telefono dee te·*le*·fo·no telephone number
nuotare nwo·*ta*·re swim
nuoto ⓜ *nwo*·to swimming
Nuova Zelanda ⓕ *nwo*·va dze·*lan*·da New Zealand
nuovo/a ⓜ/ⓕ *nwo*·vo/a new
nuvola ⓕ *noo*·vo·la cloud
nuvoloso/a ⓜ/ⓕ noo·vo·*lo*·zo/a cloudy

O

obiettivo ⓜ o·bye·*tee*·vo lens • objective
occhiali ⓜ pl o·*kya*·lee glasses (spectacles)
— da sci da shee goggles (skiing)
— da sole da *so*·le sunglasses
occhio ⓜ *o*·kyo eye
oceano ⓜ o·*che*·a·no ocean
odore ⓜ o·*do*·re smell
oggetti ⓜ pl o·*je*·tee articles • things
— d'artigianato dar·tee·ja·*na*·to handicrafts
— di valore dee va·*lo*·re valuables
— in ceramica een che·*ra*·mee·ka pottery
oggi *o*·jee today

olio ⓜ *o*·lyo oil
— d'oliva do·*lee*·va olive oil
oliva ⓕ o·*lee*·va olive
ombra ⓕ *om*·bra shadow • shade
ombrello ⓜ om·*bre*·lo umbrella
omeopatia ⓕ o·me·o·pa·*tee*·a homeopathy
omosessuale ⓜ&ⓕ o·mo·se·*swa*·le homosexual
onda ⓕ *on*·da wave
opera ⓕ *o*·pe·ra work (of art)
— lirica *lee*·ree·ka opera
operaio/a ⓜ/ⓕ o·pe·*ra*·yo/a factory worker
operatore/operatrice ⓜ/ⓕ o·pe·ra·*to*·re/o·pe·ra·*tree*·che operator
opinione ⓕ o·pee·*nyo*·ne opinion
oppure o·*poo*·re or • otherwise • or else
ora ⓕ *o*·ra hour
orario ⓜ o·*ra*·ryo timetable
— di apertura dee a·per·*too*·ra opening hours
— ridotto ree·*do*·to part-time
orchestra ⓕ or·*kes*·tra orchestra
ordinare or·dee·*na*·re order
ordinario/a ⓜ/ⓕ or·dee·*na*·ryo/a ordinary
ordine ⓜ *or*·dee·ne order
orecchini ⓜ pl o·re·*kee*·nee earrings
orecchio ⓜ o·*re*·kyo ear
originale ⓜ/ⓕ o·ree·jee·*na*·le original
oro ⓜ *o*·ro gold
orologio ⓜ o·ro·*lo*·jo clock • watch
orrendo/a ⓜ/ⓕ o·*ren*·do/a awful
ospedale ⓜ os·pe·*da*·le hospital
ospitalità ⓕ os·pee·ta·lee·*ta* hospitality
ossigeno ⓜ o·*see*·je·no oxygen
osso ⓜ *o*·so bone
ostello ⓜ **della gioventù** os·*te*·lo *de*·la jo·ven·*too* youth hostel
osteria ⓕ os·te·*ree*·a pub
ostrica ⓕ *o*·stree·ka oyster
ottimo/a ⓜ/ⓕ *o*·tee·mo/a excellent • great
ovest ⓜ *o*·vest west

P

pacchetto ⓜ pa·*ke*·to parcel • packet • package
pace ⓕ *pa*·che peace
padella ⓕ pa·*de*·la frying pan
padre ⓜ *pa*·dre father
padrone/padrona ⓜ/ⓕ **di casa** pa·*dro*·ne/pa·*dro*·na dee *ka*·za landlord/landlady
paese ⓜ pa·*e*·ze country (nation)
Paesi Bassi ⓜ pl pa·*e*·zee *ba*·see Netherlands
pagamento ⓜ pa·ga·*men*·to payment
pagare pa·*ga*·re pay
pagina ⓕ *pa*·jee·na page
paio ⓜ *pa*·yo pair (couple)
palazzo ⓜ pa·*la*·tso palace
palcoscenico ⓜ pal·ko·*she*·nee·ko stage
palestra ⓕ pa·*le*·stra gym
palla ⓕ *pa*·la ball (sports)
pallacanestro ⓕ pa·la·ka·*ne*·stro basketball
pallamuro ⓕ pa·la·*moo*·ro handball
pallavolo ⓕ pa·la·*vo*·lo volleyball
pallone ⓜ pa·*lo*·ne ball (inflated)
pancetta ⓕ pan·*che*·ta bacon
pane ⓜ *pa*·ne bread
— a pasta acida a *pas*·ta *a*·chee·da sourdough bread
— di segala dee *se*·ga·la rye bread
— integrale een·te·*gra*·le wholemeal bread
— tostato tos·*ta*·to toast
panetteria ⓕ pa·ne·te·*ree*·a bakery
panino ⓜ pa·*nee*·no roll (bread)
panna ⓕ *pa*·na cream (food)
— acida *a*·chee·da sour cream
pannolino ⓜ pa·no·*lee*·no diaper • nappy
pantaloncini ⓜ pl pan·ta·lon·*chee*·nee shorts

P

pantaloni ⓜ pl pan·ta·*lo*·nee pants • trousers
pap test ⓜ pap test pap smear
papà ⓜ pa·*pa* dad
parabrezza ⓜ pa·ra·*bre*·dza windscreen
parcheggio ⓜ par·*ke*·jo carpark
parco ⓜ *par*·ko park
— nazionale na·tsyo·*na*·le national park
— giochi *jo*·kee playground
parlamentare ⓜ&ⓕ par·la·men·*ta*·re member of parliament
parlamento ⓜ par·la·*men*·to parliament
parlare par·*la*·re speak • talk
parola ⓕ pa·*ro*·la word
parrucchiere ⓜ pa·roo·*kye*·re beauty salon
parrucchiere/a ⓜ/ⓕ pa·roo·*kye*·re/a hairdresser
parte ⓕ *par*·te part
partenza ⓕ par·*ten*·tsa departure
partire par·*tee*·re depart • leave
partita ⓕ par·*tee*·ta game • match
partito ⓜ par·*tee*·to party (politics)
Pasqua ⓕ *pas*·kwa Easter
passaggio ⓜ pa·*sa*·jo pass (sport) • passage
passaporto ⓜ pa·sa·*por*·to passport
passatempo ⓜ pa·sa·*tem*·po hobby
passato ⓜ pa·*sa*·to past
passeggero/a ⓜ/ⓕ pa·se·*je*·ro/a passenger
passeggiata ⓕ pa·se·*ja*·ta walk
passo ⓜ *pa*·so pass (mountain)
pasta ⓕ *pas*·ta pasta • noodles
pasticceria ⓕ pa·stee·che·*ree*·a cake shop
pasto ⓜ *pas*·to meal
— freddo *fre*·do buffet (meal)
patata ⓕ pa·*ta*·ta potato
paté ⓜ pa·*te* pate (food)
patente ⓕ **(di guida)** pa·*ten*·te (dee *gwee*·da) drivers licence
pavimento ⓜ pa·vee·*men*·to floor
pazzo/a ⓜ/ⓕ *pa*·tso/a crazy
pecora ⓕ *pe*·ko·ra sheep
pedale ⓜ pe·*da*·le pedal
pedone ⓜ/ⓕ pe·*do*·ne pedestrian
pelle ⓕ *pe*·le skin
pellicola ⓕ pe·*lee*·ko·la film (for camera)
pene ⓜ *pe*·ne penis
penicillina ⓕ pe·nee·chee·*lee*·na penicillin
penna ⓕ **(a sfera)** *pe*·na (a *sfe*·ra) pen (ballpoint)
pensare pen·*sa*·re think
pensionato/a ⓜ/ⓕ pen·syo·*na*·to/a pensioner • retired
pensione ⓕ pen·*syo*·ne guesthouse • boarding house
pentola ⓕ *pen*·to·la pan
pepe ⓜ *pe*·pe pepper
peperoncino ⓜ pe·pe·ron·*chee*·no chilli
peperone ⓜ pe·pe·*ro*·ne capsicum
per per for • to • through • by
— esempio e·*zem*·pyo for example
— sempre *sem*·pre forever
pera ⓕ *pe*·ra pear
percentuale ⓕ per·chen·*twa*·le percentage
perché per·*ke* why • because
perdere *per*·de·re lose
perdonare per·do·*na*·re forgive
pericoloso/a ⓜ/ⓕ pe·ree·ko·*lo*·zo/a dangerous • unsafe
permanente ⓜ/ⓕ per·ma·*nen*·te permanent
permesso ⓜ per·*me*·so permission • permit
perso/a ⓜ/ⓕ *per*·so/a lost
persona ⓕ per·*so*·na person
personale ⓜ/ⓕ per·so·*na*·le personal
pesante pe·*zan*·te heavy
pesca ⓕ *pe*·ska fishing • peach
pesce ⓜ *pe*·she fish (food)
pesce/pesci ⓜ sg/pl *pe*·she/*pe*·shee fish (alive)
pescheria ⓕ pe·ske·*ree*·a fish shop

peso ⓜ *pe*·zo weight
petizione ⓕ pe·tee·*tsyo*·ne petition
pettine ⓜ *pe*·tee·ne comb
petto ⓜ *pe*·to chest
pezzo ⓜ *pe*·tso piece
— di antiquariato dee an·tee·kwa·*rya*·to antique
— d'artigianato dar·tee·ja·*na*·to craft (product)
piacere pya·*che*·re like
pianeta ⓜ pya·*ne*·ta planet
piano ⓜ *pya*·no floor (storey)
pianta ⓕ *pyan*·ta map • plant
piatto ⓜ *pya*·to plate
— fondo *fon*·do bowl
piatto/a ⓜ/ⓕ *pya*·to/a flat
piazza ⓕ *pya*·tsa square (town)
picchetti ⓜ pl pee·*ke*·tee pegs (tent)
piccolo/a ⓜ/ⓕ *pee*·ko·lo/a small
piccone ⓜ pee·*ko*·ne pickaxe
piccozza ⓕ pee·*ko*·tsa ice axe
pidocchi ⓜ pl pee·*do*·kee lice
piede ⓜ *pye*·de foot
pieno/a ⓜ/ⓕ *pye*·no/a full
pietra ⓕ *pye*·tra stone
pignatta ⓕ pee·*nya*·ta pot (ceramics)
pigro/a ⓜ/ⓕ *pee*·gro/a lazy
pila ⓕ *pee*·la battery
pillola ⓕ *pee*·lo·la pill • the Pill
— anticoncezionale an·tee·kon·che·tsyo·*na*·le the Pill
— del mattino dopo del ma·*tee*·no *do*·po morning after pill
ping-pong ⓜ peeng·*pong* table tennis
pinzette ⓕ pl peen·*tse*·te tweezers
pioggia ⓜ *pyo*·ja rain
piombo ⓜ *pyom*·bo lead
piscina ⓕ pee·*shee*·na swimming pool
pisello ⓜ pee·*ze*·lo pea
pista ⓕ *pee*·sta trail • track (sports) • racetrack • slope
pittore/pittrice ⓜ/ⓕ pee·*to*·re/pee·*tree*·che painter
pittura ⓕ pee·*too*·ra painting (the art)
più pyoo more
plastica ⓕ *pla*·stee·ka plastic
un po' oon po (a) little
poco/a ⓜ/ⓕ *po*·ko/a few
poesia ⓕ po·e·*zee*·a poetry
politica ⓕ po·*lee*·tee·ka politics
politico ⓜ po·*lee*·tee·ko politician
polizia ⓕ po·lee·*tsee*·a police (civilian)
polline ⓜ *po*·lee·ne pollen
pollo ⓜ *po*·lo chicken
polmoni ⓜ pl pol·*mo*·nee lungs
polso ⓜ *pol*·so wrist
polvere ⓕ *pol*·ve·re powder
pomeriggio ⓜ po·me·*ree*·jo afternoon
pomodoro ⓜ po·mo·*do*·ro tomato
pompa ⓕ pom·*pa* pump
pompelmo ⓜ pom·*pel*·mo grapefruit
ponte ⓜ *pon*·te bridge
popolare po·po·*la*·re popular
porro ⓜ *po*·ro leek
porta ⓕ *por*·ta door
portacenere ⓜ por·ta·*che*·ne·re ashtray
portafoglio ⓜ por·ta·*fo*·lyo wallet
portare por·*ta*·re bring • carry
portatile ⓜ por·*ta*·tee·le laptop
portatile por·*ta*·tee·le portable
porto ⓜ *por*·to harbour • port
posate ⓕ pl po·*za*·te cutlery
possibile po·*see*·bee·le possible
posta ⓕ *pos*·ta mail
— elettronica e·le·*tro*·nee·ka email
— ordinaria or·dee·*na*·rya surface mail
— prioritaria pree·o·ree·*ta*·rya express mail
— raccomandata ⓕ ra·ko·man·*da*·ta registered mail
posteggio ⓜ **di tassì** po·*ste*·jo dee ta·*see* taxi stand
posto ⓜ *pos*·to place • seat
— di polizia dee po·lee·*tsee*·a police station
potabile po·*ta*·bee·le drinkable

potere ⓜ po·*te*·re power (strength)
potere po·*te*·re can
povero/a ⓜ/ⓕ *po*·ve·ro/a poor
povertà ⓕ po·ver·*ta* poverty
pranzo ⓜ *pran*·dzo lunch
praticare pra·tee·*ka*·re play (sport)
— il surf eel soorf surf
prima colazione ⓕ *pree*·ma ko·la·*tsyo*·ne breakfast
preferire pre·fe·*ree*·re prefer
preferito/a ⓜ/ⓕ pre·fe·*ree*·to/a favourite
pregare pre·*ga*·re worship (pray)
preghiera ⓕ pre·*gye*·ra prayer
prendere *pren*·de·re take
— in affitto een a·*fee*·to rent
— in prestito een *pres*·tee·to borrow
prenotare pre·no·*ta*·re book (make a booking)
prenotazione ⓕ pre·no·ta·*tsyo*·ne reservation
preoccupato/a ⓜ/ⓕ pre·o·koo·*pa*·to/a worried
preparare pre·pa·*ra*·re prepare
preservativo ⓜ pre·zer·va·*tee*·vo condom
presidente ⓜ/ⓕ pre·zee·*den*·te president
pressione ⓕ pre·*syo*·ne pressure
— del sangue del *san*·gwe blood pressure
presto ⓜ/ⓕ *pres*·to early
prete ⓜ *pre*·te priest
prezioso/a ⓜ/ⓕ pre·*tsyo*·zo/a valuable
prezzemolo ⓜ pre·*tse*·mo·lo parsley
prezzo ⓜ *pre*·tso price
— d'ingresso deen·*gre*·so admission price
prigione ⓕ pree·*jo*·ne prison
prigioniero/a ⓜ/ⓕ pree·jo·*nye*·ro/a prisoner
prima *pree*·ma before
— classe ⓕ *kla*·se first class
— colazione ⓕ ko·la·*tsyo*·ne breakfast

primavera ⓕ pree·ma·*ve*·ra spring (season)
primo ministro ⓜ/ⓕ *pree*·mo mee·*nee*·stro prime minister
primo/a ⓜ/ⓕ *pree*·mo/a first
principale preen·chee·*pa*·le main
privato/a ⓜ/ⓕ pree·*va*·to/a private
problema ⓜ pro·*ble*·ma problem
— cardiaco kar·*dee*·a·ko heart condition
produrre pro·*doo*·re produce
profesore/profesoressa ⓜ/ⓕ pro·fe·*so*·re/pro·fe·so·*re*·sa teacher (general)
profitto ⓜ pro·*fee*·to profit
profondo/a ⓜ/ⓕ pro·*fon*·do/a deep
profumo ⓜ pro·*foo*·mo perfume
programma ⓜ pro·*gra*·ma program
proiettore ⓜ pro·ye·*to*·re projector
promessa ⓕ pro·*me*·sa promise
pronto/a ⓜ/ⓕ *pron*·to/a ready
pronto soccorso ⓜ *pron*·to so·*kor*·so first-aid
proprietario/a ⓜ/ⓕ pro·prye·*ta*·ryo/a owner
proroga ⓕ *pro*·ro·ga extension (visa)
prosciutto ⓜ **(cotto)** pro·*shoo*·to (*ko*·to) ham (boiled)
prossimo/a ⓜ/ⓕ *pro*·see·mo/a next
proteggere pro·*te*·je·re protect
protetto/a ⓜ/ⓕ pro·*te*·to/a protected
protestare pro·tes·*ta*·re protest
provare pro·*va*·re try (attempt)
provviste ⓕ pl pro·*vee*·ste provisions • supplies
— alimentari a·lee·men·*ta*·ree food supplies
prugna ⓕ *proo*·nya plum • prune
prurito ⓜ proo·*ree*·to itch
pugilato ⓜ poo·jee·*la*·to boxing
pulce ⓕ *pool*·che flea
pulito/a ⓜ/ⓕ poo·*lee*·to/a clean
pulizia ⓕ poo·lee·*tsee*·a cleaning
pullman ⓜ *pool*·man bus (coach)
punteggio ⓜ poon·*te*·jo score

punto ⓜ *poon*·to point
puntura ⓕ poon·*too*·ra bite (insect)
puro/a ⓜ/ⓕ *poo*·ro/a pure

Q

quaderno ⓜ kwa·*der*·no notebook
quadro ⓜ *kwa*·dro painting (canvas)
qualcosa kwal·*ko*·za something
qualcuno/a ⓜ/ⓕ kwal·*koo*·no/a someone
qualità ⓕ kwa·lee·*ta* quality
quando *kwan*·do when
quantità ⓕ kwan·tee·*ta* amount • quantity
quanto/a ⓜ/ⓕ *kwan*·to/a how much
quarantena ⓕ kwa·ran·*te*·na quarantine
quaresima ⓕ kwa·*re*·zee·ma Lent
quartiere ⓜ kwar·*tye*·re suburb
quarto ⓜ *kwar*·to quarter
questo/a ⓜ/ⓕ *kwe*·sto/a this (one)
questura ⓕ kwes·*too*·ra police headquarters
qui kwee here
quota ⓕ *kwo*·ta altitude

R

racchetta ⓕ ra·*ke*·ta racquet
raccogliere ra·*ko*·lye·re pick (up)
raccomandare ra·ko·man·*da*·re recommend
raccomandata ⓕ ra·ko·man·*da*·ta registered mail
raccontare ra·kon·*ta*·re tell
racconto ⓜ ra·*kon*·to story
radiatore ⓜ ra·dya·*to*·re radiator
rafano ⓜ *ra*·fa·no horseradish
raffreddore ⓜ ra·fre·*do*·re cold (illness)
ragazza ⓕ ra·*ga*·tsa girl(friend)
ragazzo ⓜ ra·*ga*·tso boy(friend)
ragione ⓕ ra·*jo*·ne reason
ragno ⓜ *ra*·nyo spider
rapido/a ⓜ/ⓕ *ra*·pee·do/a quick
rapinare ra·pee·*na*·re rob
rapporti ⓜ pl **protetti** ra·*por*·tee pro·*te*·tee safe sex
rapporto ⓜ ra·*por*·to relationship
raro/a ⓜ/ⓕ *ra*·ro/a rare
rasatura ⓕ ra·za·*too*·ra shave
rasoio ⓜ **(elettrico)** ra·*zo*·yo (e·*le*·tree·ko) razor
ravanello ⓜ ra·va·*ne*·lo radish
razzismo ⓜ ra·*tseez*·mo racism
re ⓜ re king
realistico/a ⓜ/ⓕ re·a·*lee*·stee·ko/a realistic
recente re·*chen*·te recent
recinzione ⓜ re·cheen·*tsyo*·ne fence
regalo ⓜ re·*ga*·lo present (gift)
— di nozze dee *no*·tse wedding present
reggiseno ⓜ re·jee·*se*·no bra
regina ⓕ re·*jee*·na queen
regione ⓕ re·*jo*·ne region
regista ⓜ&ⓕ re·*jee*·sta director (films)
registrazione ⓕ re·jee·stra·*tsyo*·ne check-in (hotel)
regolare re·go·*la*·re regular
regole ⓕ pl *re*·go·le rules
religione ⓕ re·lee·*jo*·ne religion
religioso/a ⓜ/ⓕ re·lee·*jo*·zo/a religious
reliquia ⓕ re·*lee*·kwee·a relic
remoto/a ⓜ/ⓕ re·*mo*·to/a remote
respirare res·pee·*ra*·re breathe
resto ⓜ *res*·to change (money)
rete ⓕ *re*·te net
ricco/a ⓜ/ⓕ *ree*·ko/a rich (wealthy)
ricetta ⓕ ree·*che*·ta prescription
ricevere ree·*che*·ve·re receive
ricevuta ⓕ ree·che·*voo*·ta receipt
richiedere ree·*kye*·de·re ask (for something)
riciclabile ree·chee·*kla*·bee·le recyclable
riciclare ree·chee·*kla*·re recycle
ricordino ⓜ ree·kor·*dee*·no souvenir
ridere *ree*·de·re laugh
rifiutare ree·fyoo·*ta*·re refuse

rifugiato/a ⓜ/ⓕ ree·foo·*gya*·to/a refugee
rifiuti ⓜ pl ree·*fyoo*·tee rubbish
rilassarsi ree·la·*sar*·see relax
rimborso ⓜ reem·*bor*·so refund
ringraziare reen·gra·*tsya*·re thank
riparare ree·pa·*ra*·re repair
ripido/a ⓜ/ⓕ *ree*·pee·do/a steep
riposare ree·po·*za*·re rest
riscaldamento ⓜ rees·kal·da·*men*·to heating
— centrale chen·*tra*·le central heating
rischio ⓜ *rees*·kyo risk
riscuotere un assegno ree·*skwo*·te·re oon a·se·nyo cash a cheque
riso ⓜ *ree*·zo rice
— integrale een·te·*gra*·le brown rice
risposta ⓕ rees·*pos*·ta answer
ristorante ⓜ rees·to·*ran*·te restaurant
ritardo ⓜ ree·*tar*·do delay
ritiro ⓜ **bagagli** ree·*tee*·ro ba·*ga*·lyee baggage claim
ritmo ⓜ *reet*·mo rhythm
ritornare ree·tor·*na*·re return
ritorno ⓜ ree·*tor*·no return
rivista ⓕ ree·*vee*·sta magazine
roba ⓕ *ro*·ba stuff (belongings) • dope (drugs)
roccia ⓕ *ro*·cha rock • rock climbing
romantico/a ⓜ/ⓕ ro·*man*·tee·ko/a romantic
romanzo ⓜ ro·*man*·dzo novel
rompere *rom*·pe·re break
rosa ⓜ/ⓕ *ro*·za pink
rossetto ⓜ ro·*se*·to lipstick
rosso/a ⓜ/ⓕ *ro*·so/a red
rotonda ⓜ ro·*ton*·da roundabout
rotondo/a ⓜ/ⓕ ro·*ton*·do/a round
rotto/a ⓜ/ⓕ *ro*·to/a broken
roulotte ⓕ roo·*lot* caravan
rovine ⓕ pl ro·*vee*·ne ruins
rubare roo·*ba*·re steal
rubato/a ⓜ/ⓕ roo·*ba*·to/a stolen
rubinetto ⓜ roo·bee·*ne*·to faucet
rullino ⓜ roo·*lee*·no film (roll for camera)
rumoroso/a ⓜ/ⓕ roo·mo·*ro*·zo/a noisy
ruota ⓕ *rwo*·ta wheel
ruscello ⓜ roo·*she*·lo stream

S

sabato ⓜ *sa*·ba·to saturday
sabbia ⓕ *sa*·bya sand
sacchetto ⓜ sa·*ke*·to bag (shopping)
sacco ⓜ *sa*·ko sack • bag
— a pelo a *pe*·lo sleeping bag
sala ⓕ *sa*·la room • hall
— di transito dee *tran*·zee·to transit lounge
— d'aspetto das·*pe*·to waiting room
salame ⓜ sa·*la*·me salami
salario ⓜ sa·*la*·ryo wage
saldi ⓜ pl *sal*·dee sales
saldo ⓜ *sal*·do balance (account)
sale ⓜ *sa*·le salt
salire sa·*lee*·re climb • go up
— su soo board (a plane, ship)
salmone ⓜ sal·*mo*·ne salmon
salsa ⓕ *sal*·sa sauce
salsiccia ⓕ sal·*see*·cha sausage
saltare sal·*ta*·re jump
salumeria ⓕ sa·loo·me·*ree*·a delicatessen
salute ⓕ sa·*loo*·te health
salva slip ⓜ pl *sal*·va sleep panty liners
San Silvestro ⓜ san seel·*ves*·tro New Year's Eve
sandali ⓜ pl *san*·da·lee sandals
sangue ⓜ *san*·gwe blood
santo/a ⓜ/ⓕ *san*·to/a saint
santuario ⓜ san·too·*a*·ryo shrine
sapere sa·*pe*·re know (how to)
sapone ⓜ sa·*po*·ne soap
sardine ⓕ pl sar·*dee*·ne sardines
sarto/a ⓜ/ⓕ *sar*·to/a tailor
sauna ⓕ *sow*·na sauna
sbagliato/a ⓜ/ⓕ sba·*lya*·to/a wrong
sbaglio ⓜ *sba*·lyo mistake
scacchi ⓜ pl *ska*·kee chess

scala ⓕ **mobile** *ska*·la *mo*·bee·le escalator
scalare ska·*la*·re climb
scale ⓕ pl *ska*·le stairway
scanner ⓜ *ska*·ner scanner
scarafaggio ⓜ ska·ra·*fa*·jo cockroach
scarpe ⓕ pl *skar*·pe shoes
scarpette ⓕ pl skar·*pe*·te boots (soccer)
scarponi ⓜ pl skar·*po*·nee boots (hiking, ski)
scatola ⓕ *ska*·to·la box • carton • can • tin
scatoletta ⓕ ska·to·*le*·ta tin • can
scheda ⓕ **telefonica** *ske*·da te·le·*fo*·nee·ka phone card
scherma ⓕ *sker*·ma fencing (sport)
scherzo ⓜ *sker*·tso joke
schiena ⓕ *skye*·na back (body)
sci ⓜ shee skiing • ski(s)
— acquatico a·*kwa*·tee·ko waterskiing
sciare shee·*a*·re ski
sciarpa ⓕ *shar*·pa scarf
scienza ⓕ *shen*·tsa science
sciopero ⓜ *sho*·pe·ro strike
sciovia ⓕ shee·o·*vee*·a ski-lift
sciroppo ⓜ shee·*ro*·po syrup
— per la tosse per la *to*·se cough medicine
scogliera ⓕ sko·*lye*·ra cliff
scommessa ⓕ sko·*me*·sa bet
scomodo/a ⓜ/ⓕ *sko*·mo·do/a uncomfortable
sconosciuto/a ⓜ/ⓕ sko·no·*shoo*·to/a stranger
sconto ⓜ *skon*·to discount
scorie ⓕ pl *sko*·rye waste (rubbish)
— radioattive ra·dyo·a·*tee*·ve nuclear waste
— tossiche *to*·see·che toxic waste
scottatura ⓕ sko·ta·*too*·ra sunburn
Scozia ⓕ *sko*·tsya Scotland
scrittore/scrittrice ⓜ/ⓕ skree·*to*·re/skree·*tree*·che writer
scrivere *skree*·ve·re write
scultura ⓕ skool·*too*·ra sculpture
scuola ⓕ *skwo*·la school
— superiore soo·pe·*ryo*·re high school
scuro/a ⓜ/ⓕ *skoo*·ro/a dark
se se if
seccato/a ⓜ/ⓕ se·*ka*·to/a cross (angry)
secchio ⓜ *se*·kyo bucket
secco/a ⓜ/ⓕ *se*·ko/a dry
seconda classe ⓕ se·*kon*·da *kla*·se second class
(di) seconda mano ⓜ/ⓕ (dee) se·*kon*·da *ma*·no secondhand
secondo ⓜ se·*kon*·do second
secondo/a ⓜ/ⓕ se·*kon*·do/a second
sedere se·*de*·re sit
sedia ⓕ *se*·dya chair
— a rotelle a ro·*te*·le wheelchair
sedile ⓜ se·*dee*·le seat (chair)
seggiolino ⓜ se·jo·*lee*·no child seat
seggiovia ⓕ se·jo·*vee*·a chairlift (skiing)
segnale ⓜ se·*nya*·le signal • dial tone
— acustico a·*koos*·tee·ko dial tone
segnare se·*nya*·re score
segno ⓜ *se*·nyo sign
segretario/a ⓜ/ⓕ se·gre·*ta*·ryo/a secretary
seguire se·*gwee*·re follow
sella ⓕ *se*·la saddle
semaforo ⓜ se·*ma*·fo·ro traffic lights
semplice ⓜ/ⓕ *sem*·plee·che simple
sempre *sem*·pre always
senape ⓕ *se*·na·pe mustard
seno ⓜ *se*·no breast
sensuale ⓜ/ⓕ sen·soo·*a*·le sensual
sentiero ⓜ sen·*tye*·ro path • track • trail
— di montagna dee mon·*ta*·nya mountain path
sentimenti ⓜ pl sen·tee·*men*·tee feelings
sentire sen·*tee*·re feel • hear
senza *sen*·tsa without
— piombo *pyom*·bo unleaded
senzatetto ⓜ&ⓕ sen·tsa·*te*·to homeless

separato/a ⓜ/ⓕ se·pa·*ra*·to/a separate
sera ⓕ *se*·ra evening
serie ⓕ **(televisiva)** *se*·ree·e (te·le·vee·*see*·va) (TV) series
serio/a ⓜ/ⓕ *se*·ryo/a serious
serpente ⓜ ser·*pen*·te snake
serratura ⓕ se·ra·*too*·ra lock (door)
servizi ⓜ pl **igienici** ser·*vee*·tse ee·*je*·nee·chee toilets
servizio ⓜ ser·*vee*·tsyo service • service-charge
— militare mee·lee·*ta*·re military service
sessismo ⓜ se·*seez*·mo sexism
sesso ⓜ *se*·so sex
seta ⓕ *se*·ta silk
settimana ⓕ se·tee·*ma*·na week
— santa *san*·ta Holy Week
sfogo ⓜ *sfo*·go rash
— da pannolino da pa·no·*lee*·no nappy rash
sfruttamento ⓜ sfroo·ta·*men*·to exploitation
sì see yes
sicuro/a ⓜ/ⓕ see·*koo*·ro/a safe
sidro ⓜ *see*·dro cider
sieropositivo/a ⓜ/ⓕ sye·ro·po·zee·*tee*·vo/a HIV positive
sigaretta ⓕ see·ga·*re*·ta cigarette
sigaro ⓜ *see*·ga·ro cigar
simile ⓜ/ⓕ *see*·mee·le similar
simpatico/a ⓜ/ⓕ seem·*pa*·tee·ko/a nice (person)
sinagoga ⓕ see·na·*go*·ga synagogue
sindaco ⓜ *seen*·da·ko mayor
sinistra ⓕ see·*nee*·stra left (direction)
sintetico/a ⓜ/ⓕ seen·*te*·tee·ko/a synthetic
siringa ⓕ see·*reen*·ga syringe
slitta ⓕ *slee*·ta sleigh • toboggan
soccorso ⓜ so·*kor*·so help • aid
socialista ⓜ&ⓕ so·cha·*lee*·sta socialist
socio/a ⓜ/ⓕ *so*·cho/a member
soffice ⓜ/ⓕ *so*·fee·che soft
sognare so·*nya*·re dream
sogno ⓜ *so*·nyo dream
soldato ⓜ sol·*da*·to soldier
soldi ⓜ pl *sol*·dee money • cash
sole ⓜ *so*·le sun
soleggiato/a ⓜ/ⓕ so·le·*ja*·to/a sunny
solo *so*·lo only
— andata ⓕ an·*da*·ta one-way
sonniferi ⓜ pl so·*nee*·fe·ree sleeping pills
sonno ⓜ *so*·no sleep • sleepiness
sopra *so*·pra above • over
soprannome ⓜ so·pra·*no*·me nickname
sordo/a ⓜ/ⓕ *sor*·do/a deaf
sorella ⓕ so·*re*·la sister
sorpresa ⓕ sor·*pre*·sa surprise
sorridere so·*ree*·de·re smile
sostenitore/sostenitrice ⓜ/ⓕ sos·te·nee·*to*·re/sos·te·nee·*tree*·che supporter
sotto *so*·to below
sottoaceti ⓜ pl so·to·a·*che*·tee pickles
sottotitoli ⓜ pl so·to·*tee*·to·lee subtitles
spacciatore/spacciatrice ⓜ/ⓕ spa·cha·*to*·re/spa·cha·*tree*·che drug dealer
Spagna ⓕ *spa*·nya Spain
spago ⓜ *spa*·go string
spalla ⓕ *spa*·la shoulder
spazio ⓜ *spa*·tsyo space
spazzatura ⓕ spa·tsa·*too*·ra rubbish • garbage
spazzolino ⓜ **da denti** spa·tso·*lee*·no da *den*·tee toothbrush
specchio ⓜ *spe*·kyo mirror
speciale spe·*cha*·le special
specialista ⓜ&ⓕ spe·cha·*lee*·sta specialist
specie ⓕ *spe*·che species • type
— in via di estinzione een *vee*·a dee es·teen·*tsyo*·ne endangered species

— **protetta** pro·*te*·ta protected species
spermicida ⓕ sper·mee·*chee*·da spermicide
spesso *spe*·so often
spesso/a ⓜ/ⓕ *spe*·so/a thick
spettacolo ⓜ spe·*ta*·ko·lo show • performance
spiaggia ⓕ *spya*·ja beach
spiccioli ⓜ pl *spee*·cho·lee loose change
spina ⓕ *spee*·na plug (electricity)
— **multipla** *mool*·tee·pla adaptor
spinaci ⓜ pl spee·*na*·chee spinach
spingere *speen*·je·re push
spirale ⓕ spee·*ra*·le IUD
spogliatoio ⓜ spo·lya·*to*·yo change room (sport)
sporco/a ⓜ/ⓕ *spor*·ko/a dirty
sportivo/a ⓜ/ⓕ spor·*tee*·vo/a sportsperson
sposalizio ⓜ spo·za·*lee*·tsyo wedding
sposare spo·*za*·re marry
sposato/a ⓜ/ⓕ spo·*za*·to/a married
spremuta ⓕ spre·*moo*·ta fruit juice (fresh)
— **d'arancia** da·*ran*·cha orange juice (fresh)
spuntino ⓜ spoon·*tee*·no snack
squadra ⓕ *skwa*·dra team
stadio ⓜ *sta*·dyo stadium
stagione ⓕ sta·*jo*·ne season
stampante ⓕ stam·*pan*·te printer (computer)
stanco/a ⓜ/ⓕ *stan*·ko/a tired
stanza ⓕ *stan*·tsa room
stasera sta·*se*·ra tonight
Stati Uniti d'America ⓜ pl *sta*·tee oo·*nee*·tee da·*me*·ree·ka USA
stato ⓜ **civile** *sta*·to chee·*vee*·le marital status
statua ⓕ *sta*·too·a statue
stazione ⓕ sta·*tsyo*·ne (train) station
— **d'autobus** *dow*·to·boos bus station
— **della metropolitana** *de*·la me·tro·po·lee·*ta*·na metro station
— **di servizio** dee ser·*vee*·tsyo petrol station • service station
— **ferroviaria** fe·ro·*vyar*·ya train station
stelle ⓕ pl *ste*·le stars
stendersi *sten*·der·see lie (not stand)
sterlina ⓕ ster·*lee*·na pound (money)
stesso/a ⓜ/ⓕ *ste*·so/a same
stile ⓜ *stee*·le style
stipendio ⓜ stee·*pen*·dyo salary
stitichezza ⓕ stee·tee·*ke*·tsa constipation
stivali ⓜ pl stee·*va*·lee boots
stoffa ⓕ *sto*·fa fabric
stomaco ⓜ *sto*·ma·ko stomach
stordito/a ⓜ/ⓕ stor·*dee*·to/a dizzy
storia ⓕ *sto*·rya history • story
storico/a ⓜ/ⓕ *sto*·ree·ko/a historical
storta ⓕ *stor*·ta sprain
strada ⓕ *stra*·da road • street
straniero/a ⓜ/ⓕ stra·*nye*·ro/a foreign
strano/a ⓜ/ⓕ *stra*·no/a strange
strato ⓜ **d'ozono** *stra*·to do·*dzo*·no ozone layer
stretto/a ⓜ/ⓕ *stre*·to/a tight
studente/studentessa ⓜ/ⓕ stoo·*den*·te/stoo·den·*te*·sa student
stufa ⓕ *stoo*·fa heater • stove
— **a gas** a gaz gas stove
stupido/a ⓜ/ⓕ *stoo*·pee·do/a stupid
stupro ⓜ *stoo*·pro rape
stuzzicadenti ⓜ stoo·tsee·ka·*den*·te toothpick
su soo on • up
succo ⓜ *soo*·ko juice
— **d'arancia** da·*ran*·cha orange juice (bottled)
— **di frutta** dee *froo*·ta fruit juice (bottled)
sud ⓜ sood south
sugo ⓜ *soo*·go sauce
suocera ⓕ *swo*·che·ra mother-in-law
suocero ⓜ *swo*·che·ro father-in-law
suonare (la chitarra) swo·*na*·re (la kee·*ta*·ra) play (guitar)

suora ⓕ *swo*·ra nun
supermercato ⓜ soo·per·mer·*ka*·to supermarket
superstizione ⓕ soo·per·stee·*tsyo*·ne superstition
surf ⓜ **da neve** soorf da *ne*·ve snowboarding
surgelati ⓜ pl soor·je·*la*·tee frozen foods
sussidio ⓜ **di disoccupazione** soo·*see*·dyo dee dee·zo·koo·pa·*tsyo*·ne unemployment benefit
sveglia ⓕ *sve*·lya alarm clock
svegliarsi sve·*lyar*·see wake up
Svizzera ⓕ svee·*tse*·ra Switzerland

T

tabaccheria ⓕ ta·ba·ke·*ree*·a tobacconist
tabacco ⓜ ta·*ba*·ko tobacco
tabellone ⓜ **segnapunti** ta·be·*lo*·ne se·nya·*poon*·tee scoreboard
tacchino ⓜ ta·*kee*·no turkey
tachimetro ⓜ ta·*kee*·me·tro speedometer
taglia ⓕ *ta*·lya size (clothes)
tagliare ta·*lya*·re cut
tagliaunghie ⓜ ta·lya·*oon*·gye nail clippers
taglio ⓜ **di capelli** *ta*·lyo dee ka·*pe*·lee haircut
tamponi ⓜ pl tam·*po*·nee tampons
tappa ⓕ *ta*·pa leg (in race or journey) • stage (in race)
tappeto ⓜ ta·*pe*·to mat • rug
tappi ⓜ pl **per le orecchie** *ta*·pee per le o·*re*·kye earplugs
tappo ⓜ *ta*·po plug (bath)
tardi *tar*·dee late
targa ⓕ *tar*·ga number plate
tariffa ⓕ **postale** ta·*ree*·fa pos·*ta*·le postage
tasca ⓕ *tas*·ka pocket
tassa ⓕ *ta*·sa tax
tassì ⓜ ta·*see* taxi
tasso ⓜ **di cambio** *ta*·so dee *kam*·byo exchange rate
tastiera ⓕ tas·*tye*·ra keyboard
tavola ⓕ *ta*·vo·la table
— da surf da soorf surfboard
tazza ⓕ *ta*·tsa cup
tè ⓜ te tea
teatro ⓜ te·*a*·tro theatre
— dell'opera del·o·per·a opera house
telecomando ⓜ te·le·ko·*man*·do remote control
telefonare te·le·fo·*na*·re telephone
telefonata ⓕ te·le·fo·*na*·ta phone call
telefono ⓜ te·*le*·fo·no telephone
— cellulare che·loo·*la*·re mobile/cell phone
— diretto dee·*re*·to direct-dial
— pubblico *poo*·blee·ko public telephone
telegramma ⓜ te·le·*gra*·ma telegram
telenovela ⓕ te·le·no·*ve*·la soap opera
teleobiettivo ⓜ te·le·o·bye·*tee*·vo telephoto lens
telescopio ⓜ te·le·*sko*·pyo telescope
televisione ⓕ te·le·vee·*zyo*·ne television
temperatura ⓕ tem·pe·ra·*too*·ra temperature (weather)
temperino ⓜ tem·pe·*ree*·no penknife
tempio ⓜ *tem*·pyo temple
tempo ⓜ *tem*·po time • weather
— pieno *pye*·no full-time
temporale ⓜ tem·po·*ra*·le storm
tenda ⓕ *ten*·da tent
tensione ⓕ **premestruale** ten·*syo*·ne pre·me·*stroo*·a·le premenstrual tension
Terra ⓕ *te*·ra Earth
terra ⓕ *te*·ra land
terremoto ⓜ te·re·*mo*·to earthquake
terribile ⓜ/ⓕ te·*ree*·bee·le terrible
terzo/a ⓜ/ⓕ *ter*·tso/a third
tessera ⓕ *te*·se·ra pass (document)
test ⓜ **di gravidanza** test dee gra·vee·*dan*·tsa pregnancy test kit

testa Ⓕ *tes*·ta head
tiepido/a Ⓜ/Ⓕ *tye*·pee·do/a warm
tifoso/a Ⓜ/Ⓕ tee·*fo*·zo/a fan (person) • supporter
timido/a Ⓜ/Ⓕ *tee*·mee·do/a shy
tipico/a Ⓜ/Ⓕ *tee*·pee·ko/a typical
tipo Ⓜ *tee*·po type
tirare tee·*ra*·re pull
titolo Ⓜ *tee*·to·lo title
titoli Ⓜ pl **di studio** *tee*·to·lee dee *stoo*·dee·o qualifications
toboga Ⓜ to·*bo*·ga toboggan • sledge
toccare to·*ka*·re touch
tomba Ⓕ *tom*·ba grave
tonno Ⓜ *to*·no tuna
topo Ⓜ *to*·po mouse (rodent) • rat
torcia Ⓕ **elettrica** *tor*·cha e·*le*·tree·ka torch (flashlight)
torre Ⓕ *to*·re tower
torta Ⓕ *tor*·ta cake • pie
tossico/a Ⓜ/Ⓕ *to*·see·ko/a toxic
tossicodipendenza Ⓕ to·see·ko·dee·pen·*den*·tsa drug addiction
tossire to·*see*·re cough
tostapane Ⓜ tos·ta·*pa*·ne toaster
tovaglia Ⓕ to·*va*·lya tablecloth
tovagliolo Ⓜ to·va·*lyo*·lo napkin
tradurre tra·*doo*·re translate
traffico Ⓜ *tra*·fee·ko traffic
traghetto Ⓜ tra·*ge*·to ferry
tram Ⓜ tram tram
tramezzino Ⓜ tra·me·*dzee*·no sandwich
tramonto Ⓜ tra·*mon*·to sunset
tranquillo/a Ⓜ/Ⓕ tran·*kwee*·lo/a quiet
trasporto Ⓜ tras·*por*·to transport
travestito Ⓜ tra·ves·*tee*·to drag queen
treno Ⓜ *tre*·no train
triste *tree*·ste sad
troppo (caro/a) *tro*·po (*ka*·ro/a) too (expensive)
troppo/a Ⓜ/Ⓕ *tro*·po/a too much • too many
trovare tro·*va*·re find
trucco Ⓜ *troo*·ko make-up
tu inf too you
tubo Ⓜ **di scappamento** *too*·bo dee ska·pa·*men*·to exhaust (car)
tuffi Ⓜ pl *too*·fee diving (in pool)
turista Ⓜ&Ⓕ too·*ree*·sta tourist
tutti/e Ⓜ/Ⓕ pl *too*·tee/*too*·te all
tutto Ⓜ *too*·to everything
tutto/a Ⓜ/Ⓕ sg *too*·to/a all

U

ubriaco/a Ⓜ/Ⓕ oo·bree·*a*·ko/a drunk
uccello Ⓜ oo·*che*·lo bird
ufficio Ⓜ oo·*fee*·cho office
— del turismo del too·*reez*·mo tourist office
— oggetti smarriti o·*je*·tee sma·*ree*·tee lost property office
— postale pos·*ta*·le post office
ultimo/a Ⓜ/Ⓕ *ool*·tee·mo/a last
un po' oon po (a) little
una volta Ⓕ *oo*·na *vol*·ta once
università Ⓕ oo·nee·ver·see·*ta* university
universo Ⓜ oo·nee·*ver*·so universe
uomo Ⓜ *wo*·mo man
— d'affari da·*fa*·ree businessman
uovo Ⓜ *wo*·vo egg
urgente Ⓜ&Ⓕ oor·*jen*·te urgent
urlare oor·*la*·re shout
usare oo·*za*·re use
usa e getta *oo*·za e *je*·ta disposable
uscire con oo·*shee*·re kon go out with • date
uscita Ⓕ oo·*shee*·ta exit
utile *oo*·tee·le useful
uva Ⓕ pl *oo*·va grapes
— passa *pa*·sa raisin

V

vacanza Ⓕ va·*kan*·tsa holiday • vacation
vacanze Ⓕ pl va·*kan*·tse holidays
vaccinazione Ⓕ va·chee·na·*tsyo*·ne vaccination

vagone ⓜ va·*go*·ne carriage • wagon
— letto *le*·to sleeping car
valigetta ⓕ va·lee·*je*·ta briefcase
— del pronto soccorso del *pron*·to so·*kor*·so first-aid kit
valigia ⓕ va·*lee*·ja suitcase
valle ⓕ *va*·le valley
valore ⓜ va·*lo*·re value (price)
vanga ⓕ *van*·ga spade
vecchio/a ⓜ/ⓕ *ve*·kyo/a old
vedere ve·*de*·re see
vedovo/a ⓜ/ⓕ ve·*do*·vo/a widower/widow
veduta ⓕ ve·*doo*·ta lookout
vegetariano/a ⓜ/ⓕ ve·je·ta·*rya*·no/a vegetarian
velenoso/a ⓜ/ⓕ ve·le·*no*·zo/a poisonous
veloce ve·*lo*·che fast
velocità ⓕ ve·lo·chee·*ta* speed
vendere *ven*·de·re sell
vendita ⓕ *ven*·dee·ta sale
venire ve·*nee*·re come
ventilatore ⓜ ven·tee·la·*to*·re fan (machine)
vento ⓜ *ven*·to wind
verde *ver*·de green
verdura ⓕ ver·*doo*·ra vegetable
vero/a ⓜ/ⓕ *ve*·ro/a true
vescica ⓕ ve·*shee*·ka blister
vetro ⓜ *ve*·tro glass
via ⓕ *vee*·a way
— aerea a·*e*·re·a airmail
viaggiare vee·a·*ja*·re travel
viaggio ⓜ vee·*a*·jo trip
— d'affari da·*fa*·ree business trip
viale ⓜ vee·*a*·le avenue
vicino/a ⓜ/ⓕ vee·*chee*·no/a close • nearby
vicino (a) vee·*chee*·no (a) near (to)
vicolo ⓜ *vee*·ko·lo lane
videonastro ⓜ vee·de·o·*nas*·tro video tape
videoregistratore ⓜ vee·de·o·re·jee·stra·*to*·re video
vigna ⓕ *vee*·nya vineyard • wine cellar
vigneto ⓜ vee·*nye*·to vineyard
villaggio ⓜ vee·*la*·jo village
vincere *veen*·che·re win
vincitore/vincitrice ⓜ/ⓕ veen·chee·*to*·re/veen·chee·*tree*·che winner
vino ⓜ *vee*·no wine
— bianco *byan*·ko white wine
— rosso *ro*·so red wine
— spumante spoo·*man*·te sparkling wine
viola vee·*o*·la purple
virus ⓜ *vee*·roos virus
visita ⓕ *vee*·zee·ta visit • tour • medical examination
— guidata gwee·*da*·ta guided tour
vista ⓕ *vee*·sta view
visto ⓜ *vee*·sto visa
vita ⓕ *vee*·ta life
vitamine ⓕ pl vee·ta·*mee*·ne vitamins
vitello ⓜ vee·*te*·lo veal
vitto ⓜ *vee*·to food
vivere *vee*·ve·re live
vocabolarietto ⓜ vo·ka·bo·la·*rye*·to phrasebook
vocabolario ⓜ vo·ka·bo·*la*·ryo dictionary
voce ⓕ *vo*·che voice
volare vo·*la*·re fly
volere vo·*le*·re want
volo ⓜ *vo*·lo flight
volta ⓕ *vol*·ta time • turn
volume ⓜ vo·*loo*·me volume
vomitare vo·mee·*ta*·re vomit
votare vo·*ta*·re vote
vuoto/a ⓜ/ⓕ *vwo*·to/a empty

Z

zaino ⓜ *dzai*·no backpack • knapsack
zanzara ⓕ tsan·*tsa*·ra mosquito
zenzero ⓜ *dzen*·dze·ro ginger
zia ⓕ *tsee*·a aunt
zucca ⓕ *tsoo*·ka pumpkin
zucchero ⓜ *tsoo*·ke·ro sugar

Index

l'indice

For topics that are covered in several sections of this book, we've indicated the most relevant page number in bold.

A

abbreviations ... 3
accidents ... 51, **146**, 147
accommodation ... **58**, 95
addresses ... 48, **55**, 112
addressing people ... 21, 78, **106**
adjectives (grammar) ... 14
admission (going out) ... 123
admission (sightseeing) ... 94
adverbs (grammar) ... 14
age ... **108**, 111
airplane ... 40
alcoholic drinks ... 172
allergies ... 155, 181
alphabet (Italian) ... 12
amounts ... 33, 177
animals ... 144
appointments ... 92, 126
architecture ... 93, **97**
area codes ... 82
art ... 96
articles (grammar) ... 15
assaults ... 148
ATMs ... 89

B

babies ... 101
baggage ... **45**, 65
bags (shopping) ... **72**, 177
banking ... 87
bar ... 123, **173**
bargaining ... 74
be (verb) ... 16
beach ... 142
beer ... 172, 173
beliefs ... 133
bicycle ... 51
bill (general) ... 87
bill (restaurant) ... 163, **169**
blind travellers ... 99
boat ... 40
body language ... 112
body parts (diagram) ... 157
books ... 76
border crossing ... 53
breakfast ... 59, 60, **160**
breaking up (romance) ... 132
bus ... 40, **45**
business ... 53, **91**, 110, 162

C

cafe ... 123, 161, 171
calendar ... 35
cameras ... 75, **77**, 86
camping ... 66
car ... 49
car parts (diagram) ... 50
cell phone ... **84**, 113
centuries ... 38
changing money ... 63, **87**
check (banking) ... 87
check (restaurant) ... 163, **169**
checking in ... 59
checking out ... 65
cheering (sport) ... **137**, 139
chemist ... 150, **156**
children ... **101**, 110, 111
cinema ... **116**, 123
civilities ... 104

clothes ... 74
coffee ... 125, 171, **172**
communications ... 80
community issues ... 119
computers ... **85**, 92
concerts ... 115, 123, 125
consonant sounds ... 11
consulates ... 149
contact details ... 81, 92, **112**
contraception ... 130, **154**
conversation ... **107**, 109
cooking classes ... 95
cooking utensils ... 180
cost (accommodation) ... **59**, 67, 68
cost (bicycle) ... 51
cost (car & motorbike) ... 49
cost (food) ... 177
cost (general) ... 71, **87**
cost (internet) ... 86
cost (sightseeing) ... 94, 95
cost (sporting equipment) ... 137
cost (taxi) ... 48
cost (telephone) ... 82, 84
countries (nationalities) ... 108
credit cards ... 87, 90
cultural differences ... 134
customs (border crossing) ... 54
customs (traditions) ... 134
cycling ... 51

D

dancing ... 115, 125, 128
dates (calendar) ... 35
dating (romance) ... 128
days of the week ... 35
demonstratives (grammar) ... 18
dentist ... 150, **157**
dialects (local) ... 31
diets (special) ... 181
directions ... 55
disabled travellers ... 99
discounts ... 8, **94**, 101
diving ... 142
doctor ... 146, **150**
drinks ... 8, 125, 128, 163, 164, **171**
driving ... 49
drugs (illegal) ... 127

E

eateries ... 161
eating in ... 176
eating out ... **160**, 181, 184
elevators ... 62, 99
email ... **85**, 112
embassies ... 149
emergencies ... 146
endearments ... 132
English, use of ... **30**, 54, 76, 93, 101, 116, 149, 150, 163
entertainment ... **122**
entertainment guide ... 76, 123
environment ... 121
etiquette tips ... 74, 92, 109, 112
exchange rates ... 89
exhibitions ... 97

F

false friends ... 7
family ... 101, **110**
faulty things ... 71
feelings ... 118
film (camera) ... 77
film (cinema) ... **116**, 123
food (eating out) ... 159
food (glossary) ... 184
food (preparation) ... **166**, 180
food (self-catering) ... 176
food (shopping) ... 176
football (soccer) ... 138
foreign exchange office ... 89
formal speech ... 7, **21**, 78, 107
future (grammar) ... 27
future (time) ... 37

G

galleries ... 96
gas (petrol) ... 50, **51**
gay travellers ... 123
gender (grammar) ... **19**, 130
going out ... 122
goodbyes ... 105, **112**
grammar ... 14
greetings ... 105

INDEX

guarantees (shopping) ... 71
guide dogs ... 99
guidebooks ... 93
guides (hiking) ... 141
guides (sightseeing) ... 93, 94

H

have (verb) ... 19
health ... 150
hiking ... 140
hire (bicycle) ... 51
hire (car & motorbike) ... 49
hire (sports equipment) ... 138
hobbies ... 114
holidays ... 53, **107**
homestays ... 68
hospital ... 150
hotel ... 58
hotel room (diagram) ... 62

I

idioms ... 9, 111, 113, 147
illnesses ... **150**, 152
informal speech ... 7, **21**, 107
injuries ... **146**, 152
insurance ... 49, 148, 152
interests ... 114
internet ... 62, 82, **85**, 92
interpreter ... **30**, 92
introductions (meeting people) ... 106
invitations ... **124**, 128
Italian-speaking countries ... 6

K

keys ... 64
kissing ... **112**, 130, 131

L

language classes ... 95
language difficulties ... **30**, 131
laundry (hotel) ... 62, 63
lawyer ... 149
lesbian travellers ... 123
lifts (elevators) ... 62, 99
local expressions ... 9, 111, 113, 147
local food ... 8, 162, 164, 168, 176, **184**
lockers (luggage) ... 45
lost (items) ... 45, **148**
lost (way) ... 96, 141, **147**
love ... 131
luggage ... **45**, 65

M

mail ... 80
maps ... 55, 93, 140
marriage ... 111
meals ... 125, **160**, 175, 184
mechanic (car) ... 50
medications ... 152, 154, **156**
meeting people ... 104
meeting up ... 8, 92, **126**
meetings (business) ... 91
menu decoder ... 184
menus ... **163**, 165, 167, 170, 172, 184
messages ... 63, 64, 83
meter (taxi) ... 48
mobile phone ... **84**, 113
money ... 87
months ... 35
motorbike ... 49
museums ... 96
music ... 76, 115

N

names ... 92, **106**, 111
nationalities ... 108
negatives (grammar) ... 20
nightclubs ... 123, **125**
nonalcoholic drinks ... 171
nonsmoking (seat) ... 45, 163
numbers ... 32

O

occupations ... 109
older people ... 94, **99**
opinions ... 119
optometrist ... **150**, 151, 152
organic food ... 183
outdoors ... 140

P

parking (car)...................**50**, 59, 100
parties (entertainment)......... 123, 126
parties (politics)...........................120
passports...............................**53**, 66
past (grammar)..............................27
past (time)....................................37
pasta 170
paying the bill (general)..................87
paying the bill (restaurant)....165, **169**
petrol......................................50, **51**
pharmacist 150, **156**
phone.......................... 62, **81**, 84, 147
photography........................**77**, 85, 94
pick-up lines 128
plane 40
plants 144
plurals (grammar) **23**, 97
police 146, **148**
polite speech.................. 7, **21**, 78, 107
politics 119
possessives (grammar)..................23
post office.................................... 80
prepositions (grammar)..................24
prescriptions (medical).........149, **156**
present (grammar).........................26
present (time)................................36
price .... see *cost*
pronouns (grammar)...................... 21
pronunciation (Italian)....................10

Q

quantities.............................. 33, 177
questions (grammar) 25

R

rape..148
reading (books)..............................76
reading Italian 12
receipts..............................**72**, 88, 152
recycling 121
refunds... 88
rejections................................8, 129
religion 133
renting (accommodation)............. 68
repairs (bicycle) 51
repairs (general) 75
reservations (accommodation).**59**, 61
reservations (restaurant).............162
reservations (taxi) 65
reservations (tickets) 41
responses (invitations).................126
restaurant........ 123, 125, 162, **163**, 181
restaurant table (diagram)............169
road signs 52
robbery 45, 146, **148**
romance 128
room (diagram)...............................62
room (hotel) **59**, 61, 64

S

safe sex.................................**130**, 154
safe travel 146
school 110, 111
scoring (sport) 136
sea..142
seasons..36
seating 41, 45, 102, 163
self-catering 176
senior travellers 94, **99**
sex..130
shopping (food) 176
shopping (general) 8, **70**, 73
sightseeing.....................................93
signs (border crossing)...................54
sizes (clothes).................................75
signs (general) 71, 98, 100, 143, 168
signs (road) 52
signs (shops)................................ 178
smoking.. 127
soccer 138
social issues 119
social networking..........................113
souvenirs 78
sports...135
street (diagram)..............................56
studies 109
swearing 147
swimming 137, 142

T

taxi **48**, 65, 100, 175
tea 171
telephone.................... 62, **81**, 84, 147
theatre **116**, 123

theft 45, 146, **148**
tickets 8, **41**, 43
time..34
titles (addressing people) 92, **106**
toilets 55, 64, 67, 100, **147**
tongue twisters 174
tours... 63, **95**
train...40, **46**
transport **40**, 95
travellers cheques..................... 88, 89
trekking..140

V

vaccinations 151
valuables.................................. 45, 66
vegetarian food 181
verbs (grammar)............................26
visas 54
vowel sounds..................................10

W

walking.................... 95, 100, 125, 140
water (drinkable) 67, 141, 142, **171**
weather..143
well-wishing.................................. 110
wheelchairs 99
wine...173
women travellers 8, 138, **154**
word order (grammar) 28
word stress (pronunciation) 13
work 53, **91**, 109
writing Italian.................................. 12

10 Ways to Start a Sentence

When's (the next flight)?	A che ora è (il prossimo volo)?	a ke *o*·ra e (eel *pro*·see·mo *vo*·lo)
Where's (the station)?	Dov'è (la stazione)?	*do*·ve (la sta·*tsyo*·ne)
I'm looking for (a hotel).	Sto cercando (un albergo).	sto cher·*kan*·do (oon al·*ber*·go)
Do you have (a map)?	Ha (una pianta)?	a (*oo*·na *pyan*·ta)
Is there (a toilet)?	C'è (un gabinetto)?	che (oon ga·bee·*ne*·to)
I'd like (a coffee).	Vorrei (un caffè).	vo·*ray* (oon ka·*fe*)
I'd like to (hire a car).	Vorrei (noleggiare una macchina).	vo·*ray* (no·le·*ja*·re *oo*·na *ma*·kee·na)
Can I (enter)?	Posso (entrare)?	*po*·so (en·*tra*·re)
Could you please (help me)?	Può (aiutarmi), per favore?	pwo (a·yoo·*tar*·mee) per fa·*vo*·re
Do I have to (book a seat)?	Devo (prenotare un posto)?	*de*·vo (pre·no·*ta*·re oon *po*·sto)